D0204277

Policy Analysis for Educational Leaders

POLICY ANALYSIS FOR EDUCATIONAL LEADERS

A STEP-BY-STEP APPROACH

Nicola A. Alexander
University of Minnesota

Boston   Columbus   Indianapolis   New York   San Francisco   Upper Saddle River
Amsterdam   Cape Town   Dubai   London   Madrid   Milan   Munich   Paris   Montreal   Toronto
Delhi   Mexico City   São Paulo   Sydney   Hong Kong   Seoul   Singapore   Taipei   Tokyo

Vice President and Editorial Director: Jeffery W. Johnston
Senior Acquisitions Editor: Meredith D. Fossel
Associate Editor: Anne Whittaker
Editorial Assistant: Andrea Hall
Vice President, Director of Marketing: Margaret Waples
Marketing Manager: Christopher Barry
Senior Managing Editor: Pamela D. Bennett
Production Editor: Kerry Rubadue
Production Manager: Susan Hannahs
Senior Art Director: Jayne Conte
Cover Designer: Karen Noferi
Cover Art: Fotolia
Full-Service Project Management: Nitin Agarwal, Aptara®, Inc.
Composition: Aptara®, Inc.
Text and Cover Printer/Binder: Courier/Westford
Text Font: Palatino LT Std

Every effort has been made to provide accurate and current Internet information in this book. However, the Internet and information posted on it are constantly changing, so it is inevitable that some of the Internet addresses listed in this textbook will change.

Library of Congress Cataloging-in-Publication Data

Alexander, Nicola A.
  Policy analysis for educational leaders : a step-by-step approach/Nicola A. Alexander.
   p. cm.
  1. Education and state—United States—Evaluation—Textbooks.   2. Educational leadership—Study and teaching—United States—Textbooks.   I. Title.
  LC89.A575 2013
  379.73—dc23

                                                                                            2011042243

10 9 8 7 6 5 4 3 2 1

ISBN-10:   0-13-701600-X
ISBN-13: 978-0-13-701600-6

Dedication

To Alexis, for whom I always want to make a difference

ABOUT THE AUTHOR

Nicola A. Alexander (Ph.D., University at Albany) is an Associate Professor in the Department of Organizational Leadership, Policy, and Development at the University of Minnesota. She is also co-coordinator of its Educational Administration Program. Her formal education background is in public administration and policy. She is particularly interested in issues of adequacy, equity, and productivity as they relate to PreK–12 education. Dr. Alexander's overriding concern revolves around notions of fairness, and she examines the potentially different impact of education policies on diverse groups. She maintains that as policymakers and analysts, we need to ensure that policy supports student success.

Dr. Alexander is a former board member of the American Education Finance Association and presently serves as a board member of the National Education Finance Association. She has served on the editorial board of *Educational Administration Quarterly* and has published articles and presented on issues of adequacy, equity, and productivity as they relate to PreK–12 education. She has published in books, monographs, and journals, including *American Educational Research Journal, Educational Policy, Journal of School Business Management*, and *Journal of Education Finance.*

PREFACE

RATIONALE FOR THIS TEXT

I have taught courses in policy analysis for over a decade both in schools of public policy and in a department of educational policy and administration. I teach now in a department of organizational leadership and development. While teaching the required graduate courses in education policy, I realized that there was no analytical policy text that matched the needs of my students.

My students require a methods course on how to *do* policy analysis. The difficulty is that although many educational texts discussed and evaluated existing education policy they did not teach students *how* to complete the necessary analytical steps. Indeed, education policy texts are often a survey of the literature on policy studies. The policy analysis texts that take a methodological approach are often grounded in economic analysis. They typically do not provide enough background and foundational knowledge to education administrators and policymakers on how to complete an analysis of policy. I found that, to fulfill the objectives of my class, I relied on various texts that I borrowed from several sources, and I supplemented those materials with personal knowledge and expertise.

While it is good to have a variety of perspectives and pedagogical tools, I kept thinking that having one text that addressed the needs of the students would make their policy analytical journey go more smoothly. I also began to think that education leaders in the field would find the content of a practical text valuable. *Policy Analysis for Educational Leaders: A Step-by-Step Approach* is a culmination of years of my telling colleagues and students that I think a policy analytical book that covered all the topics that I wanted would be a welcome addition to the field.

The approach of *Policy Analysis for Educational Leaders* is a synthesis of the approaches that worked well with the various texts that I used in my policy analysis classes. I found the educational and practical focus of some texts on policy analysis to be useful in offering insight into policy making and the politics of education. These texts formed a useful backdrop to analysis, but I needed to gear their content toward the method of policy analysis rather than the process of policy making. A methodological focus was a key part of the book that I imagined.

I also liked texts that emphasized the theoretical framework of policy analysis, but students sometimes found their content to be abstract and difficult to apply. I wanted to make these materials more readable and readily applicable for education practitioners. Practicality was also a key aspect of the book I imagined.

Several texts provided excellent analytical guidelines but did so from an economic perspective. I wanted to make those books more accessible to education administrators and to provide to education leaders more of an explanation of the underlying economic principles that undergird those discussions. Making the necessary connections for education leaders was an important part of the book I imagined.

In the end, I imagined a book that would offer a practical guide to policy analysis, include educational content, and be filled with education examples. I wanted to go beyond the typical policy steps that stopped at recommendation and to include implementation, monitoring, and evaluation. I hope that, on reading *Policy Analysis for Educational Leaders*, you find it as I imagined it, and that it offers practical guidance to education leaders in their effort to make the world a better place.

ORGANIZATION OF THE TEXT

This book is organized into 13 chapters. The text begins by laying the groundwork for policy analysis. Chapter 1 offers a rationale for the importance of policy analysis and why education leaders would be interested in this topic. It highlights the importance of values and philosophy in the policy analysis process as a starting point in thinking about the development of policy. Chapter 2 continues this theme by pointing out that policy analysis is essentially problem analysis and introduces the steps necessary to conduct effective policy analysis. It also provides a discussion on how policy analysis fits in with the broader stages of the policy-making process. The overview of the steps provided in Chapter 2 is expanded upon in the remaining chapters, where each step has an individual chapter devoted to it. (The last chapter—Chapter 13—synthesizes all the steps of the process by applying them to the introduction and progress of the Elementary and Secondary Education Act, reauthorized in 2002 as the No Child Left Behind Act.)

Chapter 3 focuses on the definition of the problem. It gives clear guidance on how to structure a problem and create a policy statement. It includes a description of the steps necessary in creating a problem statement and the difficulties therein. It also discusses the goals that arise from the identification of the problem. By defining the problem, education leaders focus attention on the social condition that must be changed in order to improve society.

Chapter 4 offers a discussion on how education leaders can make the case that the facts support their description of the world and, ultimately, their solution to what they find wrong with it. It is not enough to point out problems and to identify solutions if others are not persuaded by one's analysis. This chapter gives guidance on how to assemble facts in a meaningful way so that they become transformed into persuasive evidence.

Chapter 5 discusses the importance of establishing driving values in the choices education leaders make regarding problem definitions, alternatives, and implemented strategy. Determining evaluative criteria requires looking at the cost of various alternatives, the net benefits associated with the outcomes, the administrative ease associated with implementing that alternative, and so on. In essence, the criteria selected say something about the assumptions regarding the role of society, government, and the economy.

Chapter 6 describes the interventions that need to be considered to resolve or alleviate the negative condition identified by education leaders. Alternatives are not to be confused with the outcomes sought and are always a *means* to an end; they are not an end in and of themselves. This chapter examines the process for developing alternatives.

Chapter 7 offers guidelines on how to consider and articulate the rationale used to weigh the policy options (or alternatives) and their outcomes against the criteria that were established. The explicit evaluation of alternatives is an important policy analytical step because, if the decision-making process is covert and intuitive, it is more likely to reduce accountability. Reduced accountability reduces the credibility of the results stemming from the policy analysis process. Moreover, reduced credibility often lessens the ability of education leaders to persuade community members that the path chosen is the appropriate one.

Chapter 8 is an explicit discussion of the process of deciding on the appropriate policy option, not just weighing how the policy options compare on the various criteria. This chapter focuses on the steps needed to test the credibility of the results of the previous steps. This discussion also delves more deeply into the appropriate role of policy analysts in this process once they have evaluated the alternatives.

Chapter 9 focuses on persuading relevant stakeholders on the appropriateness of a decision once it has been made. This chapter looks closely at the best way to communicate that information. It provides advice on the structure of policy arguments and information about the different modes of policy arguments, and it tries to teach education leaders to have a better understanding of their audience.

Chapter 10 is an explicit recognition that, for policies to have meaningful impact, they must be carried out. This chapter focuses on the implementation process and offers guidance to help education leaders anticipate challenges that may arise. The discussion includes an overview of the stages of implementation, the hurdles of implementation, leadership challenges, and a guide to creating an implementation plan.

Chapter 11 is a discussion of the monitoring process. By monitoring behavior and outputs associated with tackling the problem, education leaders provide data for evaluation and prediction that informs knowledge about whether and why a policy produced the desired results. Monitoring offers information on what happened and informs analytical decisions on how it happened and why. It is the penultimate step in the policy analytical process and connects the actions outlined in the implementation plan with policy objectives.

Chapter 12 examines the evaluation process, the last formal step in the policy analysis process. Evaluation focuses on the achievement of goals and objectives. It is the production of information about the value of policy outcomes. While actual evaluation occurs after implementation, it is imperative to have an evaluation plan from the outset. This step is essential for education leaders to consider because it offers them an opportunity to provide clear guidance on what constitutes an improvement of the problematic condition.

Chapter 13 offers concluding remarks. In this chapter, I reiterate the importance of the policy analysis process, especially for education leaders. I summarize the steps in the policy analysis process and apply it to a substantive education policy in the United States, the No Child Left Behind Act.

The text also includes a removable field guide: "Pullout Field Guide for Educational Leaders: Summary of Checklist of Each Step of the Policy Analytical Process." This pullout feature is a quick overview of the entire process and offers easy-to-access guidance on all ten policy analytical steps contained in *Policy Analysis for Educational Leaders*.

DISTINGUISHING FEATURES

My experience points to the need for a text that is methodological in focus and educational in context. This text meets the needs of aspiring and practicing educational administrators and policy leaders. To make sure the steps of policy analysis are clear, I use chapter objectives and education vignettes to open each chapter. The substance of each chapter is interwoven with multiple education examples, and with figures and tables summarizing and highlighting many of the chapter's main points. Each chapter closes with a summary, reflective questions, news story for analysis, and selected references and websites. Each of the selected references and websites includes an explanation about why education leaders would find the source to be of interest.

ACKNOWLEDGMENTS

Policy Analysis for Educational Leaders: A Step-by-Step Approach is the culmination of years of interaction with students in policy classes. I would like to thank all those who encouraged me to write this book, including colleagues and students who insisted not only that there was a need for this book but that I should be the one to write it. I thank Peg Sherven especially for putting me in contact with a representative from Pearson.

I would like to thank the people at Pearson Education and the reviewers of the manuscript at various stages: Charles M. Achilles, Seton Hall University; Dannielle J. Davis, Alabama State University; Charles P. Gause, University of North Carolina at Greensboro; Martha McCarthy, Indiana University; Ronae Gibbs; Paul E. Pitre, Washington State University; and Jesulon Sharita, South Carolina State University. I also want to mention Steve Dragin, who gave me encouragement on an earlier draft, and Meredith Fossel, who gave me encouragement on later ones. I would like to thank especially Anne Whittaker, who gave me helpful feedback on how to make the book better. I also would like to express my appreciation for all those who granted me permission to use their materials as part of this text. My thanks as well to Marianne L'Abbate, who provided thoughtful copyediting in the final stages of the manuscript.

Finally, I would like to acknowledge the cheering committee of my daughter, Alexis; sister, Marie; and mother, Monica, who assured me that I would complete this book. I would be remiss if I did not mention my brothers, Neville, Christopher, Gregory, and Wellesley, and their respective families. I also want to mention my dad, Neville Alexander, who always encouraged us to value education and the difference it can make. I also think of Uncle Hume, who was looking forward to an autographed copy. Sorry that it took so long . . .

BRIEF CONTENTS

Chapter 1   Laying the Groundwork 1

Chapter 2   Getting Started at the Beginning: Thinking of Policy Analysis as Problem Analysis 28

Chapter 3   Taking the First Step: Define the Problem 48

Chapter 4   Make the Case by Assembling the Evidence 64

Chapter 5   Establish Your Driving Values 79

Chapter 6   Develop Alternatives 101

Chapter 7   Weigh the Options: Evaluating Alternatives 115

Chapter 8   Make Recommendations 128

Chapter 9   Persuade Your Audience 140

Chapter 10 Implement the Solution 153

Chapter 11 Monitor Outputs 165

Chapter 12 Evaluate Outcomes 178

Chapter 13 Concluding Remarks 192

Pullout Field Guide for Educational Leaders: Summary of Checklist of Each Step of the Policy Analytical Process

References *201*

Index *207*

CONTENTS

Preface   *vii*

Chapter 1   **LAYING THE GROUNDWORK   1**
Chapter Objectives   1
Education Vignette   1
Why Should Leaders Study Policy Analysis?   2
   Players on the Leadership Landscape   2
   What Policy Analysis Can Do   2
   The Role of Persuasion   2
Users of Policy Analysis   3
Why Use This Text?   5
What Is Policy Analysis?   5
   A Brief Definition   5
   Why Policy Analysis?   5
   The Goal of Policy Analysis   6
Types of Policy Analysis   6
   Ex Post and Ex Ante Analysis   7
   Forecasting, Prescribing, Monitoring, Evaluating   7
   Rational Lens, Structural Lens, and Cultural Lens   8
   Transparency Versus Objectivity   8
Philosophies of Education   9
   Values: Cornerstone of Worldviews and Philosophies   10
   Brief Overview of Worldviews   10
   Eight Common Values   11
   Defining Philosophy   14
   Key Philosophies and Their Role in Education Policy   14
      IDEALISM   14
      REALISM   15
      PRAGMATISM   16
      PHENOMENOLOGY AND EXISTENTIALISM   17
      CONFLICT THEORY   17
      POSTMODERNISM AND CRITICAL THEORY   20
   Policy Values in Action   21
      Chapter Summary   *24*
      Review Questions   *24*
      News Story for Analysis   *24*

Discussion Questions 26

Selected Websites 26

Selected References 27

Chapter 2 GETTING STARTED AT THE BEGINNING: THINKING OF POLICY ANALYSIS AS PROBLEM ANALYSIS 28

Chapter Objectives 28

Education Vignette 28

Where Do You Start? 29

The Role of Leaders 29

Policy Analysis as Problem Analysis 29

The Problem is the Beginning of Analysis 29

Differences Among Conditions, Policy Problems, and Policy Issues 29

The Policy Analysis Process 31

THE COMPLEXITIES OF POLICY ANALYSIS 31

Policy Analysis Versus Policy Making 32

The Role of Policy Analysts 32

Phases in Policy Making 33

PROBLEM STREAM 33

POLITICS STREAM 34

POLICY STREAM 34

Stages of the Policy-Making Process 35

Issue Definition 35

Agenda Setting 36

Policy Formulation 36

Policy Adoption 37

Policy Implementation 37

Policy Evaluation 37

Policy Analysis is Not Policy Evaluation 38

Focusing on the Problem 38

Policy Evaluation 39

POLICY EVALUATION AS FEEDBACK 39

POLICY EVALUATION AS SUMMATIVE JUDGMENT 39

Going Beyond Evaluation 40

The Steps to Policy Analysis 41

The Craft of Policy Analysis 41

Key Questions of the Policy Analysis Process 41

Creating a Policy Analysis Roadmap 41

TEN STEPS OF POLICY ANALYSIS 42

Stepping-Stones of Policy Analysis   44
    Chapter Summary   44
    Review Questions   44
    News Story for Analysis   45
    Discussion Questions   46
    Selected Websites   46
    Selected References   47

Chapter 3   TAKING THE FIRST STEP: DEFINE THE PROBLEM   48

Chapter Objectives   48

Education Vignette   48

Structuring the Problem   49

  Writing a Clear Description of the Problem   49
    DIFFERENT PHASES IN PROBLEM STRUCTURING   49

  Problematic Characteristics of Policy Problems   49
    PERSONAL VERSUS POLICY PROBLEM   50
    INTERDEPENDENCE OF PROBLEMS   50
    SUBJECTIVITY AND ARTIFICIALITY OF STRUCTURING POLICY PROBLEMS   51
    DYNAMIC NATURE OF POLICY PROBLEMS   52

  Building on Your Condition Statement   52

Making the Condition a Problem   53

Scope of the Problem   54

  Bounding the Problem   54
    WHO IS INCLUDED?   54

  Causes of the Problem   55
    RATIONAL PERSPECTIVE   56
    INSTITUTIONAL PERSPECTIVE   56
    CULTURAL PERSPECTIVE   56

Goals and Objectives of Solving the Problem Identified   58

  The Goal is the Obverse of the Problem   58

  Objectives are Working Definitions of Goals   58
    OBJECTIVES VERSUS ALTERNATIVES   59
    Chapter Summary   60
    Review Questions   60
    News Story for Analysis   60
    Discussion Questions   62
    Selected Websites   62
    Selected References   63

Chapter 4   MAKE THE CASE BY ASSEMBLING THE EVIDENCE   64

Chapter Objectives   64

Education Vignette   64

Purpose of Assembling the Evidence   65

Functions of Research   65

Transforming Data into Evidence   65

LAYING THE FOUNDATION   65

ASSESSING THE NATURE AND EXTENT OF THE PROBLEM   66

ASSESSING THE PARTICULAR FEATURES OF AN IDENTIFIED POLICY SITUATION   67

ASSESSING PAST POLICIES   67

Using the Purpose of the Evidence to Determine What Is Needed   67

Evidence for Monitoring   68

Evidence for Prescription   68

Evidence for Evaluation   69

Evidence for Forecasting   70

Determining the Value of Specific Data   70

How Do You Make Good Use of Data?   71

BUILDING YOUR ARGUMENT   71

ASSESSING DATA CONTEXTS   71

How to Locate Relevant Sources   72

People and Documents are Key   72

COLLECTION STRATEGIES   72

DATA FROM PEOPLE WITHIN AND OUTSIDE YOUR ORGANIZATION   72

DATA FROM DOCUMENTS WITHIN AND OUTSIDE YOUR ORGANIZATION   73

How to Categorize Types of Data   73

Quantitative or Qualitative Debate   73

Chapter Summary   74

Review Questions   75

News Story for Analysis   75

Discussion Questions   76

Selected Websites   76

Selected References   77

Chapter 5   ESTABLISH YOUR DRIVING VALUES   79

Chapter Objectives   79

Education Vignette   79

What Do You Care About?   80

Establish Evaluative Criteria   80

Relationship Between Values and Criteria   80

What Does Success Look Like?   81

What Are the Specific Criteria That Frame Policy Decisions?   82

Does It Work?   82

HOW WILL YOU KNOW?   82

Is It Fair?   83

Horizontal Equity   84
Vertical Equity   84
Transitional Equity   86
Ability to Pay   86
Benefits Principle   87

Can We Afford It?   87

What Is the Role of Economics?   87
Opportunity Costs   88
Private Versus Public Benefits   88
Provision Versus Production   89
Counting the Costs   90
Costs versus Benefits   90
Decision Tools   91
How Can You Tell?   91
Using the Economic Tools   91
Cost-Benefit Analysis   92

Will People Support It?   92

How Acceptable Is the Alternative to Different Groups?   93

What Factors Influence the Political Acceptability of Policy?   93

How Can You Measure the Acceptability of a Policy?   93

How Can You Change the Acceptability of a Policy
Intervention?   94

Who Will Implement It?   94

Is There Sufficient Administrative Capacity?   94
What Are the Major Organizational Limitations?   94
How Can You Tell?   94

What If the Criteria Conflict?   96

Chapter Summary   96
Review Questions   97
News Story for Analysis   97
Discussion Questions   99
Selected Websites   99
Selected References   100

Chapter 6   DEVELOP ALTERNATIVES   101

Chapter Objectives   101

Education Vignette   101

What Are Alternatives?   102

Alternatives Are Not Outcomes   102

Alternatives Are Not Implementation Plans   102

Basic Alternatives and Their Variants   102

Developing Alternatives by Modeling the System   103

The Metaphor of the Market   103

The Production Metaphor   103

Evolutionary Models   104

Doing Nothing Different   104

How Do You Generate Alternatives?   **104**

Sources of Alternatives   105

GENERIC ALTERNATIVES   105

CUSTOMIZING POLICY INTERVENTIONS   106

Policy Types   **107**

Policy Mechanisms and Best-Practice Context   **107**

Inducements   108

Capacity-Building Policies   108

System Change Policies   109

Mandates   109

Hortatory Policies   109

Chapter Summary   *110*

Review Questions   *111*

News Story for Analysis   *111*

Discussion Questions   *113*

Selected Websites   *113*

Selected References   *114*

Chapter 7   WEIGH THE OPTIONS: EVALUATING ALTERNATIVES   115

Chapter Objectives   **115**

Education Vignette   **115**

How Do You Weigh Your Options?   **116**

Anticipating the Future   117

SAFEGUARDS IN FORECASTING   117

Discussing Relevant Criteria   117

MEASURING EFFECTIVENESS   118

MEASURING EQUITY   119

MEASURING COSTS   119

MEASURING POLITICAL FEASIBILITY   120

MEASURING THE ABILITY OF AN ALTERNATIVE TO BE IMPLEMENTED   120

Packaging Your Alternatives   121

Distinguishing Among Alternatives   121

Using Quick Quantitative Analysis   **122**

Creating a Scorecard   122

Evaluating Alternatives: The Single-Step, Norm-Based
Approach   123

Evaluating Alternatives: The Two-Step, Criterion-Based Approach   124

Chapter Summary   125
Review Questions   125
News Story for Analysis   126
Discussion Questions   126
Selected Websites   127
Selected References   127

Chapter 8   MAKE RECOMMENDATIONS   128

Chapter Objectives   128
Education Vignette   128
Transforming Trade-Offs into Preferred Results   128

Beyond Eeny, Meeny, Miny, Moe   129

Role of the Analyst   130

Transform Values into Results   130
Education Leader as Researcher, Bureaucrat, or Entrepreneur?   130
Policy Analyst as Adviser and Decision Maker   131

Need for Advocacy   131

Value-Laden Arguments   131
Ethically Complex Arguments   132
Is There One Best Way?   133

Refine Approaches to Recommendation   134

Testing the Credibility of Your Recommendation   134

Chapter Summary   135
Review Questions   136
News Story for Analysis   136
Discussion Questions   137
Selected Websites   138
Selected References   138

Chapter 9   PERSUADE YOUR AUDIENCE   140

Chapter Objectives   140
Education Vignette   140
The Art of Communication   141

How to Convey Your Analysis   141

Who Is Your Audience?   142
Expectations of Audience   142
Audience Knowledge and Understanding   142
Audience Response to the Solution   143

AUDIENCE FORUM   143
HOMOGENOUS OR DIVERSE   143
COMPLETE OR ABRIDGED ANALYSIS   143
TIME   144

Making the Policy Argument   144
AUTHORITY   144
METHOD   144
GENERALIZATION   144
CLASSIFICATION   146
CAUSE   146
SIGN   146
MOTIVATION   147
INTUITION   147
ANALOGY   147
PARALLEL CASE   147
ETHICS   147

Checklist for Communicating Analysis   148

Timeliness   148

Clarity of Findings   148

So What?   149
Chapter Summary   149
Review Questions   149
News Story for Analysis   150
Discussion Questions   151
Selected Websites   151
Selected References   151

Chapter 10   IMPLEMENT THE SOLUTION   153

Chapter Objectives   153

Education Vignette   153

Setting the Stage for Change   154

Why Won't It Work   154

Creating an Implementation Plan   154
OUTLINE THE PLAN   154
EXPAND THE OUTLINE   155
CHECK YOUR PLAN   157

Implementing Strategically   158

Major Implementation Challenges   158
HUMAN (PEOPLE-RELATED) PROBLEMS   158
PROCESS (PROGRAM-RELATED) PROBLEMS   159
STRUCTURAL (SETTING-RELATED) PROBLEMS   159
INSTITUTIONAL (PROGRAM-RELATED OR SETTING-RELATED)
    PROBLEMS   159

Stages in Implementation   160

Mobilization   160

Implementation Proper   160

Institutionalization   160

Chapter Summary   161

Review Questions   161

News Story for Analysis   161

Discussion Questions   163

Selected Websites   163

Selected References   163

Chapter 11   MONITOR OUTPUTS   165

Chapter Objectives   165

Education Vignette   165

What Is Monitoring?   166

Functions of Monitoring   166

Compliance   167

Accounting   167

Auditing   167

Explanation   168

What Should We Track?   168

Functions, Data, and Data Sources   168

Three Key Monitoring Questions   170

WHY SHOULD WE TRACK THESE DATA?   171

WHO SHOULD TRACK THE REQUIRED DATA?   171

HOW OFTEN SHOULD WE TRACK THESE DATA?   171

Methods of Tracking   172

Establishing Baselines   172

Determining What Change Is Being Measured   173

MEASUREMENT ACROSS SPACE AND TIME   173

UNITS OF ANALYSIS   173

DISPLAYING DATA   173

Chapter Summary   174

Review Questions   174

News Story for Analysis   174

Discussion Questions   175

Selected Websites   176

Selected References   176

Chapter 12   EVALUATE OUTCOMES   178

Chapter Objectives   178

Education Vignette   178

Evaluating Versus Monitoring   179

Focus of Evaluation   179

Types and Purposes of Evaluation   180

Formative Evaluations   180

Summative Evaluations   180

Users of Evaluation   181

Approaches to Evaluation   181

Methods of Evaluation   182

Components of an Evaluation Plan   182

Analytical Considerations   183

Common Methods of Assessment   184

RANDOMIZED CONTROL TRIALS   184

DIRECT CONTROLLED TRIALS   185

QUASI-EXPERIMENTS   185

MATCHING   185

BEFORE-AND-AFTER COMPARISONS   185

WITH-AND-WITHOUT COMPARISONS   186

NONEXPERIMENTAL DIRECT ANALYSIS   186

NONEXPERIMENTAL INDIRECT ANALYSIS   186

Political Considerations   186

Chapter Summary   187

Review Questions   188

News Story for Analysis   188

Discussion Questions   189

Selected Websites   190

Selected References   190

Chapter 13   CONCLUDING REMARKS   192

Chapter Objectives   192

Education Vignette   192

Remember Why We Do Policy Analysis   192

Policy Analysis and You   193

Policy Analysis and the Community   193

Policy Analysis and Change   194

Policy Analysis and Evaluation   194

The Steps in Policy Analysis Using an Existing Policy Example   194

Elementary and Secondary Education Act (ESEA)   194

DEFINE THE PROBLEM   195

MAKE THE CASE   195

ESTABLISH YOUR DRIVING VALUES   195

DEVELOP ALTERNATIVES   196

WEIGH THE OPTIONS   196

Make Recommendations   196
Persuade Your Audience   196
Implement the Solution   196
Monitor Outputs   196
Evaluate Outcomes   196
Chapter Summary   197
Review Questions   197
News Story for Analysis   197
Discussion Questions   199
Selected Websites   199
Selected References   200

PULLOUT FIELD GUIDE FOR EDUCATIONAL LEADERS: SUMMARY OF CHECKLIST OF EACH STEP OF THE POLICY ANALYTICAL PROCESS

References   201
Index   207

1

Laying the Groundwork

CHAPTER OBJECTIVES

After reading this chapter, you will be able to:

- Describe why policy analysis is important for education leaders
- List the basic principles of policy analysis
- Describe various types of policy analysis and recognize their application(s)
- Identify the key philosophies of education and their basic principles
- Give an example of how philosophy has shaped worldviews

EDUCATION VIGNETTE

You are the new U.S. secretary of education. You have received contrasting reports on the state of education in the United States. Some herald it as the most accessible system; others lament reduced opportunities for vulnerable student populations. Some point to the dominance of U.S. universities on the international stage; others complain about the low ranking of the United States in the report of Trends in International Mathematics and Science Study. *Some complain that the standards of education are too low; others worry about the repercussions of high-stakes testing. Some point to the high rate of return on investment if students participate in some postsecondary options; students of higher education complain that they are burdened with debt that they incurred attending postsecondary institutions. Some college and university presidents want to hold secondary schools more accountable for what high school graduates know. On the other hand, they worry that the federal government is expanding its oversight of colleges to include defining what a credit hour means. Some complain about too much federal involvement; others want more. Some business leaders decry the cost of training high school and college graduates entering the workforce. Others worry that schools are not educating citizens but training cogs in a machine.*

What do you think? Is there a problem in education? If you think there is a problem, what do you do?

WHY SHOULD LEADERS STUDY POLICY ANALYSIS?

Players on the Leadership Landscape

The leadership landscape is filled with complications. Leaders must voice ideas, convey dreams, create workable ideals, establish goals, solve problems, offer alternatives, and get others to agree. By definition, you are not much of a leader if no one is following. The complexities of leadership are particularly apparent in education policy, where leadership takes several forms, from the teacher in the classroom to the principal of a building, to the administrators of a school district, to the school board members to whom they answer (or not), to the policymakers at the state level or their peers in the federal government. Add to this list members of think tanks, community groups, students of higher education, funders of foundations, nongovernmental organizations, and parents, and one has a sense of how challenging it is for education leaders to persuade others to follow a recommended course.

What Policy Analysis Can Do

Different policies are often tried repeatedly because of their popularity rather than their effectiveness. One must also contend with policy revision, policy rejection, and policy cynicism on the part of key players needed to enact, support, and promote change. Broaden the perspective even further by including those stakeholders primarily interested in higher education, education for sustainable development, and international contexts, and one may wonder why education systems are not more chaotic. Even more surprising is the fact that certain leaders are able to forge agreements that lead to substantive transformation or improvement in the field. Think of the work of Geoffrey Canada, who created the Harlem Children Zone to end the cycle of generational poverty by addressing the needs of the entire community, not just the child in school. Reflect on the dream of Wendy Kopp, who created Teach for America based on her senior thesis at Princeton. She believed that a strong cadre of high-quality teachers would improve student achievement and that the teaching profession could attract top college graduates if it had the appropriate structure. Consider even more mundane changes. A principal of a small public elementary school in Minneapolis who persuaded parents to pick up their children in a location different from the one that they had been using for several years. The principal was concerned about the safety of the students with the increase in the number of parents picking up their children. The principal worried that the original pickup location had become too crowded. Being able to persuade others to embrace change and to do things differently is an important skill for leaders. You have a powerful tool when you are able to rebut the phrase, "That's how we have always done it" or "That's not how we do things around here."

The Role of Persuasion

Some may argue that there is not much need for persuasion in education settings because education organizations are hierarchical structures. They think that leaders of these institutions are able to rely on the authority of their position to get things done. However, while many organizations in the education setting have clear titular heads, the system itself is rather open. That is, each entity within the education arena is relatively independent: Teachers close their doors and teach; principals emphasize some directives and downplay others; district and state administrators target their own priorities; and so on. This openness is even more apparent in higher education, where there is a high degree of autonomy among faculty and staff members in those institutions. Buy-in among personnel is essential for meaningful change to occur. Trying to lead in global contexts also has its sets of challenges as leaders from multiple organizations and societies try to get their voices heard and their dreams realized. Despite the theoretical ability possessed by organizational and governmental leaders simply to tell people what to do, to get things done, leaders still have to persuade.

Persuasion is not just born of rhetoric but also of transparency and reflection. How many times have you made a decision that you have instantly regretted? These regrets are often accompanied by the phrase, "If only I had known," yet many times you did know. You knew the facts but may not have realized that those facts were relevant, or you did not do a good job persuading your constituents of the relevancy of those facts. This is not to say that the inclusion of relevant data will always lead to the most favored outcome. This text is not about making perfect decisions; it is about making thoughtful, informed ones. It is about following a process of decision making that allows you to persuade others and yourself about the appropriateness of your actions. Strong leaders are not only able to envision a better place, they are also able to persuade others of its existence, and through that persuasion, they transform their environment.

To transform your environment, you need to be a reflective, action-oriented leader. You must think about the needs of the organization or community that you lead, and you do what you must to allow your ideas for improvement or sustainability to become a reality. Consequently, your daily context requires you to be engulfed in policies, either reacting to them or creating them. After all, what is policy but a call to action? You will find that if people understand the rationale for your call and the basis for your decision, they are more likely to implement your ideas. This text provides a methodological scheme that allows you to develop a system of decision making that enables you to justify your actions, not just rationalize them. Justifying your actions is a function of leadership; policy analysis allows you to fulfill that function.

USERS OF POLICY ANALYSIS

Administrators, policymakers, and academics may be interested in different stages of the policy analysis process and may not find each aspect of the process equally relevant to their day-to-day lives or responsibilities. Practitioners, for instance, may not want to focus their efforts on the definition of the policy problem if they have to accept the problematic condition that they have already been given. They may argue that the formulators of policies do not seek their input in identifying what is wrong with the world and the reason that the problem exists. I would argue that even with a problem already defined, practitioners still have an important role to play in selecting among the multiple ways that the condition can be alleviated (e.g., Kingdon, 1995). For example, it matters that education leaders in Massachusetts have created different regulations in response to federal mandates than their peers in Alabama. A key part of pursuing the appropriate strategy is to have an understanding of what caused the problem in the first place.

If we look at the No Child Left Behind Act of 2001,[1] we may see that this is a policy in which federal policymakers have defined at least two problems: (1) Students are not all performing proficiently, and (2) different student groups present marked differences in their performance. According to the law, educators have the responsibility of addressing those ills and eliminating marked differences in the proficiencies of different student groups so that all students perform at proficient levels. What actions can and should education practitioners take to fulfill that responsibility? The response of administrators to this question is aligned to the action-oriented nature of the policy analysis process. For practitioners, this text may be particularly useful because it provides guidance in the systematic framing of strategies and assistance in making the case for the policy path chosen. This text also facilitates the communication of ideas and the delineation of tasks that are useful in the implementation and evaluation of policies.

Policymakers are also action-oriented in their focus on the policy process; however, the actions they seek or require must be rooted in how they see the problem and in their understanding of that problem. For policymakers, the most important aspect of the policy process may be in their definition and structuring of the problem and the flexibility that they give administrators to pursue solutions. The guidance provided in this book will be particularly useful for policymakers because it emphasizes and guides the appropriate structuring of policy problems. Appropriate problem structuring is essential in solving the right problem and in conducting effective policy evaluation (e.g., Dunn, 2004; Patton & Sawicki, 1993).

As education scholars, we may focus more on understanding policy analysis than on the development of appropriate actions. If we divorce theory from practice, however, we lose key elements of the phenomenon and its underlying construct. This limits our understanding and our ability to add to the knowledge in the field. While scholars may be more interested in resolving a knowledge gap, doing so requires an examination of the realities in which policy actions take place.

Whether you are in the school building, in the policy arena, or in academe, analyzing policy is fraught with challenges for a variety of reasons. For instance, problems are often not well defined (e.g., Heck, 2004; Dunn, 2004). Even if they are well defined, we may not come up with a perfect solution for resolving them. And even if we have a perfect solution in theory, in practice, we may face many high hurdles putting the solution in place. That is, defining the problem well does not necessarily mean implementing its solution appropriately. We do not have absolute standards to consider when we decide which conditions are problematic and which are not. There is often no dominant solution, even if we are in agreement about what the problem

---

[1]The title of this act is misleading because President George W. Bush signed it into law in January 2002. However, the act itself indicates that its short title should be the No Child Left Behind Act of 2001 (see P.L. 107–110—Jan. 8, 2002 115 Stat. 1425). Given its official title, that is the way I chose to describe it in the text, with the acknowledgment that it was not actually signed until the subsequent year.

is. All we have are guidelines that provide our constituents—as well as ourselves—with a roadmap to the decisions that we have made and the reasons that we chose the paths that we did.

WHY USE THIS TEXT?

This text has an educational and practical focus geared toward the actual policy analytical method rather than the policy-making process. Its practical applications are grounded in a strong theoretical framework that is readable and readily applicable for education practitioners and policy leaders. It includes guidelines for analysis that are especially geared toward practicing or aspiring education administrators; thus, it incorporates more of an explanation of the underlying economic focus than traditional policy analytical texts. This text is a practical guide to policy analysis; it includes strong education content and step-by-step guidance, from problem definition to implementation and evaluation. This text is methodological in focus and educational in context. Its reliance on a step-by-step method to policy analysis, accompanied by education vignettes, makes this text unique to the field of policy studies. Now that you have a sense of why you should study policy analysis and why this text is helpful in that endeavor, let us cover some basic points.

WHAT IS POLICY ANALYSIS?

A Brief Definition

Policy analysis is a method of inquiry, a process by which we try to make the world a better place. It is a journey that begins with identifying something wrong with our surroundings, and it ends with a resolution or alleviation of that problematic condition. Policy analysis is analogous to the change process described in Duke (2004), which involves both an understanding and achievement of educational change. The step-by-step approach to policy analysis offered in this text calls for both action and reflection, and it can serve as a useful guide for education leaders at all levels of the policymaking process—teachers, principals, policymakers, researchers, and evaluators—as well as scholars in the field. While the guide offered here is linear and described in steps, it is important to recognize that the process is organic and is often iterative in reality (Bardach, 2009; Duke, 2004).

Why Policy Analysis?

Problems exist if your ideal differs from the reality you face. Thus, problems arise when a specific set of circumstances does not meet your desires or expectations, or if it conflicts with your values. Because people's ideals differ, the same set of facts may present itself as different problems to different people. However, not all problematic conditions rise to the level of policy problems. The fact that I am not an independently wealthy person may be problematic for me, but this fact does not warrant the consideration of the collective. That is, not all negative conditions are worthy of being addressed by leaders. Thus, the good news is that you need not trouble yourself to create utopia, where everything is perfect. Focus your efforts on solvable conditions that have substantive consequences for the community that you lead.

Policy problems are not static and may change over time, across places, and among different policymakers. Heck (2004) notes that "policy problems by nature are public, consequential, complex, dominated by uncertainty, and affected by disagreement about the goals to be pursued" (p. 8). Policy analysis is the process by which one can bridge the divide between what is and what should be. Scholars agree that policy analysis is about making a choice among alternatives; however, what one considers a preferred option is a subjective decision. Where there is subjectivity, there is a role for politics to determine whose values rule. While I recognize that policy analysis is not a neutral endeavor, there are right and wrong ways to approaching analysis. Consequently, the purpose of this text is not to give you the right answers to policy problems but to put you on the right path for addressing them.

As education leaders, we constantly face situations that are less than ideal. For example, if you were the president of a college, you may wonder if your status according to *U.S. News and World Report* is good enough. You may consider the graduation rates of students as being too low. You may wonder about the richness of the course offerings. You may worry about your label as a "party school." You may hear a lot of complaints about parking. You may even lament the climate in which your institution finds itself. Some conditions you cannot change and some conditions are not worth changing even if you could. Consequently, a key component of policy analysis is distinguishing among a condition, a policy problem and a policy issue. Determining what conditions are worthy of being defined as problems, and what problems are worthy policy issues depend on the values that you bring to the fore. **Conditions** simply describe the world around you. **Policy problems** are those conditions that you do not like and you think can be changed, should be changed, and should be changed using the resources of the collective. **Policy issues** are policy problems for which there is disagreement on the appropriate solution. This distinction is an important underpinning of the process and underlies the discussion throughout the text.

The Goal of Policy Analysis

The goal of policy analytical research is to provide an analysis of fundamental social problems and to offer practical alternatives for solving them. Policy analysis arms leaders and other policymakers with facts in order to make rational decisions on the best way to alleviate a policy issue. That is, policy analysis supplies practical, actionable information. The process is descriptive with prescriptive results. It presumes certain relationships, is creative in its identification of problems and alternatives, and is grounded in plausible beliefs (Dunn, 2004). The purpose of this discussion is to set the stage for understanding the process of policy analysis by providing an overview of the process.

TYPES OF POLICY ANALYSIS

Several schools of thought exist in the field of policy, and we often group policy research based on the different perspectives that dominate the analytical process. These perspectives focus on the timing of the analysis, the purpose of the analysis, the disciplinary perspective underlying the analysis, and the transparency of the analysis.

Ex Post and Ex Ante Analysis

This grouping of policy research is based on whether we conduct analysis with the assumption that the chosen policy has already been or has not yet been implemented (Odden & Picus, 2009; Patton & Sawicki, 1993). If the policy has already been undertaken, we refer to these studies as **ex post analysis**. Ex post studies presume that the major tasks that lie ahead are the monitoring and evaluation of the outcomes of previously made decisions. Work done by analysts in the federal Government Accountability Office (GAO) typifies this category. Another example is the feedback offered by principals on the progress made by teachers in their schools. However, education leaders need to lead, and consequently they also need to be proactive rather than simply react to policies already in place. Consequently, many education leaders will find it useful to conduct ex ante analysis.

Ex ante analysis takes place before the actual implementation of policy. By relying on ex ante analysis, we can examine how a possible solution would work in theory and can anticipate and address potential challenges to successful resolution of the policy issue. Ex ante analysis allows one the freedom to explore all stages of the policy analysis process and the potential to think beyond the solutions that have already been tried. However, it is not enough simply to dream. While I encourage students to think creatively, they must be clear how their recommendations will address some of the constraints that exist and not simply wish them away (e.g., Bardach, 2009).

Forecasting, Prescribing, Monitoring, Evaluating

We may also group policy analytical research by the primary aim of the analysis. Dunn (2004) and Heck (2004) argue, for example, that the policy analysis process consists of four key actions: forecasting, prescribing, monitoring, and evaluating.

Forecasting allows policy scholars to make assertions about the future, either by making projections based on data, predictions based on theory, or conjectures based on intuition. Economists tend to use the first two methods, while storytellers and futurists tend to rely on the last one. Because ex ante analysis is, by its very nature, future-oriented, there needs to be clear and dependable ways of coming to a conclusion of likely outcomes of particular actions. Without being able to talk about the future in a meaningful way, we abdicate one of our major responsibilities as education leaders.

Prescribing or recommending policy must be grounded in our expectations of the future. In policy analysis, we assume that we will prescribe adoption and implementation of the policies that balance everyone's concerns the best and recommend rejection of those policies that do not.

In policy analytical research, **monitoring** requires the collection of data that will allow evaluation of whether the chosen strategy led to alleviation or resolution of the problem defined. Monitoring is essentially a descriptive process that deals with what is. For example, did scores go up, did they go down, or did they stay the same? Do gaps in performance exist between or among different student groups? While what one chooses to monitor is tied to the policy issue and in this way is grounded in values, the monitoring process itself is empirical, not normative. That is, monitoring allows for factual assertions based on data (**empirical**) and is not designed to be the last word on a program's success or lack thereof (**normative**).

Evaluating goes beyond monitoring. While monitoring provides information on what exists, evaluation requires considered assessment about whether the outcomes are good or bad. Much of policy analytical research has been in the field of evaluation where analysts have passed judgment on the outcomes of particular policies. These judgments are largely based (or should be) on the relationship between the actual and intended effects of a particular policy or program. These results can then inform assertions regarding the future, and the cycle of policy analysis is started once again (Dunn, 2004).

These policy analytical actions coincide with key aspects of theorizing, which are to describe, explain, predict, and prescribe. Description entails the documentation of facts and context. Explanation highlights connections between and among key variables and identifies patterns that may exist. These explanations and patterns can inform what we expect to happen in the future (allowing predictions). Based on these predictions, we can formulate prescriptions: We can prescribe certain actions if we want to obtain certain outcomes. Thus, the study of policy analysis offers a sound bridge on which to make the journey from theory to practice, and then back again.

Rational Lens, Structural Lens, and Cultural Lens

Another way in which to categorize research in the field is the disciplinary perspective on which we rely to define policy issues. Heck (2004) notes that there are three major lenses: the rational, the structural, and the cultural. The **rational lens** emphasizes the importance of the internal motivations of individuals in the establishment and pursuit of policy goals. The **structural lens** places an emphasis on structures and systems. It explicitly recognizes the potential impact of institutions on the actions of individuals and the policy outcomes produced. The **cultural lens** emphasizes relationships. Culturalists acknowledge the context of policies and the importance of environment, relationships, time, and values in creating that context (Heck, 2004).

These three perspectives certainly overlap, but the crux of the problem would be viewed differently from each one, and thus the solutions offered by proponents of each perspective may also differ. For example, education leaders may agree that an important policy issue is that "too many students in higher education do not earn a bachelor's degree in 4 years." From a rational perspective, the reason for that problem may be that insufficient incentives exist for students to finish on time (e.g., Hanushek, Heckman, & Neal, 2002). From a structural perspective, the root of the problem might be insufficient organizational structures that would allow students to finish within 4 years because classes are filled, and so on (e.g., Alexander, 2004). A cultural perspective might claim that insufficient relationships and bonds are formed between students and the broader university community (e.g., Tinto, 1997).

Transparency Versus Objectivity

The definition of policy issues and resulting alternatives offered are grounded in values, so it is important to note from the outset that the policy analysis process is not objective. This does not mean that it should not be grounded in data and logical arguments. It is the subjectivity of the policy analytical process that makes it all the more important to ground assertions and to make clear for the readers the choices being made and why.

In the past, researchers sought in vain to make the policy analysis process more objective. However, the importance of underlying values in both the definition of the problem and the solutions sought means that policy scholars have increasingly rejected the characterization of policy analysis as objective or that it should be (e.g., Dunn, 2004; Heck, 2004). Instead, the subjectivity in conducting policy analysis should be emphasized. The key is not to be objective but to be **transparent**, which means making the assumptions and the values underlying your decision explicit. Thus, an important benefit of the process is a clear rationale for conclusions: from the definition of the problem to the alternatives recommended to resolve it, to the strategy chosen to put the solution in place, to conclusions regarding whether the policy worked. In policy analysis, we need to be clear about the relationships we are assuming. Our assumptions regarding presumed relationships explain who, what, when, where, why, how, and with what consequences an event occurs and how likely we are to recommend and accept particular solutions. In discussing policy-relevant information for research, Dunn (2004) raises five important questions: (1) What is the nature of the problem? (2) What present and past policies have been established to address the problem? (3) How valuable are these outcomes in solving the problem? (4) What policy alternatives are available to address the problem and what are their likely future outcomes? and (5) What alternatives should be acted upon to solve the problem? Policymakers and other leaders grapple with the answers to these questions. Their responses reflect their values, the subject of the next section.

PHILOSOPHIES OF EDUCATION

Leaders do not define problems or propose solutions blindly or in a vacuum. Whether they do it consciously or not, they bring with them a host of experiences and expertise that shape their view of the world. Their assumptions are grounded in beliefs regarding the nature of reality. When U.S. federal policymakers enacted the No Child Left Behind Act of 2001, their explicit assumption was that all children can perform at specified levels and if they do not, it is the fault of key professionals in the system. When federal administrators recommend increased oversight of vocational, nondegree, career-training programs, the assumption is that students and the federal government are bearing too much of the risks of funding these postsecondary programs. On a global level, when leaders of the World Bank invest in education, it is based on their assumption that education is an important tool for ending global poverty.

This section orients readers to the policy analysis process by focusing explicitly on values. The rest of this discussion describes various philosophies of education, ethical foundations, and accompanying worldviews. Part of this discussion entails an examination of intrinsic and extrinsic values in order to stimulate your thinking on the important role that values play in your analysis of public policy. That is, values and philosophy influence one's definition of problems, recommendations of actions, implementation of policy, and the evaluation of that policy.

Values: Cornerstone of Worldviews and Philosophies

According to Ellis (1998), no policy can be justified without both a value belief and a factual belief on how the value in question can be achieved effectively. He further asserts that we can categorize our values as being intrinsic or extrinsic. With **intrinsic values**, we want a particular outcome for its own sake. With **extrinsic values**, we want a particular outcome for what we think that it can get us. As you read through these definitions, think about what that may mean for us as individuals and as leaders in the education arena. For example, do we value diversity because we think that diversity in schools is good in and of itself, or do we value diversity because we think that it can improve our standing in an increasingly globalized world? If we choose the first response, diversity is an intrinsically held value; if we choose the latter response, we think of diversity as an extrinsic value. Our answer to this and other value-laden questions reflect our worldview and how we organize our intrinsic versus extrinsic values.

Brief Overview of Worldviews

Ellis (1998) lists six basic types of value systems or worldviews. They are egoistic hedonism, utilitarianism, distributive justice, retributive justice, personalism, and ethical relativism. For leaders, what is important to note is the different priorities and intrinsic values dominating each view. This discussion helps us to reflect on our own choices and to clarify what people would be willing to give up if values come into conflict with each other, as they often do in complex arenas such as schools.

The brief discussion of the worldviews that I provide here does not do justice to the thorough treatise provided by Ellis (1998) in his full-length text. For our purposes, however, what is important is an understanding of the choices proponents of various worldviews are likely to make if they have to choose among a variety of options for resolving a problem. It is especially important to be aware of these choices because policy analysis becomes relevant only when a choice is required among policy alternatives.

For those subscribing to the view of **egoistic hedonism**, the priority is the policy that increases the well-being of the individual making the decision. As leaders of an organization, you may seek out those policies that advance your career, augment your power, or enhance your prestige. In **utilitarianism**, the priority is the policy that leads to the greatest good for the greatest number of individuals in the community considered. Utilitarian leaders favor policies that maximize scores, optimize overall achievement, and lead to high averages. For the supporter of **distributive justice**, the priority should be to increase the well-being of those who receive the least benefit from the present system. Leaders oriented toward distributive justice favor programs that benefit the most vulnerable members of the community. They prefer policies that enhance opportunities for those at the lowest end of the performance spectrum, mitigate the challenges of poverty, and focus on the needs of those most at risk of failing. The proponent of **retributive justice** favors policies that strengthen or establish connections between action and consequence. Leaders guided by retributive justice favor policies that are incentives-based, tie effort to outcomes, and tie merit to reward. Leaders advocating **personalism** favor policies that target the self-actualization of individuals and the enlightenment of society. Leaders who advocate **ethical relativism** reject the belief that one guiding principle works universally well or that one priority should be privileged over another.

Eight Common Values

According to Fowler (2009), many of us share the same values; what often distinguishes us is how we prioritize these values. She suggests eight key values that we all care about; we just care about them differently, which leads to different worldviews and philosophical orientations.

The first of these values is **individualism**, which reflects a value for the individual human being and can be expressed in terms of an individual reaching his or her own personal pinnacle (self-actualizing) or in the individual economic freedoms that are allowed. Leaders oriented toward egoistic hedonism, personalism, and utilitarianism would have this value high on their list of priorities. The second value is **order**, in which there is recognition that society needs rules to function and to balance the different needs of the people within it. Leaders often value order for the stability it provides so that they can pursue other goals. For instance, the establishment of zero-tolerance policies was to ensure the safety of students. Research studies showed that children learn better when they are not in a chaotic atmosphere or living in fear. The increased use of school climate on school report cards demonstrates the increasing attention that society is giving to the connection between order and the learning environment.

The next three values, **liberty**, **fraternity**, and **equality**, are taken from the French Revolution, where the freedom, brotherhood, and equality of the members of the community were prized. Fowler categorizes these three values as democratic values and says that fraternity is different from equality in that there is a sense of a brotherhood rather than equality for the community at large. She defines freedom in its literal sense as having no restriction on action. She equates equality with equity, where it refers primarily to members of society having equality of opportunity. For example, proponents of distributive justice would likely prioritize fraternity and equality as top values to pursue.

The next three values, economic growth, efficiency, and quality, are grouped together under economic values, where the growth of the economy, efficiencies, and high-quality outcomes are favored. Prioritizing **economic growth** suggests that leaders will favor policies that lead to an overall increase in gross domestic product, an increase in personal income, low rates of unemployment and inflation, and other indicators of a strong economy. **Efficiency** refers to absence of waste; leaders would propose policies that give the most bang for a buck, even if that may result in unequal distributions of wealth or other desired resources. **Quality** is a nebulous term. Fowler explicitly ties it to economic values, but it could be construed to have a broader meaning. For example, federal policymakers use this term repeatedly by requiring that there be a "high-quality" teacher in every classroom.

How you prioritize these and other values provides a useful roadmap to the possible solutions you feel are available to solve the problems identified. The key philosophies undergirding education policy may include all of the above values, albeit in different order of significance.

Table 1.1 Values Orientation Self-Assessment Worksheet

Below are six columns characterizing values. Choose the values that best describe your orientation. Working across each row, rate the degree to which you identify with each of the six statements by giving it a score from 0 to 10 (0 meaning you do not identify at all with this statement, and 10 meaning you identify completely with this statement). The scores across the row must add up to 10 (for example, 10, 0, 0, 0, 0, 0; or 1, 1, 1, 1, 1, 5; or 2, 2, 1, 1, 2 ,2). In other words, the numbers across the row can be any combination of six numbers that add up to 10.

I prefer policies that make life better for me.	I prefer policies that lead to the betterment of the whole.	I prefer policies that help those who are served the least by society.	I prefer policies that link action and consequences.	I prefer policies that promote self-actualization.	I prefer policies that are contextually bound.
It is important for policies to augment my power in the organization.	It is important for policies to optimize the overall effectiveness of the group.	It is important for policies to enhance opportunities for the most vulnerable.	It is important for policies to link rewards to meritorious actions.	It is important for policies to enhance the enlightenment of the community.	It is important for policies to be based on individual environments.
I really care that my actions advance my career.	I really care that my actions focus on the greatest good.	I really care that my actions help those most in need of help.	I really care that my actions punish bad behavior.	I really care that my actions lead individuals to greater personal reflection	I really care that my actions respect the different values of others.
Society is better off when it values individual interests.	Society is better off when it values the good of the whole.	Society is better off when it values those who are the least powerful.	Society is better off when it values talent.	Society is better off when it values enlightenment.	Society is better off when it values differences.

It is important for me to enhance my prestige.	It is important for me to improve the overall standing of the group.	It is important for me to improve the status of the disadvantaged.	It is important to me that genius is rewarded.	It is important to me that everyone reaches his or her potential.	It is important to me that everyone has a say.
▮	▮	▮	▮	▮	▮
Schools should promote individualized programs.	Schools should promote high performance standards.	Schools should promote support services for those who need them.	Schools should promote tracking and classrooms based on skills.	Schools should promote a program of philosophy.	Schools should promote a program in the humanities.
▮	▮	▮	▮	▮	▮
Others are helped if I help myself.	The greatest good for the greatest number is the way to go.	I am helped if I help others.	One good turn deserves another is a good credo.	It is better to be an unhappy human being than a happy pig.	Live and let live should be how we live our lives.
▮	▮	▮	▮	▮	▮
Total column 1	**Total column 2**	**Total column 3**	**Total column 4**	**Total column 5**	**Total column 6**
▮	▮	▮	▮	▮	▮

After you have rated each of the six items across all seven rows, total the numbers for each column.

Interpretation:

If your highest column total is in column 1, then your values orientation is **egoistic hedonism.**

If your highest column total is in column 2, then your values orientation is **utilitarianism.**

If your highest column total is in column 3, then your values orientation is **distributive justice.**

If your highest column total is in column 4, then your values orientation is **retributive justice.**

If your highest column total is in column 5, then your values orientation is **personalism.**

If your highest column total is in column 6, then your values orientation is **ethical relativism.**

Defining Philosophy

A common view of philosophy is that it is a pursuit for people in berets sipping coffee and contemplating the state of the world; in other words, it is an activity for thinkers, not doers. *Merriam-Webster's Collegiate Dictionary*, 11th Edition, defines philosophy as "2 . . . **b:** a search for a general understanding of values and reality by chiefly speculative rather than observational means **c:** an analysis of the grounds of and concepts expressing fundamental beliefs." Both these definitions may give you the misguided belief that an understanding of philosophy is the purview of those who simply want to think, that it is not something for action-oriented individuals, perhaps like yourself. You may even think that as a leader (practicing or aspiring), you do not have the luxury of such reflection. However, reflection is crucial to sound leadership. Whether you are leading communities, classrooms, schools, districts, states, or the nation, the grounding of your philosophy influences the conditions that you identify as problematic and the solutions that you find palatable.

You cannot be all things to all people. Similarly, schools cannot be all things to all people (Frase & Streshly, 2000; Spring, 2005). Choices are made, priorities are set, and your prioritizing of values gives important clues to your philosophy of education. The history of education in the United States provides an interesting backdrop to the panoply of values that leaders emphasized over time. Policymakers have used schools to achieve a variety of goals—to build leaders, to address poverty, to challenge the status quo, to preserve the status quo, to build self esteem, to sort children, to stimulate the economy, to develop a skilled workforce, to promote an informed citizenry, and so on. However, resources are scarce and policymakers eventually must choose the focus of education through the programs they are willing to fund. With the tightening of resources, the influence of philosophy and values becomes even more pertinent.

The discussion in this chapter may seem like one of those quizzes found in popular magazines. It presents the ideal of each category. If you find yourself drawn primarily to the tenets of any one philosophy, this affinity shows that you have a strong tendency to align yourself with that particular group. Note, however, that the labels themselves are not particularly important but are useful terms that summarize certain priorities and understandings so that you are aware of the grounding of your position. You may find traces of yourself in multiple descriptions. The purpose of this discussion is not to pigeonhole you or have you worry that you don't fit any one category. Rather, I want you to question the assumptions that you make and to strengthen your willingness and ability to engage others in useful discourse on how society may be improved.

Key Philosophies and Their Role in Education Policy[2]

IDEALISM. Do you think that there is a universal truth unbound by contextual restrictions? If you do, you might be an idealist. You are more likely to believe that schools and education are about ideas and that they are separate from the broader

---

[2]Much of this discussion is based on Sadovnik, Cookson, and Semel (2001) and Noll (2009).

community. You believe eternal ideas are the bases of knowledge and that absolute ideals and universal standards should prevail. You reject the notion that truth is to be found in the world of matter or that schools should have a social agenda beyond the transmission of academic knowledge. Rather, you advocate an abstract process of discovering truth. In your mind, education should maximize abstract and higher-order thinking.

If you are an idealist, you are less likely to promote actions that draw on social agendas beyond the transmission of academic knowledge. You define your purpose as ensuring that children can read and know the classics. You place little priority on changing the neighborhood or family from which the children come. Your leadership is marked by advocacy of education institutions that maximize abstract and higher-order thinking. You probably have a poster of Plato hanging on your dorm wall or a book of his quotes on your bookshelf.

Given this philosophy, you may consider that a problem with schools is their lack of a universal approach to knowledge. For example, Hutchins (1953, cited in Noll, 2009) asserts that the problem with schools stems from "the triviality of that [education] produced by the doctrines of adaptation, of immediate needs, of social reform, or of the doctrine of no doctrine at all" (p. 13). If you are a disciple of this philosophy, you are likely to base solutions to the problem of schooling on greater reliance on a traditional curriculum. This is a common theme of proponents of "back to basics" and is reflected in the U.S. No Child Left Behind (NCLB) Act. Aspects of NCLB epitomize an idealistic education philosophy because of its assumption about the existence of universal knowledge that can be systematically measured through the use of standardized tests. The goal of 100 percent student proficiency also suggests that there is a belief that knowledge is abstract, universal, and obtainable by all. The rise of curriculum standards and the expansion of high-stakes standardized tests across the United States are partially grounded in the reemergence of leaders ascribing to this philosophy. Kentucky provides another example of idealism underlying education policy. In that state, each high school must offer a core curriculum of advanced placement, International Baccalaureate, dual enrollment, or dual credit courses.

REALISM. If you believe in universal truth but are drawn to a systematic theory of logic in which the world of matter is very important, you are probably a realist. You base much of your assumptions of reality and human nature in the findings of nature and the natural world. Your assumptions regarding knowledge are based on the fixed laws of nature, and thus scientific investigation is an important cornerstone for providing effective education to students. You lead with the understanding that individuals should be able to use education to enhance their reasoning and to choose a path of moderation.

Do you start your quest for truth with a logical mapping of the world and then test that understanding in reality? Is Aristotle your hero? If so, you are showing all the signs of a realist. You may also find yourself trying to balance the world of faith with the world of reason. Unlike idealists, you do not promote ideas for ideas' sake, but in order to have a better understanding of the world and thus to improve it. You support curricula that are steeped in practical and applied courses like the sciences and languages. While you would agree that schools are to develop the intellect of individuals for the good of society, you do not think that communities are an extension of schools, or vice versa. Like idealists, you advocate policies that maintain a wall between the community and schools, and schools should be touted as places of learning. You are convinced that education is a matter of science and rigor, not building esteem and holistic development. This philosophy is consistent with the emphasis on scientific-based research permeating many recent federal education policies, such as the requirement that quantitative analysis and traditional, experimentally designed research be used to assess the success of federal programs. It is also reflected in the increased emphasis on math and science courses in both state and federal legislation. For example, in 2006, policymakers in Utah recently increased the number of science classes needed for graduation from high school. In addition, this policy outlines core curriculum requirements for K–12; it increases the state minimum required units of credit for high school graduation in language arts from 3 to 4, and in mathematics and science from 2 to 3, effective for students graduating in the 2010–2011 school year.

PRAGMATISM. Do you think that education is more about the learning process than it is about the learning outcome? If you answered yes, you might be a pragmatist. You are not fond of the widespread use of high-stakes, standardized tests. Instead, you are more interested in the application of contemporary issues in student learning and rely on inductive approaches, where one goes from the specific to the general. In this philosophy, a problem sparks speculative thought, which leads to action of some sort, which in turn ultimately yields results. You live by the belief that schools are intricately tied to student experiences and their broader community. You are a fan of John Dewey, and you think he helped move education light years ahead. You are a firm supporter of lab schools, and you advocate tying research, pedagogy, and individual experience to the process of learning. You are convinced that environment and experience are essential to the learning process (e.g., project learning). In your mind, the problem with schools is their reliance on static rather than on dynamic and developing knowledge. You favor a working relationship between school and society and might consider that the key to schooling is developing knowledge by doing.

You view children as organic beings whose course of study should reflect their particular stage of development. You assert that ideas are not separate from social condition and that schools should function as preparation for life in a democratic society. Consequently, you believe that a prime purpose of education is to socialize diverse groups into a cohesive democratic community, and that the role of school is to integrate children into a democratic society, where cooperation and community are desired ends. With that understanding, you lead schools with the belief that they can be agents of social reform. In your mind, the problem with education is that it relies too heavily on lockstep, rote memorization rather than on an individualized, problem-solving approach to learning. With the push for easily measured accountability, widespread school programs grounded in this philosophy have fallen out of political favor on the state and national stage. A key exception is the Harlem Children Zone led by Geoffrey Canada. This program takes a holistic approach to child development and learning. Other policy examples include the use of service learning projects. For example, a Minnesota law signed in May 2009 established requirements that schools must meet to receive revenue for students enrolled in a public school in a project-based program. The bill defines a project-based instructional program as primarily student-led coursework for credit that may be completed on site, in the community, or online and that is available to all or only some students and grades in a school.

PHENOMENOLOGY AND EXISTENTIALISM. Do you believe that knowledge is individually centered? If your answer is yes, you might be a phenomenologist or an existentialist. If your focus is on individual consciousness, perception, and meaning as they arise in a particular individual's experience, then you are more closely associated with phenomenologists. If you are more concerned with the impact of knowledge on the lives of individuals, then you are oriented toward existentialism. Your leadership is grounded in the view that the purpose of education is to stress individuality by discussing the nonrational as well as the rational world. You believe that education problems arise in schools when teachers do not pose questions, generate activities, and work together with students. You support a curriculum that is based on the humanities. You worry that, with federal education policy requiring testing in math and science, there is less emphasis on courses that are not tested. Tightening budgets have led many school leaders to cut music and art from the regular curriculum. Your views regarding the importance of the individual in the construction of his or her own knowledge do not dominate the current national discourse on education policy. For example, in Minnesota, policymakers enacted the Profile of Learning in 1998 as part of the state's high school graduation standards. It included state-suggested curriculum packages, a state-mandated methodology for the classroom, and an emphasis on hands-on and group projects. Though it seemed quite prescriptive in tone, it sought to promote a constructivist view on learning. Opponents viewed this policy as an attack on academic rigor, and Minnesota policymakers eventually repealed the law in 2003.

CONFLICT THEORY. Do you think that the role of education is to give students insight on how to demystify dominant ideology and to help them become agents of radical educational and social change? If you answered yes, you might be a conflict theorist or radical progressive. If your definition of education problems is grounded in your belief that class struggles are an important undercurrent in most education problems, you may feel an affiliation to this group of scholars. Your leadership promotes supporting professional development that encourages teachers to be transformative intellectuals who can understand the innate bias of the curriculum and existing educational structure. This is typically marked by workshops centered on conversations about race and class, and the role of racism in student outcomes. With the rise of political groups on the right, recent challenges to the curriculum have been that it is not sufficiently open to religious (read "Christian") values (e.g., Spring, 2005). Groups and individuals with a variety of political views have tried to use policy to transform the system and to change the educational status quo. An example of recent policy intended to facilitate educators changing the

Table 1.2 Education Philosophy Self-Assessment Worksheet

Below are six columns describing philosophical characteristics. Choose the values that best describe your beliefs. Working across each row, rate the degree to which you identify with each of the six statements by giving it a score from 0 to 10 (0 meaning you do not identify at all with this statement, and 10 meaning you identify completely with this statement). The scores across the row must add up to 10 (for example, 10, 0, 0, 0, 0, 0; or 1, 1, 1, 1, 1, 5; or 2, 2, 1, 1, 2, 2). In other words, the numbers across the row can be any combination of six numbers that add up to 10.

I think that truth is universal and unchanging.	I think that truth can be found in the logic of the world.	I think that truth is dynamic and is better understood if it is tied to your everyday experiences.	I think that truth is in the eye of the beholder.	I think that truth is dominated by the elite.	I think that truth is what one makes of it.
Education is about abstract ideas, not about fixing the community.	Education is about discovering what is real from the laws of nature.	Education is more about the learning process, not the learning outcome.	Education is about focusing on individual consciousness and meaning.	Education is about making students aware of oppressive forces.	Education is about creating critical thinkers.
Schools should set high standards for its students.	Schools should enhance the reasoning skills of students.	Schools should rely on inductive approaches to enhance learning.	Schools should focus on individuality.	Schools should focus on social change.	Schools should focus on connecting theory and practice.
Students would be better educated if they were taught core knowledge.	Students would be better educated if they were grounded in scientific investigation.	Students would be better educated if schools connected knowledge to their reality.	Students would be better educated if they made meaning of the nonrational as well as the rational world.	Students would be better educated if the inherent biases in education systems were removed or challenged.	Students would be better educated if schools focused more on the creation of a democratic education.
Knowledge is found in the ideals that we set, not in the world of matter.	Knowledge should promote a better understanding of the world.	Knowledge is best developed by students doing.	Knowledge occurs only when students are allowed to construct their own knowledge of the world.	Knowledge should be about the creation of transformative intellectuals.	Knowledge should be about building a more democratic society.

Schools should promote higher-order thinking.	Schools should promote practical and applied courses.	Schools should tie together research, pedagogy, and individual experiences.	Schools should promote the humanities.	Schools should enhance the ability of students to be critical consumers of existing school structures.	Schools should promote policies that make them more welcoming for all families.
Schools should be in the business of educating children, not reforming the ills of society.	Schools should be a place for science and learning, not building self-esteem.	Schools should actively build a working relationship with the broader community.	Schools should promote pedagogy where teachers pose questions, generate activities, and work together with students.	Schools should be in the business of transforming society.	Schools should be in the business of supporting democracy.
Total column 1	**Total column 2**	**Total column 3**	**Total column 4**	**Total column 5**	**Total column 6**

After you have rated each of the six items across all seven rows, total the numbers for each column.

Interpretation:

If your highest column total is in column 1, then your values orientation is **idealism.**

If your highest column total is in column 2, then your values orientation is **realism.**

If your highest column total is in column 3, then your values orientation is **pragmatism.**

If your highest column total is in column 4, then your values orientation is **phenomenology/existentialism.**

If your highest column total is in column 5, then your values orientation is in **conflict theory.**

If your highest column total is in column 6, then your values orientation is in **critical theory.**

nature of relationships within the existing school structure is North Dakota Law HB 1566, adopted in August 2009. This act requires that the commissioner of higher education in that state study the interplay between the state university system and tribally controlled community colleges. Specifically, it requires the commissioner to address ways in which the North Dakota university system as a whole and the individual campuses can better interact with tribally controlled community colleges through improved communication, collaboration, and relationship-building activities. In addition, the commissioner is called on to focus on ways in which tribally controlled community colleges can encourage American Indians to pursue options in higher education. The policy hopes to bring economic benefit to American Indian families and communities and to develop ways in which the university system and the individual campuses can work with tribally controlled community colleges.

POSTMODERNISM AND CRITICAL THEORY. Do you think that schools should emphasize reason and stress principles of equality, liberty, and justice? A yes answer means that you might be a postmodernist or critical theorist. Your leadership is grounded in the belief that the role of education is to promote localized and particular theories rather than to espouse the values of a universal truth. You think that the solution to the problems of society rest in the connection between theory and practice. This connection can act as a corrective to the separation of ideas and practical applications in much modernist deliberations. You likely think that the key education policy problem is the absence of the development of democratic education. You argue that schools are a strong transmitter of culture, and teachers are either agents of the status quo or agents of change. By and large, in the United States, the political culture of the local communities dictates which form an educator's transmission of culture is allowed to take (e.g., Fowler, 2009; Spring, 2005). **Political culture** refers to the broad set of actions that are considered acceptable by a community. Leaders who are oriented toward this philosophy often require policies that make schools more welcoming for families not currently well served by the system. For example, part of Kentucky law 704 KAR 3:390, which was adopted in February 2009, requires districts to solicit input from parents and the community and to identify potential barriers to participation. The law also requires that the barriers identified are addressed through engagement with community partners or off-campus locations of after-school, weekend, or evening services.

It is not always easy to predict which conditions will be defined as policy issues or which policies will be enacted based on conventional wisdom regarding political ideology or philosophy. For example, many liberal and conservative groups are equally vocal in their opposition to what they perceive as an unwelcoming school environment and an unacceptable status quo. Although their assumptions and goals may differ, groups from different philosophical camps may find themselves supporting or opposing the same policy. For example, there was multifaceted support for the parental choice program in Milwaukee, Wisconsin, and there is pluralistic opposition to NCLB. Liberals often oppose this federal reform because they fear it is an opening salvo to promote choice, introduce vouchers, and ultimately to end public schools and their commitment to the common good. Conservatives often oppose this legislation because of the increased role of the federal government in state and local education matters.

Still, the choice of what conditions will spark discontent and the identification of a solvable negative condition is grounded in the balance and priorities of values that decision makers hold.

Table 1.3 categorizes the key philosophies identified in this chapter and offers a description of the concomitant assumptions of reality, purpose of education, and the role of schooling. The first column highlights important philosophical schools of thought, from idealism to postmodernism. For pedagogical purposes, we have categorized the "pure" forms of these beliefs in individual cells, but as noted previously, education leaders may find themselves drawn to multiple philosophical camps. The table also contains examples of problems that are generated from these assumptions and possible solutions. In the last column are real-life examples of specific policies that reflect aspects of the identified philosophies.

Policy Values in Action

This section of the chapter provides an example of how one education leader articulates her intrinsic values and how they inform her analysis of education policy. In a 1990 article, Yale University president Amy Gutmann highlighted two policy values in particular that are at the heart of creating policy guidelines in education: individual freedom and civic virtue. **Individual freedom** refers to the absence of barriers to individual action and thought. **Civic virtue** refers to the existence of individual responsibility to the broader community. She posits that the important question for educators is "not whether to maximize freedom or to inculcate virtue, but how to combine freedom with virtue" (Gutmann, 1990, p. 11). Gutmann contends that the very essence of the education process requires the privileging of values and a conception of a good society. She asserts, "The content of public school cannot be neutral among competing conceptions of the good life, and if it could, we would not and should not care to support it" (p. 16). The practical application of this philosophy requires education policies to be bounded by the principles of nonrepression and nondiscrimination. That is, Gutmann argues that education should enhance the freedom of rational inquiry (**nonrepression**) and the inclusion of all children in educational contexts (**nondiscrimination**) unless there is a legitimate rationale to do otherwise.

With these guidelines, Gutmann contends that a major problem with schools is the lack of democratic institutions, and she argues for a reorientation from conventional goals. Her ordering of values calls her to reject tracking, sexist education, racial segregation, and narrowly defined vocational education as a means of solving the problem of schools. She concludes that "[d]emocratic education empowers citizens to make their own decisions on how to combine freedom with virtue [thereby authorizing] people to direct their individual and collective destinies" (p. 19).

As education leaders, you will likely develop your own set of rules regarding the appropriate ordering of values for the identification of problems and the discovery of solutions. That reflective process will underlie much of your work in policy analysis. As education leaders, however, you are not only called on to be thoughtful, but also to act. This text provides a systematic way for you to be reflective, define a policy issue, and offer appropriate reasoned arguments for its resolution.

Table 1.3 Educational Philosophies in Schools

Philosophy	Purpose of Education	Role of Schooling	Educational Problem	Possible Solutions
Idealism	Uncover truth through ideas for the sake of understanding ideas and the goal of transforming lives.	To provide a venue through which individuals can move toward the common good but through different means, where ability plays a role in the curriculum to which one is exposed.	There is too little reliance on a core curriculum.	Increase reliance on core curriculum through the use of cultural literacy and curriculum performance standards. In Kentucky, for example, each high school is mandated to "offer a core curriculum of advanced placement, International Baccalaureate, dual enrollment, or dual credit courses, using either or both on-site instruction or electronic instruction through the Kentucky Virtual High School or other on-line alternatives."
Realism	Help individuals understand and apply scientific principles to make the world a better place.	To enhance the ability of children to reason through their study of the material world and thus allow them to choose appropriate life paths.	There is too little emphasis on the sciences in the regular curriculum.	Increase requirements for science classes in the curriculum. For example, Utah's 2006 law R277-700 outlines core curriculum requirements for K–12, and increases the state minimum required units of credit for high school graduation in language arts from 3 to 4, and in mathematics and science, from 2 to 3. It is effective for students graduating in the 2010–2011 school year. See http://www.rules.utah.gov/publicat/code/r277/r277-700.htm
Pragmatism	To balance the broader needs of society with the more personal needs of individuals so that children can learn to cooperate and succeed in a democratic society.	To encourage students to find processes that work to achieve desired ends.	Students are not sufficiently engaged in their learning.	Increase the use of service learning projects. For example, Minnesota law H.F. No. 2, signed in May 2009, defines a project-based instructional program as primarily student-led coursework for credit that may be completed on site, in the community, or online and is available to all or only some students and grades in a school. It also establishes requirements that schools must meet to receive revenue for students enrolled in a public school and in a project-based program. See https://www.revisor.leg.state.mn.us/bin/bldbill.php?bill=H0002.5.html&session=ls86

Existentialism and phenomenology	To focus on the needs of individuals.	To allow individuals to make sense of themselves and their world.	Children are not sufficiently exposed to the humanities.	Increase the role of music, art, and drama in schools. Section 25 of Texas Law HB 3, signed in June 2009, requires the state board to adopt rules requiring students in Grades 6–8 to complete at least one fine arts course. See http://www.legis.state.tx.us/tlodocs/81R/billtext/pdf/HB00003F.pdf
Conflict theory	To provide children with the tools to understand the weaknesses in the dominant ideology and to change the status quo.	To provide teachers who are transformative intellectuals and who engage students in a critical examination of the world.	Too many structural inequities are reproduced in schools.	Provide educators with information that allows them to be critical consumers of existing school structure. For example, part of North Dakota law HB 1566, adopted in August 2009, requires that the commissioner of higher education study the interplay between the state university system and tribally controlled community colleges. Specifically, the law requires the commissioner to address ways in which the North Dakota university system as a whole and the individual campuses can better interact with tribally controlled community colleges through improved communication, collaboration, and relationship-building activities. In addition, the commissioner has to focus on ways in which tribally controlled community colleges can encourage American Indians to pursue options in higher education. This will result in bringing economic benefit to American Indian families and communities. It also provides ways in which the university system and the individual campuses can work with tribally controlled community colleges to provide tutoring, mentoring, and other types of assistance necessary to ensure that the retention rates and graduation rates of American Indian students are increased. The law requires that the commissioner report any findings and recommendations, along with any legislation required to implement the recommendations, to the 62nd legislative assembly. See http://www.legis.nd.gov/assembly/61-2009/bill-text/JBPS0300.pdf
Postmodernism and critical theory	To provide a venue for teachers to explore the differences between what may seem to be inherently contradictory theories and to achieve understanding and change through that exploration.	To provide critical pedagogy and to provide a venue for political action.	Schools are often unwelcoming places for families without privilege.	Require policies that make schools more welcoming for families not currently well served by system. For example, part of Kentucky law 704 KAR 3:390, adopted in February 2009, requires districts to solicit input from parents and the community to identify potential barriers to participation. It also requires that the identified barriers be addressed through engagement with community partners or off-campus locations of after-school, weekend, and/or evening services.

Source: Compiled by author based primarily on Sadovnik, Cookson, and Semel (2001) and Noll (2009), with examples of policies taken from Education Commission of the States, downloaded at http://www.ecs.org. Note that labeling of policies is provided by the author and is not part of the ECS document.

Chapter Summary

This chapter lays the groundwork for policy analysis. It opens with a rationale for leaders to study the field. It makes the point that the focus of this text is not to give you right answers but to offer you a right path for getting those answers. It presents a basic overview of the policy analysis process and continues with a systematic way of categorizing the field. By the end of this chapter, you should be aware of different ways of categorizing the field and how your work will fit in the broader policy context.

This text focuses on ex ante analysis, with the presumption that, as an education leader, you will have to propose strategies, not simply respond to them. By relying on ex ante analysis, we can examine how a possible solution would work in theory and can anticipate and address potential challenges to successful resolution of the policy issue.

It is important to note from the outset that the policy analysis process is not objective. This does not mean that the process should not be grounded in data and logical arguments, but the subjectivity of the policy analytical process makes it all the more important to ground assertions and to make clear for readers the choices being made and why. Decision making is grounded in the values that we bring and the philosophies to which we subscribe.

This chapter offers a systematic way of determining how values and policy intersect. That intersection frames the philosophy of education that you hold. Amy Gutmann's prescriptive treatise offers a guide for developing education policy for the good of a democratic society. As an education leader, you will ultimately accept or reject her treatise, perhaps modifying her guidance to come up with a philosophy of your own. From these reflections, you can better inform your thinking of how problems are defined and solutions are found in the policy analysis process. You are now ready to jump into the heart of the text, which details the steps in the policy analysis process.

Review Questions

1. Why is policy analysis important for education leaders?
2. Is leadership different from management? How does policy analysis allow managers to lead?
3. Fowler identifies eight fundamental values that she asserts individuals share: (1) individualism, (2) order, (3) equality, (4) liberty, (5) fraternity, (6) economic growth, (7) efficiency, and (8) quality. Do you think Fowler's list is accurate? Explain.
4. Review the section describing the key philosophies of education. Which of the eight values identified by Fowler would dominate each of the philosophies described?
5. How would you describe your philosophy of education? What are your intrinsic values?
6. How would your philosophy of education influence your response to the questions raised in the chapter-opening education vignette?

News Story for Analysis

"Calgary school to deploy 'Go Grrrl' philosophy." National Post *(Canada). December 4, 2002, Wednesday All but Ottawa Edition.* SOURCE: National Post. BYLINE: *Heather Sokoloff.* SECTION: *News; Pg. A1.*

Alberta is poised to accept a proposal to open the country's first all-girls public school that would operate with a curriculum based on a philosophy called "Go Grrrl."

About 100 Calgary parents are pushing for the school, where classes will use a program developed by two Arizona researchers called the "Go Grrrl" curriculum.

Central to it is a "Grrrls Bill of Rights," which emphasizes bringing female professionals into the classroom to talk about their jobs, examining the media's role in constructing a girl's image of herself, and teaching the importance of female friendships.

Students will be encouraged to direct much of their own learning to build decision-making skills and learn to look after themselves.

Ultimately, the girls should graduate understanding the importance of economic independence, said Lynn Bosetti, an education professor at the University of Calgary who wants to send her 10-year-old daughter to the school.

"That doesn't mean that a girl who wants to be a homemaker can't come to this school. She would be encouraged to be a great homemaker, and make the best decisions to get her there."

Students will be taught to question the images and interpretations of women. In art class, students might be asked to find out why Degas chose to depict so many ballerinas. "We want them to understand the baggage and the benefits that come with being a woman," Dr. Bosetti said.

The curriculum is crafted to give students an understanding of women's role in history, art and literature as preparation for careers in such male-dominated fields as business, science and engineering.

But the school founders are split over whether to term the school philosophy "feminist."

"What we are wanting is for girls to have all the opportunities they can possibly have. If that is considered feminist by some people, well, then I guess you can call it feminist," said Liz LoVecchio, the parents' spokeswoman and a graduate of an all-girls school.

"But it's not a word I am comfortable using because it sets out certain connotations."

The term does not matter much to Jane Cawthorne, a girls-school graduate and the mother of a 10-year-old girl. Ms. Cawthorne said feminists might object to the proposal, saying the separation of boys and girls leaves young women ill-equipped to deal with men in the real world.

"That's not my concern right now. My concern is getting her through these crucial years," she said.

Giving girls their own school is the best way to avoid the self-esteem crash that often occurs when girls begin their adolescent years, Ms. Cawthorne said.

"Girls are faced with 2,000 media images a day and they are all told they have to look a certain way, wear certain clothes, be a certain weight. There has to be ways we can counter that."

Parents say they warmed to the idea of single-sex education after noticing their pre-teen daughters were paying more attention to boys than school work.

Ms. Cawthorne is also concerned about research that indicates teachers call on boys more often than girls in class, take their questions more seriously and devote class time to dealing with their discipline problems.

She is also well aware of research from the 1980s and 1990s that shows girls perform better academically in single-gender institutions. "This will be an environment that is really nurturing for young girls, that tells them all possibilities are open to them."

The group is also taking the unusual step of proposing that parents and students have the right to evaluate their teachers and principal, as well as experiment with the use of merit pay to reward outstanding teaching.

That part of their plan has put the group at odds with the Calgary Board of Education. The public school board is enthusiastic about creating an all-girls school but is bound by the teachers union's collective agreement, which forbids parents from playing a role in teacher evaluation.

School board officials are hoping the parents will forgo the teacher evaluation scheme and open up as an alternative public school next September.

"Teachers being evaluated by non-professionals is inappropriate," said Kally Krylly, coordinator of program renewal at the public school board. "The program itself is something that we can accept. Particular aspects, such as merit pay, we cannot do that."

The parents will have to submit their proposal directly to Lyle Oberg, Alberta's Minister of Education, if the school board officially rejects the plan, which it is expected to do. The parents will formally submit their proposal at a school board meeting on Dec. 17.

Dr. Oberg can permit the parents to create a charter school, meaning the school would receive public funding but be run independently by parents.

"I think they will get it, one way or another," he said during an interview last night.

He added he is "intrigued" by the teacher evaluation proposal, although he will need assurances from the parents that teachers interested in working at the school have agreed to the conditions.

"I think it's very interesting and actually quite exciting. What they are doing is trying to assure that their children receive the best teaching, and no one can argue with a parent's desire to do that."

Although common in the Catholic and private sectors, single-sex public schools are a rarity.

The Nellie McClung Girls Junior High Program in Edmonton is the only one in Canada. Founded in 1995 with 70 students, enrollment mushroomed to more than 500 girls this year.

More than 100 Calgary parents have signed the proposal to create a new facility for girls in Grades 4 through 7. Subsequent grades would be added later if the plan is accepted.

Source: Material reprinted with the express permission of: "National Post Inc."

Discussion Questions

1. What are the philosophies of education that are apparent in this article? How do they influence education policies that emerge?
2. Would you want to lead a school like this? Explain.
3. If you were leading this school, what policy direction would you set?
4. Is there a role for state (provincial) or school board leaders in providing oversight for this school? If yes, what is it? If no, why not? Explain your response.
5. Distinguish between the intrinsic and extrinsic values of the various stakeholders described in the article. How do you know which values are described and who holds them?

Selected Websites

Philosophy of Education Society of Great Britain. Available at

https://www.philosophy-of-education.org/useful_websites.asp.

This is the homepage for the Philosophy of Education Society of Great Britain. Its useful links offer a great search engine for looking up a variety of philosophical terms in its field guide to the nomenclature of philosophy.

Education Commission of the States. Available at

http://www.ecs.org.

This is the homepage of The Education Commission of the States (ECS). This organization was created in 1965 to improve public education by facilitating the exchange of information, ideas, and experiences among state policymakers and education leaders. It is a nonprofit, nonpartisan organization involving key leaders from all levels of the education system, and builds partnerships, shares information, and promotes the development of policy based on available research and strategies. The website contains comprehensive packages of information on a growing number of early learning, K–12, and postsecondary issues in the United States, ranging from broad overviews to in-depth policy analyses.

U.S. Department of Education. No Child Left Behind Act of 2001. Available at

http://www.ed.gov/policy/elsec/leg/esea02/index.html.

This is the official government website detailing the goal and objectives of the federal No Child Left Behind Act of 2001. It contains the full 670 pages of the act. It is also delineated by sections and titles so that particular sections may be reviewed. This site is useful because as education leaders it is important to separate fact from fiction. This site provides the contents of the law and is not tempered by anyone's views of it.

Selected References

Frase, L. E., & Streshly, W. (2000). *Top 10 myths in education: Fantasies Americans love to believe.* Lanham, MD: Scarecrow Press (Technomic Books).

The authors discuss various beliefs currently held by many education leaders, including the belief that education can save society and that national testing will boost achievement. This book has a strong point of view, with which you may agree or disagree. Its usefulness is in its identification of major assumptions and values in the field. It also gives readers a sense of the disagreement that exists regarding the appropriate road to education reform.

Gutmann, A. (1990). Democratic education in difficult times. *Teachers College Record, 92*(1), 7–20.

Gutmann discusses the tension between civic virtue and individual freedom and argues that this tension is a fundamental challenge for education. She proposes creating a "state of democratic education," which leaves maximum room for citizens to shape their society in an image with which they can identify their moral choices. This is a good treatise to review in terms of how you can make the philosophical arguments needed to justify the policy actions that you recommend.

Hirsch, E. D. (2010). First, do no harm [Quality Counts 2010]. *Education Week, 29*(17), 29, 31.

The author argues that language standards need to focus on academic content in literature, history, science, and the arts being taught comprehensibly and collectively. Hirsch advocates a common curriculum to which leaders of local school districts would have to adhere. This article is useful to education leaders because it offers concrete recommendations based on the author's definition of the problem of education. It would be useful to reflect on the differences (if any) between your recommendations and his based on your particular philosophy of education.

López, G. R., Scribner, J. D., & Mahitivanichcha, K. (2001, Summer). Redefining parental involvement: Lessons from high-performing migrant-impacted schools. *American Educational Research Journal, 38*(2), 253–288.

The school of pragmatism has two main categories: (1) instrumentalism and (2) experimentalism. Those who support instrumentalism strongly favor having a working relationship between school and society. This article by Lopez, Scribner, and Mahitivanichcha reflects an instrumentalist orientation. It demonstrates how having parents play a more active role in the formal education of their children can lead to positive outcomes for all those involved in the learning process: parents, children, and educators.

Noll, J. W. (2009). *Taking sides: Clashing views on educational issues* (15th ed.). Dubuque, IA: McGraw-Hill.

Noll presents current controversial issues in a debate-style format. He frames each issue with an issue summary, an issue introduction, and a postscript. This book is helpful for education leaders because of the overview it provides on the leading arguments for and against key contemporary policies.

Sadovnik, A. R., Cookson, P. W., & Semel, S. F. (2001). *Exploring education: An introduction to the foundations of education* (2nd ed.). Boston: Allyn & Bacon.

The authors provide a sound introduction to the philosophy of education that teachers and other educators would find helpful in reflecting on their profession and its reform.

Getting Started at the Beginning

Thinking of Policy Analysis as Problem Analysis

CHAPTER OBJECTIVES

After reading this chapter, you will be able to:

- Define policy analysis
- Describe the fundamental method underlying policy analysis
- Identify the six to eight key phases of policy making
- Distinguish between policy making and policy analysis
- Differentiate between policy evaluation and policy analysis
- List the steps necessary for a rational approach to developing policy

EDUCATION VIGNETTE

Dr. Know enters the district administration office. He still gets a kick out of entering the building in his new role as the new superintendent of Nikville, and he wants to lead by example by having a collaborative process for making decisions in the district. He has called together the two executive directors of his district as well as the principals of all 11 secondary schools. He asks them to brainstorm about the challenges facing secondary education in the district and ways of tackling those challenges. He goes around the room asking each participant to tell him what is the biggest problem facing the district. One by one, the participants speak up: "Unfunded mandates." "No Child Left Behind." "Budget cuts." "State standards." "Union contracts."

How would you respond to each of these ideas? How can you ensure that Dr. Know is getting at the heart of policy analysis?

WHERE DO YOU START?

The Role of Leaders

Leaders must see order in chaos, envision excellence in mediocrity, and pursue a better world. To do that, they must be able to identify what is wrong and have an idea about what "good" looks like. For example, the Reverend Martin Luther King, Jr. pointed out that the distribution of civil rights was inequitable in the United States and conceived of a time when justice would prevail. Stephen Denning, business leader and former World Bank executive, thought that there was insufficient access to the knowledge about solutions to global poverty, and he envisioned a world where that knowledge was readily accessible. Rudy Perpich, former governor of Minnesota, was perturbed about the fact that his children could not attend any public school they wanted and was instrumental in passing the first charter school laws in the United States. Kristin Waters, former principal of Bruce Randolph School in Denver, Colorado, considered that not enough students were being successful in school. By the end of her tenure, reading proficiency went up by 22 percentage points, and 97 percent of the students graduated.

What are the education conditions that you would like to change? What is your image of the future, and where would you start in pursuing it?

POLICY ANALYSIS AS PROBLEM ANALYSIS

The Problem is the Beginning of Analysis

Policy analysis may be a misleading term. The policy analysis process does not begin with policies that have already been in place; it begins with a recognition that a fundamental condition needs to be changed. An important part of that recognition is being able to tell the difference among conditions, policy problems, and policy issues. The importance of starting with the problem cannot be overstated and is an important step in making the world a better place. For example, Dunn (2004) notes that the failure of many policies lies in the misdiagnosis of the problem rather than in mistakes made in finding the right solution. A variety of policy researchers concur (Bardach, 2009; Patton & Sawicki, 1993). Many researchers agree that starting with a policy solution instead of the problem definition often limits the alternatives that are considered and leads to analysts displacing ends with a nonrational focus on means.

What does this mean for you as an education leader? You will need to start your quest for change with a simple identification of the condition that you would like to change. To do that effectively, you need to distinguish among conditions, policy problems, and policy issues.

Differences Among Conditions, Policy Problems, and Policy Issues

Conditions are basic descriptions of the world that can be supported by empirical data. For example, a basic description of a condition may be that a large proportion of third-graders are not reading at grade level. This is a condition that policymakers hope to address with the adoption of the reauthorized No Child Left Behind Act of 2001. We may note that not enough of the population has a postsecondary degree or that first-generation college students have lower persistence rates than their peers. These last two conditions are the focus of the efforts of members of the College Board's Commission on Access. Generally, these conditions can be found readily, and your readers will not have to take your word for it. You can produce data that are descriptive in nature and do not require readers to have the same belief systems that you do.

All conditions that you choose to highlight and would like to do something about are not policy problems, however. For conditions to be transformed to **policy problems**, they must contain three basic characteristics. First they must be shown to be negative. Second, they must be solvable using public resources. Third, they should be solved using public resources. If any of these elements are missing, the transformation of a condition to a policy problem is not complete, and you should revisit your identification of the policy problem. For example, the Wake County School Board in North Carolina recently took steps to reverse a longstanding policy to promote racial diversity in its schools. This suggests that education leaders in that community no longer considered a lack of racial diversity in their schools to be a policy problem. Perhaps they no longer considered the condition to be negative, solvable, or solvable using public resources. Their actions prompted a response from U.S. secretary of education Arne Duncan, appointed by President-elect Obama in 2008 and confirmed by the U.S. Senate in January 2009. He decried the move by the Wake County School Board as an action against the core values of the nation. He wrote, "In an increasingly diverse society like ours, racial isolation is not a positive outcome for children of any color or background" (Duncan, 2011). This discussion again highlights the importance of education leaders being able to persuade others on the existence of a policy problem in the first place. It also underscores the usefulness of the policy analysis process in the act of leadership.

In the same way that not all conditions rise to the level of policy problems, not all policy problems are policy issues. Policy issues are a special subcategory of policy problems. Only policy problems on which there is disagreement over the most appropriate solution are **policy issues**. Only policy issues require the full steps of the policy analysis process described herein. If there is already agreement on the most appropriate way to resolve a policy problem, there is no need to use resources to try to find out what the most appropriate resolution is because you already know. The next step would be to implement the agreed-on strategy. Let us go back to the condition of too little ethnic diversity or racial isolation among students in schools. If education leaders agreed that this condition needs to be changed and the way to address it is through the busing of students, the condition would be a policy problem, not a policy issue. One reason that the condition of student diversity at all education levels remains an issue for education leaders is that, while there is general agreement that we need to avoid racial isolation, we are not sure how. For example, the use of busing in U.S. elementary and secondary schools was a common strategy that has lost political favor in recent years because many education leaders, community activists, and researchers did not find these programs to be effective at reducing racial isolation (e.g., Orfield, Frankenberg, & Lee, 2002/2003). In higher education institutions, the use of admission quotas have similarly been challenged, and certain aspects of this strategy have been found unconstitutional by the U.S. Supreme Court.

Making sure that your policy analysis is clear about the distinction among conditions, problems, and issues has the effect of Clark Kent's transformation into Superman. When Clark Kent dons his costume and transforms himself, heroic actions follow and common citizens are willing to believe in change. Similarly, if education leaders do not transform conditions into policy problems, it is unlikely that

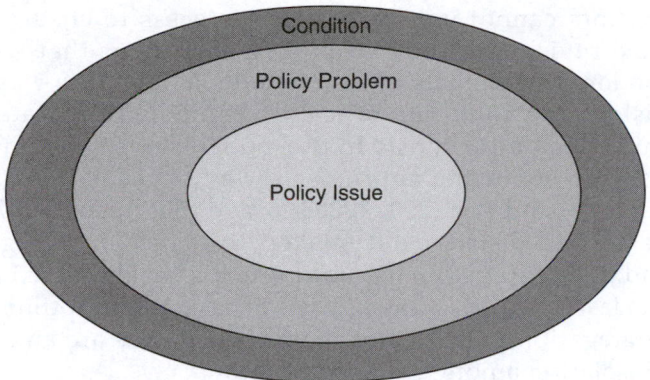

FIGURE 2.1   Relationship Among Conditions, Policy Problems, and Policy Issues

their communities will be willing to do things differently. Only when the transformation from condition to policy problems takes place are decision makers and other stakeholders willing to act. Figure 2.1 illustrates the nested nature and relationships among conditions, policy problems, and policy issues.

The Policy Analysis Process

Once you have established that you have a policy issue, the policy analytical process has begun. The definition of the policy process described by Fowler (2009 p.13) is useful here in describing what policy analysis is: "The policy process is the sequence of events that occurs when a political system considers different approaches to public problems, adopts one of them, tries it out, and evaluates it." The difficulty is how to choose among the various strategies that can be adopted to resolve a policy issue. Clearly, we can choose among options in several ways. We could flip a coin, or we could recite the time-honored eeny, meeny, miny, moe but those strategies are not as persuasive or as systematic and do not provide a transparent accounting of why we chose one strategy over another.

The policy analysis process is a good way of helping policymakers to choose the most appropriate use of limited resources given particular constraints. Those constraints may mean that politics and ideology play a big part, but even that is important to document explicitly so that the decision to choose one approach over another is clear. It is important to emphasize that, while the policy analytical process is not necessarily objective, it should be transparent.

THE COMPLEXITIES OF POLICY ANALYSIS.   As noted by Fowler (2009) and others, policy issues are, by their very nature, controversial; they are also dynamic. What sparks disagreement in a particular community and in a particular time is not fixed. Before the judges handed down their decision in *Brown v. Board of Education* in 1954, many key decision makers in the United States did not identify the differing education opportunities offered to blacks and whites as problematic. Because many leading state policymakers did not consider the gap in schooling opportunities as problematic, there was no policy issue. This does not mean that actors cannot use the political process to ensure the relabeling of conditions and revision of contexts so that conditions that were considered the norm are no longer acceptable in the public milieu. This was the case after the *Brown* decision: The condition of legally mandated separate schooling for blacks and whites was now considered a policy problem, and policymakers continue to disagree about the appropriate way of resolving it. For example, Orfield, Frankenberg, and Lee (2002/2003) argue that busing and other policies often used by state and district policymakers to reduce desegregation have not worked well and that segregation in public schools has increased rather than decreased over the last 50 years. Wraga (2006) offers a more optimistic assessment of existing desegregation policies and suggests that they are an effective way of reducing racial isolation among children of color.

No Child Left Behind (NCLB) Act of 2001 is another example of a policy that arose from key policymakers pushing for the redefinition of a condition as a problem. In the past, we generally assessed how schools are doing by their overall student performance. We considered schools that had high *overall* achievement (measured by mean student performance on standardized tests) as being effective. The adoption of No Child Left Behind in 2002 led to a national reevaluation of what goods schools look like and what effective schools do. In the new definition, federal policymakers now explicitly defined the gap between the performance of black and that of white students as problematic. While there now seems to be general agreement that the achievement gap between blacks and whites is a policy problem, deep disagreement remains among education leaders on the best way of resolving it.

POLICY ANALYSIS VERSUS POLICY MAKING

The Role of Policy Analysts

Notice that the role of policy analysts is different from that of policymakers, even though there may be some overlap. We usually think of **policy analysts** as individuals interested in the technical aspects of policy and as being removed from political turmoil, short time horizons, and the give and take of policy making. We usually associate **policymakers** with politicians, who generally want to have an immediate impact on the political system and its outcomes and who want to be in the center of the struggle to have certain values reflected in selected policy choices. Both policy analysts and policymakers are concerned about the collective, and their decisions affect the broader community. As an education leader, you will also need to worry about the broader society and the short- and long-term implications of your decisions. You will need to analyze problems and offer solutions that balance the needs of the political environment.

Education leaders will have to draw on both their analytical and political skills, but it is important to note that the process of policy analysis is different from that of policy making. **Policy analysis** is a systematic search for the appropriate solution of a policy issue that has been identified and defined. **Policy making** is essentially the struggle to have your values backed by the authoritative role of government (Wirt & Kirst, 1975). Successful policy analysis ends with the appropriate solution for the policy problem that was identified given the goals and constraints. Successful policymaking is fully anchored in the political system. It "is the dynamic and value laden process through which a political system handles a public problem" (Fowler, 2009 pp. 3–4).

Because actionable problems are largely found in the political realm, it is imperative that education leaders have a basic understanding of the policy-making process.

Phases in Policy Making

Kingdon (1995) proposes that policy is accomplished in the United States when three important streams in the policy-making process—problem stream, politics stream, and policy stream—merge. This description holds true for other democracies and may be applied to other forms of governance, too. What education leaders should take away from this discussion is the need to monitor conditions that may rise to the level of a policy problem. With the dynamic, and often chaotic, nature of the policy-making process, it is often easy to focus on existing policies, power relationships, and distribution of resources, rather than on the nature of the condition that education leaders would like to change.

PROBLEM STREAM.   As with the policy analytical process, the definition of problems in policy making is dynamic and iterative. However, there is longstanding concern among policy scholars that researched and scholarly definitions of the problem seldom make it into the policy-making arena. Heck (2004) counters that evidence of the practical influence of scholarship may be limited in the short run, but in the long run, cumulative evidence generally influences how policymakers define the policy problem in the field.

The **problem stream** essentially captures how problems are defined. Kingdon (1995) observes that indicators, focusing events, and feedback bring problematic conditions to the attention of policymakers. **Indicators** are the data that describe the magnitude of the problem. **Focusing events** are occurrences that help to transform a condition into a problem in the mind of decision makers. **Feedback** provides information on how the status of the condition has changed or remained the same. Education leaders need to be aware of these three components and be able to present information about them so that decision makers and their constituencies find them useful.

Why should education leaders care? Education leaders must try and influence the problem stream because how the problem is defined influences the nature of the solutions that will prevail. For example, in the early tenure of Steve Denning at the World Bank, key members in the organization defined the key problem facing the organization as global poverty caused by insufficient monetary resources. With the problem defined in that way, the key solution would be to increase monetary resources in the form of loans or grants. Steve Denning wanted to rediagnose the problem as one of global poverty caused by insufficient access to knowledge (Denning, 2007). This means that a key strategy to solving it would be to increase the access to knowledge. Similarly, the pro-chancellor and chair of the Governing Council of Osun State University in Osogbo, Nigeria, Professor Peter Okebukola defined a lack of high-quality teachers as a key education problem facing Nigeria. He asserted that the problem of teacher inadequacy resulted from the low prestige accorded to the teaching profession and the mass exodus of trained teachers to Europe, North America, and Asia. Given his diagnosis of the problem, it is not surprising that he wants to establish a national quality assurance and monitoring system for teachers and recommends policies that he anticipates would have an impact on teacher quality (Ogundare, 2010). Similarly, many policymakers in the United States have defined the gap between the achievement scores of white and black students as a problem. They have often diagnosed that problem as being a result of an inadequate supply of highly qualified teachers. Given that definition of the problem, it is not surprising that strategies to increase the supply of highly qualified teachers would be pursued. For example, in Minnesota, both Democratic and Republican legislators sponsored a bill in 2011 to promote alternative teacher licensure in that state.

In the examples described here, education leaders are more likely to be successful in persuading other decision makers of their view of the world if they are able to present relevant data, take advantage of pertinent events, and allow opportunity for feedback.

POLITICS STREAM. The **politics stream** details the balance of power and resources that exist in the policy-making system. This balance can influence which problem definition is carried downstream to the governmental agenda. The **governmental agenda** is a list of policy items on which decision makers are seriously considering action. This stream is a combination of partisan and electoral politics as well as the actions of special interest groups. To stay above water, education leaders need to be aware of the national mood, potential avenues of interest, group pressure, and the desires of individuals or groups with a great deal of political clout (Kingdon, 1995). This does not mean that you have to buckle under the pressure of powerful groups or individuals. It does mean, however, that you must have an understanding of political processes and the constraints that they may place on the feasibility of your decisions. The technical merit of your argument may not be sufficient in selecting the appropriate course of action. You must also consider the balance of power and values that make some choices untenable, regardless of their potential effectiveness in solving an identified problem.

Why should education leaders care? As an education leader, your framing of the policy problem can influence how the issue is viewed by those who set the legislative agenda and establish rules. If a condition is not being seriously considered by policymakers, then there is little likelihood that there will be collective action to change it. Being aware of the political dimensions of policy analysis allows you to offer meaningful problem definitions that fellow leaders consider actionable. For example, after publication of *A Nation at Risk* in 1983 (National Commission on Excellence in Education, 1983), education leaders in the United States could create more interest in addressing education problems when they framed their concern as a quest for improving student performance. Similarly, efforts to address bullying and school security received more attention after the 1999 mass shootings in a high school in Columbine, Colorado, in the United States. In addition, with the rise of standards-based accountability policies, the demand for more phonetic and less whole-language approaches to literacy has been more appealing to those who set the agenda (e.g., McDonnell, 2009).

POLICY STREAM. The **policy stream** captures the different alternatives that exist. This stream is the most easily aligned with the work of policy analysis: the quest for an alternative that improves societal conditions. It is especially important for education leaders to be active participants in this process because they have the knowledge and insight to contribute to the appropriate selection of alternatives. This stream is the one in which the skills of the policy analysis process are fully brought to bear. The plethora of ideas advanced in the problems and politics streams are sorted and organized in order to gauge which ones meet the needs of the community most appropriately. Education leaders are essential in guiding this process.

Why should education leaders care? The proposals to address policy change are dissected, analyzed, modified, discarded, or used in the policy stream. Your roles as an education leader is important in bringing to light the ideas that take into account the full needs of your community. The act of policy development, which is the work of the policy stream, allows education leaders to devise rational, persuasive arguments on the proposed alternative. As noted by Kingdon (1995), problems are less likely to be addressed if policymakers do not see viable solutions for solving them. For example, education leaders long expressed concern over the equity of school finance in the United States. However, it was not until Coons, Clune, and Sugarman (1970) provided the courts with a working definition of how to measure equity that plaintiffs in school finance lawsuits had a chance at victory (e.g., *Serrano v, Priest*, 1971).

The merging of the problem, political, and policy streams can account for the policies that are adopted. When we study and try to understand the context of the struggle in any one of these policy-making processes, understanding the politics of education and the underlying theories and applications are important. In the study of policy analysis, however, the focus is on the characterization of existing unsatisfactory conditions. The focus of education leaders interested primarily in policy analysis would be on the policy stream, where alternatives are refined.

It is important to be aware of the political phases in the policy process and to note key overlaps with policy analysis as a method. Consequently, this chapter also includes a brief discussion of the commonly accepted stages of the policy process.

STAGES OF THE POLICY-MAKING PROCESS

The policy-making process generally encompasses six to eight phases. Fowler (2009) identifies the six stages of the policy process as issue definition, agenda setting, policy formulation, policy adoption, policy implementation, and policy evaluation. Dunn (2004, p. 45) describes them more broadly and adds policy adaptation, policy succession, and policy termination among the stages completed during policy making. Dunn's last three additions differ somewhat from the rest of the process because I consider them to be subcategories of policy evaluation. That is, based on their assessment of particular programs and policies, policymakers may decide to adapt existing policy action (adaptation), redirect the goal of that action (succession), or cut the program altogether (termination).

Issue Definition

Issue definition is the start of the policy-making process as well as the policy analytical process. As noted already, not all negative conditions are policy problems or policy issues. A key transformation of a negative condition is evidence that the phenomenon actually exists and that it has sufficient negative implications for the community as a whole so that members care if it is not resolved. For example, education leaders have long had concerns about the equity of schooling offered to poor students, students with special needs, and high achievers. There is also concern about the quality of education being provided to ensure that the United States is on the top rung of the achievement ladder marking education performance. This concern has resulted in a variety of reports and policies, including the Elementary and Secondary Education Act (ESEA) in

1965, which defined the issue as poor children not doing as well in school as their more wealthy peers. It has also resulted in the Individuals with Disability Act, first authorized in 1974, which defined the problem as inappropriate education being offered to students with special needs. Definitions also include the mediocrity of the education system, as prompted by the 1983 report *A Nation at Risk*, which led to an increase in policies at all levels of governance in the United States emphasizing improved standards. This emphasis on excellence and accountability also influenced the reauthorization of ESEA in 2001 and led to the redefinition of a variety of education problems in the No Child Left Behind Act of 2001. This stage of the policy-making process takes place in the problem stream, and much of the chapter discussion of that subject applies here. It is also analogous to the problem definition step in policy analysis.

Agenda Setting

Not all policy issues are going to be acted on by a government. Kingdon (1995) notes that **visible participants** in the political system, such as politicians, are more likely to define the issue that make it to the agenda, while **hidden participants** (e.g., analysts) are more likely to influence the solutions to these problems. Visible participants are so called because their influence on policy making is public, assumed, and obvious because of their role as elected leaders. Hidden participants are so described because they are less likely to be known by the general population. Their impact on policy via their influence on proposals and underlying scholarship is often less publicized.

Education leaders may be visible or hidden participants. Visible participants include elected leaders or leaders appointed at high levels of government. For example, many governors have billed themselves as education governors; two examples are former governor Bill Clinton of Arkansas and former governor George W. Bush of Texas. In addition, elected members of school boards who are more involved in policy directives than in the day-to-day running of the district are also examples of visible participants. Examples of hidden participants are the practitioners responsible for implementing the policy, scholars who have developed proposals to address problematic conditions, and civil servants working behind the scenes. Leaders of grassroots organizations, unions, and various special interest groups may be visible or hidden depending on the publicity that surrounds their actions and analysis.

Legislators are responsible for placing policy issues on the public agenda. Policy analysts can influence the agenda by informing the definition of a policy issue adopted by policymakers. If an issue does not make it to the agenda, it will not have a policy generated explicitly to resolve it. This stage in the policy-making process is analogous to the need to make the case in the policy analysis process. However, getting an issue onto the governmental agenda is not sufficient. It does not guarantee that suitable alternatives for resolving the problematic condition will be proposed. These alternatives would have to have the appropriate words to describe what needs to be done and funding to support those actions. That is the role of policy formulation.

Policy Formulation

In this phase of the political process, officials formulate alternatives to address a problem. As noted by Dunn (2004) and Fowler (2009), these policies may be in the form of executive orders, court decisions, and statutes. The formulation of policies thus captures in writing the required approach proposed to resolve the issue being addressed. For you as an education leader, this stage in the policy-making process encompasses the policy analytical tasks of establishing your intrinsic values, thinking of alternatives, and weighing those alternatives against the considerations that you deem important. In exploring options, it is essential for education leaders to remember the condition that they would like to solve. Education leaders must continue to focus their efforts on solving the problem rather than on gaining allegiance to a particular strategy for solving that problem.

Policy Adoption

It is not enough to capture in words the recommended strategy of dealing with a policy issue. There also needs to be formal acceptance of those words by the appropriate authorizing body. In the conduct of policy analysis, the likelihood of one approach being supported or opposed is an integral part of the policy analytical process and underlies the recommendation that stems from the policy analysis process. That is, analysts need to gauge the feasibility of their proposed solution being adopted. Their assessment plays a crucial role in the recommendations made. In policy analysis, when education leaders make recommendations and persuade relevant stakeholders that their decision is the proper one, they inform the policy adoption stage in the policy-making arena.

Policy Implementation

Policy implementation is the stage of the policy process where proposed actions are finally realized. In early policy research, we often focused on the political likelihood of a policy being adopted. Less explored was its implementation. Dunn (2004) indicates, for example, that an adopted policy is carried out by administrative units. Firestone (1989) notes that the rewards and consequences for the actors in this stage of the process are different from those for key players in the policy adoption phase. This phase of policy making presents many rewards and challenges to education leaders. At this stage, leaders are better able to see if they made a difference in the community and resolved the problem identified. The implementation and monitoring plans developed by education leaders are an important analogue to the implementation stage of the policy-making process.

Policy Evaluation

Policy evaluation is the stage of the policy-making process in which the feedback loop is required for education leaders to assess if the policy change that was implemented actually worked. This part of the process calls for a clear delineation of the goals and the objectives of the policy in order to have a standard by which to determine the policy's effectiveness. Weiler (1990) asserts that policy evaluation is essentially political because evaluation requires the explicit use of values in judging whether a program was successful.

Policy evaluation allows us to answer the question, "Did it work"? Did it work? is the question that must ultimately be asked of any policy. As important as policy evaluation is to both policy making and policy analysis, however, it is not the entire process. A mistake made by many students in the policy analysis process is that they start with an existing policy. They assume that the policy analysis process simply means that they

Table 2.1 Approximate Match between Standard Phases Described in the Policy-Making Process Literature and Steps in the Policy Analysis Process

Policy-Making Phases	Steps in Policy Analysis
Issue definition	Define the problem.
Agenda setting	Make the case.
Policy formulation	Establish your driving values.
	Develop alternatives.
	Weigh the options.
Policy adoption	Make recommendations.
	Persuade your audience.
Policy implementation	Implement the solution.
	Monitor outputs.
Policy evaluation	Evaluate outcomes.

Source: Compiled by author based on literature.

conduct an assessment of whether an existing policy worked or not. However, policy analysis is more than policy evaluation; the distinction is important. Evaluation occurs toward the end of the policy analytical process and examines ways in which proposed alternatives were effective, if at all. Policy analysis goes beyond the assessment of policy proposals. At its best, it assesses the policy problem that these solutions were designed to solve.

POLICY ANALYSIS IS NOT POLICY EVALUATION

Focusing on the Problem

When students come into the policy analysis class, they are often passionate about the effectiveness, or lack thereof, of a particular policy. They are excited about documenting why they so strongly support or oppose a particular policy. Quite often, they are passionately opposed. This attention to existing policies often turns the focus of the students away from the problem that the policy was intended to solve in the first place. Instead of addressing a problem that needs resolution, the policy analysis process becomes distilled into simply being an evaluative process. Even if their evaluations are done systematically, students still have no clear rationale on why the option examined was the most appropriate solution to resolve the policy issue that they really care about. In other words, by focusing solely on one of the potential solutions to a particular problem, instead of the problem itself, students are committing what Dunn (2004) describes as a **Type III error**; that is, the students solve the wrong problem. For example, when students care about the costs of higher education but start their analysis by defining the problem as an inappropriate tax code, their efforts are focused on the wrong condition. The solution to the problem, as they state it, would be to fix the tax code. However, fixing the tax code may not lead to any change in the costs of higher education. If students really care about reducing the costs of higher education, the costs of higher education should be the start of their policy analysis. To focus on refining a solution that may not be the most appropriate for addressing the problem limits the utility of the policy analytical process.

Education leaders may complain that they do not like unfunded mandates, No Child Left Behind, budget cuts, state standards, union contracts, and so on. However, their focus should be on the conditions that they would like to change, not the strategies used to address them. By approaching policy analysis as problem analysis, education leaders can better ensure that they are not distracted by the means to a solution and can focus instead on the conditions that they would like to change.

Policy Evaluation

POLICY EVALUATION AS FEEDBACK.   When you start with an existing policy rather than the condition that you would like to change, policy evaluation can provide feedback or summative results. **Formative evaluations** are conducted when assessments provide feedback early enough in the implementation process that those who are carrying out the policy can respond. In the field of education, an example of formative evaluation is the use of computer-assisted instruction. Yeh (2006) describes the evaluative process when he illustrates how teachers can use computers to provide rapid feedback to their students. He found that investing in this reform strategy often leads to higher student motivation, less frustration, and lower failure rates. While these findings are important, it is important to distinguish between questions that ask if a policy works and questions that explore what *working* means. The answers to the latter questions require a clear definition of the problem.

POLICY EVALUATION AS SUMMATIVE JUDGMENT.   Policy evaluation may also be **summative** and used to determine if a program should be adapted, continued, or terminated. As noted earlier, policy adaptation occurs when leaders adapt the initial solution that was adopted to address a problem. For example, policymakers in Kentucky revised the funding mechanisms used for their elementary and secondary schools in response to the court's findings that the system for funding schools in that state was inadequate (see *Rose v. Council for Better Education*, 790 S.W.2d 186).

Policy succession occurs when the original problem for which a policy was proposed has evolved or disappeared. In that case, rather than getting rid of the policy altogether, policymakers may decide to direct the efforts of program administrators to resolving a new policy problem. Leaders then shift the focus of existing programs or policies to address another problematic condition. An illustrative educational example is the creation and transformation of the desegregation rule in Minnesota and its companion integration revenue program statute. In its original conceptualization, the Minnesota State Board of Education established a 30% cap on ethnic minority students for all Minnesota public schools. Schools that exceeded this ceiling were required to submit a desegregation plan to the Minnesota Department of Education or face financial sanctions. The sanctions were to dissuade district leaders from violating the rule by not having more systemic opportunities for ethnic integration. By the 1990s, demographic changes in the state's two largest school districts, Minneapolis and Saint Paul, signaled a new set of challenges to ethnic integration that would eventually affect many of the metropolitan school districts within the state. These communities experienced increasingly high proportions of students of color, and if policymakers enforced the 30% cap on minority students, then education leaders in Minneapolis and St. Paul would have had to turn away their own neighborhood students. The student population from which they drew often was more than 30% minority. To address that challenge, policymakers revised the statutes so that the integration standard would be based on the relationship of the school to the district in which it is located rather than on the school's ethnic integration vis-à-vis the state's arbitrary cap. That is, the Minnesota State Board of Education prohibited schools within a district from having a minority population that was 15% above the district's average. Consequently, rather than placing an absolute cap on the percentage of minority enrollments, schools had to ensure that their minority populations were not very different (defined as anything more than 15%) from the average of the district in which it was located. As minority populations in the metropolitan areas continued to grow dramatically, but asymmetrically within and among districts, it became increasingly difficult for policymakers to establish ethnic integration standards that could be fairly and equally addressed by all school officials. By 2002, the desegregation rule remained, but the Minnesota legislature now allowed voluntary participation of school districts into existing integration collaboratives. Along with the use of appropriation policies for state revenues designated specifically for the improvement of ethnic integration, the new goal of the desegregation rule is now simply to increase interracial contact, a term that state policymakers have not defined concretely.

Using summative evaluation, policymakers and administrators may determine that a program or policy is no longer necessary. This was the case in Wake County, North Carolina, where board members changed the law on integration. Another example of a law being terminated (repealed) is in Minnesota, where the Minnesota Board of Education had created a set of rules in 1993 labeled the profile of learning, which were officially adopted in 1998. These rules were intended to offer a set of statewide standards that would increase the quality of education offered in Minnesota by making coursework and grading more consistent across the state. By 2003, the Minnesota legislature repealed the policy because it was determined that the policy did not provide a good avenue for ensuring excellence for Minnesota students.

Going Beyond Evaluation

Policy analysis is policy evaluation, writ large. That is, policy analysis is not simply about whether a policy worked; it entails the completion of 10 essential and iterative steps, of which the evaluation of outcomes is simply one part of a very important whole. As noted by Fowler (2009) and others, the purpose of evaluation is to see if individuals are doing what they are supposed to or if policies work the way they are supposed to. The first purpose addresses simple compliance; the second addresses the question of effectiveness. However, education leaders will be unable to address the effectiveness of programs unless they are weighed against their ability to resolve the problem that they were implemented to address. This brings us back to where we started the discussion: Policy analysis should be viewed as problem analysis. The place to start is with identification of the problem. However, policy analysis is not only about pointing out what is wrong with the world. It is the process by which options to make the world better are offered. The chapter closes with an overview of the other steps in the policy analysis process.

THE STEPS TO POLICY ANALYSIS

The Craft of Policy Analysis

Many policy researchers note that policy analysis is not a science. Bardach (2009) writes that it is "more art than science" (p. xvi). Patton and Sawicki (1993) concur and add that basic policy analysis is "craft rather than science" (p. 4). These researchers and others agree that there are key steps that must be covered in order to improve the quality of the policy analytical process. The analogy that I often draw on in class is the baking of a cake. Some ingredients are key components of the cake-making process, but if a baker wants to bake a particular flavor of cake, it helps to have a recipe that can be adapted. Education leaders must be familiar with the basic policy recipe, but they must be flexible to make changes as necessary.

Key Questions of the Policy Analysis Process

It is also important to recognize that providing steps in the analytical process is a way to make that process pedagogically helpful, and it is helpful to remember that the process is invariably not as mechanistic as implied by the description. Instead, it is often organic and always iterative. Three major questions guide the policy analysis process, and they involve how, what, and who questions. The first question is, How are decisions made? That is, what process is used? For example, the process described in the book follows a rational, goal-oriented, step-by-step approach. The second question is, What criteria are used? For example, what are the driving values that will help education leaders not only define policy problems but come up with solutions? The third questions is, Who gets to make that determination? For example, as education leaders consider various constraints on resolving problems, whose values, whose benefits, and whose costs count? The answers to these three questions vary and often depend on the reason for doing the analysis in the first place.

Creating a Policy Analysis Roadmap

Researchers vary on the exact number of steps in the policy analysis process. However, the key features of the process are essentially the same. That is, a problem must be identified; you must decide how you will choose among the alternatives to solve the problem; you must identify the alternatives from which you will choose. As an analyst, you will let readers know how well each alternative fared when weighed against considerations that you (or your boss, or your constituents, or other stakeholders) think are important. Based on that analysis, you will select one of the alternatives and then, if change is to occur, you will implement the selected alternative. This process is somewhat analogous to the one used in choosing the winner on *American Idol* or *America's Next Top Model*. That is, based on your understanding of what is good or bad, you will consistently eliminate the least workable options until there is a solution that balances the criteria of a group. The benefit of learning these analytical methods in the classroom is that you have some exposure to formal policy analysis while you are still in school. For example, winter conditions do not exist in Jamaica, but members of the Jamaican bobsled team were still able to adapt the rudiments of bobsledding to the particular conditions that they face by practicing on sand instead of snow. This unusual training first came to light when the Jamaican bobsled team was the first from a tropical country

to participate in the 1988 Winter Olympics in Calgary, Canada. This story was made famous in the 1993 film *Cool Runnings*. Since then, many more participants from tropical
climates practice for and participate in the Winter Olympics. While some of these steps
may feel mechanistic and unrealistic while you are studying them in school, they will
offer the basic elements for conducting sound policy analysis and they will allow you to
make better policy decisions in the more complex conditions offered in reality.

TEN STEPS OF POLICY ANALYSIS. The 10 steps of the policy analytical process that will
be explored and described more fully in this text are (1) define the problem, (2) make the
case, (3) establish your driving values, (4) develop alternatives, (5) weigh the options,
(6) make recommendations, (7) persuade your audience, (8) implement the solution,
(9) monitor outputs, and (10) evaluate outcomes.

1. Define the Problem. The first step in the policy analysis process is define the
problem. By defining the problem, education leaders focus attention on the social condition that must be changed in order to improve society. The definition of the problem
sets the course for the goal of analysis, the viability of alternatives considered, and how
success is defined. As you define a problem, you can do so in terms of its scope: how
many people are affected and to what degree, key stakeholders, and the degree of influence that policymakers may have in making a change. This step is covered in more
detail in Chapter 3.

2. Make the Case. The essence of policy analysis is identifying choices that lead to
the optimal resolution of a problem. It is not enough, however, to point out problems
and to identify solutions if others are not persuaded by your analysis. Policymakers
often disagree about the appropriate choices to be made regarding public policy. It is
imperative that policy analysts demonstrate that the facts support their description of
the world and, ultimately, their solution to what they find wrong with it. Consequently,
policy analysis requires evidence-based strategies because it is more convincing to
point to facts than to rely on intuition. How to assemble these facts in a meaningful way
so that they become transformed into persuasive evidence is the subject of Chapter 4.

3. Establish Your Driving Values. The choices you make regarding problem definitions, alternatives, and implemented strategy will be grounded in the values that you
or other decision makers bring to the analysis. While values reflect your ideals, **criteria**
are concrete, working definitions of these ideals. In determining evaluative criteria,
you may want to look at the cost of various alternatives, the net benefits associated
with the outcomes of those evaluative criteria, the administrative ease associated with
implementing each alternative, and so on. In essence, the criteria that you select say
something about the assumptions you are making regarding the role of society, government, and the economy. The driving values that shape your choices and the criteria
derived from them are discussed more fully in Chapter 5.

4. Develop Alternatives. Alternatives are the policy options that you are considering
to resolve the problem at hand. They describe the interventions you are taking into account to resolve or alleviate the negative condition that you identified. Alternatives are
not to be confused with the outcomes sought and are always a *means* to an end; they are
not ends in and of themselves. Alternatives detail *how* you plan to mitigate the negative
condition that you have identified as a policy issue. In coming up with alternatives,

you are developing a particular action or package of actions that will help to address the problem. The process by which you develop alternatives is discussed more fully in Chapter 6.

5. Weigh the Options.   Steps 3 and 4 will result in a set of alternatives from which you will choose one based on the criteria you have deemed important. Making the evaluation of alternatives explicit is an important policy analytical step because it enhances accountability. Reduced accountability reduces the credibility of the results stemming from the policy analysis process. Reduced credibility often lessens the ability of education leaders to persuade a community that the path chosen is the appropriate one. One of the primary tasks in weighing your options is to be explicit and grounded about the rationale underlying your evaluation. Chapter 7 offers guidelines on how to consider and articulate the rationale used to weigh policy options.

6. Make Recommendations.   This step differs from simply weighing options because it incorporates the information from step 5 and provides bases by which you can indicate clearly and explicitly the preferred alternative. This step reflects the normative, multifaceted, and iterative nature of the policy analytical process. Step 5 focused on how you would *weigh* policy alternatives; this step focuses on how you would then *decide* on the appropriate policy. In essence, this step allows you to "test your work," thus ensuring the coherence of your evaluative argument. The discussion in Chapter 8 about making recommendations also delves more deeply into the appropriate role of policy analysts in this process once they have evaluated the alternatives.

7. Persuade Your Audience.   Before you can move on to implementing a policy, you have to persuade relevant decision makers about its suitability. A key step in policy analysis is *communicating* decisions to key stakeholders. Important parts of communicating your analysis are being aware of the structure of policy arguments; knowing the different modes of policy arguments; and, perhaps most important, understanding your audience. This step differs somewhat from step 2, making the case, because that step asked you to look more closely at assembling the data. This step looks more closely at communicating that information once the decision about the appropriate policy strategy is made. The art of communication is covered more fully in Chapter 9.

8. Implement the Solution.   For policies to have an impact, they must be carried out. While implementation is not equivalent to outcome, managing the implementation process bolsters the chance that the enacted policy will yield the results sought. Enacted policies are not implemented for many reasons. This step ensures that education leaders pay attention to the implementation process and anticipate challenges that may arise. A full discussion of this step, including an overview of the stages of implementation, barriers to implementation, leadership challenges, and a guide to creating an implementation plan, appears in Chapter 10.

9. Monitor Outputs.   Policy analysis is about addressing a problematic condition. To know how effective your efforts are at resolving the problem, you have to document relevant aspects of its context. Monitoring offers information on what happened and informs analytical decisions on how it happened and why. It is the penultimate step in the policy analytical process and connects the actions outlined in the implementation plan with policy objectives. Monitoring outputs is discussed more fully in Chapter 11.

10. Evaluate Outcomes.   Evaluation focuses on the achievement of goals and objectives, and produces information about the value of policy outcomes. In that process, you may revisit whether the original goals were worthwhile. However, evaluation is not necessarily about assessing the value of policy goals but gauging how well the policy actually achieved them. Revising the goals would essentially entail a reevaluation of the problem statement, which is a function of the entire policy analytic process, not just the formal evaluative step. While actual evaluation occurs after implementation (ex post), it is imperative to have an evaluation plan from the outset. This step is essential for education leaders to consider because it offers them an opportunity to provide clear guidance on what constitutes an improvement of the problematic condition. Evaluating outcomes is discussed more fully in Chapter 12.

Stepping-Stones of Policy Analysis

Education leaders should view the 10 steps as stepping-stones in the policy analysis process but not treat them as if they, or the order in which they are presented here, are set in stone. Maybe you will find it useful to think of the alternatives before you establish your driving values. Maybe you think communicating with your audience is part and parcel of making your case. The process is iterative, and you may find yourself doing the steps out of order or repeating them again and again. Follow the basic process, which will allow you to focus on the policy problem and to devise alternatives that resolve it. As you go through the details of the list, you will have a clearer idea of how the pieces of the policy analysis puzzle fit together and how they can clarify your decision process.

Chapter Summary

Policy analysis is not simply policy evaluation; it covers several steps, of which evaluation is just one part. Policy analysis is not policy making. There is overlap between the policy-making process and the policy analytical process, but they are not identical. The policy-making process is largely entrenched in politics and focuses on the decision makers and the struggle to have one's values backed by the authoritative role of government. By contrast, policy analysis is often perceived to be a more technical process and potentially less contentious, although there is disagreement in the literature on whether policy analysis is as neutral as some earlier researchers had claimed.

In this chapter, we have explored the policy analysis process. We have addressed what it is and what it is not. We have looked at how policy analysis can intersect with policy making. Next, we will discuss how to start the analytical process with the definition of the problem, which is the focus of the next chapter. In starting the analysis, remember that a policy issue is one in which there is a condition that needs to be changed, this condition can be changed using communal resources, it should be changed using communal resources, *and* for which there is disagreement about the most appropriate strategy for change.

Review Questions

1. What is policy analysis?
2. As a policy analyst, what do you think are some of the challenges in identifying education policy problems in modern society?

3. What are the steps in the policy analytical process? Are there any you would add or omit? Why?

4. How would you transform an education condition into a policy issue? Provide an example.
5. Prepare a reflective critique of the policy analysis process and your place in it using the reading materials assigned.
6. What are some of the major pitfalls in conducting policy analysis?
7. At the beginning of the chapter, you were introduced to Dr. Know and were asked how to make sure that he was getting at the heart of policy analysis. How would you have framed the problem facing the district? Has your framing changed after reading this chapter? Explain how and why.

News Story for Analysis

12-State Study Finds Falloff in Testing Gains After NCLB. Education Week. *August 1, 2007.* SECTION: *Pg. 9 Vol. 26 No. 44.*

Since the enactment of the No Child Left Behind law, test-score improvement among 4th graders in 12 states has fallen off in reading and slowed in math, according to a new study.

The paper also cites National Assessment of Educational Progress [NAEP] scores reflecting a virtual halt to progress in closing racial achievement gaps in reading since the federal law was signed in 2002.

The research, which draws on data from both state tests and the federally administered NAEP, is sure to add fuel to the heated debate over the controversial law as Congress prepares to take up its reauthorization.

"Over the past four years, 'No Child' proponents have made very strong claims that this reform is raising student achievement," said lead author Bruce Fuller, a professor of education and public policy at the University of California, Berkeley, and the director of the Policy Analysis for California Education research center based at Berkeley and Stanford University. "In fact, after NCLB, earlier progress made by the states actually petered out."

Mr. Fuller said that pattern emerged from his examination of pre-NCLB state test data as well as results from the long-term NAEP. But he does not suggest that the NCLB law is responsible for the reading-achievement stagnation and math-gain slowdown that he says occurred in the 12 states since the 1990s.

The study, published in the July issue of *Educational Researcher*, a peer-reviewed journal of the Washington-based American Educational Research Association, joins a thicket of recent reports on achievement levels since the federal law took effect.

In math, the new study found a rise in achievement since passage of the NCLB law in the 12 states studied: Arkansas, California, Illinois, Iowa, Kentucky, Massachusetts, Nebraska, New Jersey, North Carolina, Oklahoma, Texas, and Washington state.

Between 2002 and 2006, the study shows, scores on the 12 states' tests registered an unweighted mean growth rate of 2.4 percentage points in math proficiency. But the researcher noted that growth was slower after 2003 than it had been before passage of the NCLB law.

"Sustained gains in math post-NCLB offer a bright glimmer of hope that federal policy can make a difference inside classrooms," Mr. Fuller said in an e-mail.

The new research follows a June study by the Washington-based Center on Education Policy that found consistent and significant increases in state-test scores since the legislation became law in January 2002.

Mr. Fuller found fault with the CEP study's reliance on state tests alone, which he said were less trustworthy gauges of progress than long-range NAEP data—especially on reading.

When asked to comment on Mr. Fuller's new analysis, CEP President Jack Jennings defended the state tests as "more accurate barometers of whether kids are learning what the state thinks is important."

Reading Gap Sustained

Katherine McLane, the press secretary for the U.S. Department of Education, took issue with Mr. Fuller's conclusions.

"The fact is that No Child Left Behind is working," she said. "What the report seems not to account for is that a law that affects tens of thousands of schools all over America can't be implemented overnight and its effects are not immediate."

On the achievement gap, Mr. Fuller's study pointed to national NAEP data showing that in math, African-American 4th graders closed the gap with white students by more than half a grade level between 1992 and 2003. But it highlighted the fact that no further progress was made in 2005. Latino 4th graders, he observed, continued to close the math achievement gap even after passage of the federal law.

In reading, however, Mr. Fuller pointed to national NAEP data showing that black and Latino students' 4th grade reading proficiency has not appreciably narrowed the gap with white students' scores under the NCLB law.

Source: As appeared in *Education Week* (Vol. 26, Issue 44, Page 9). Reprinted with permission from Editorial Projects in Education.

Discussion Questions

1. What are the different phases of policy making implied in this news story? How do you know?
2. How are the different tasks of policy analysis reflected in the story?
3. How would you distinguish between the process of policy making and policy analysis using the information provided in this news story?
4. As an education leader, how would you use Mr. Fuller's study to inform your analysis of the policy issue and what worked?
5. How would you respond to Ms. McLane's remarks regarding the study? Would your response differ if you were primarily interested in policy making versus policy analysis? Explain.

Selected Websites

Economic Policy Institute. Available at

http://www.epi.org/research/education/.

This is the education section of the official website of the Economic Policy Institute, a nonprofit Washington, D.C., think tank. It was created in 1986 to broaden the discussion about economic policy to include the interests of low- and middle-income workers. Their analysis of policy problems is through a "living standards" lens, and they analyze the impact of policies and initiatives on the American public. The site contains leading research on education and other policy issues that may be of interest to policymakers. Education leaders should compare and contrast the definition of policy problems and recommendations offered at this site with those of the more conservative research institution, National Center for Policy Analysis.

National Center for Policy Analysis. Available at

http://www.ncpa.org/pub/?c=Education.

This is the education section of the official website of the National Center for Policy Analysis, which is a public policy research organization that develops and promotes private alternatives to government regulation and control. Their problem analysis stems from their belief that there is too much government regulation. Education leaders may find this site helpful in terms of viewing how conditions are identified and solutions proffered when approached from this perspective.

U.S. Department of Education. Available at

http://www.ed.gov.

This is the official government website of the U.S. Department of Education. It contains information on educational issues important to all levels of education, including accreditation for higher education institutions, student loans for higher education students, pedagogical strategies for elementary students, and so on. This site is useful because it offers education leaders insight on the education conditions that the president and other leaders at the federal level find problematic. It is important to know what these issues are and to be aware of policy directions and the implications of policies being considered.

U.S. Department of Education, Office of Elementary and Secondary Education. Available at *http://www2.ed.gov/about/offices/list/oese/index. html*.

This is the official website of the Office of Elementary and Secondary Education (OESE). It contains useful and timely information to enhance your knowledge of elementary and secondary education programs and issues. The office is responsible for directing, co-ordinating, and recommending policy for programs designed to assist state and local education agencies, help ensure access to services, foster educational improvement at the state and local levels, and to provide financial assistance to local educational agencies.

Selected References

Dunn, W. N. (2004). *Public policy analysis: An introduction* (3rd ed.). Upper Saddle River, NJ: Prentice Hall.

This text provides an excellent overview on the field of policy analysis. Education leaders may find it helpful for the theoretical framework that it provides. The book takes a multidisciplinary approach to analysis. Like other scholars in the field, Dunn describes the importance of starting the process with a clear definition of the problem.

Fowler, F. C. (2009). *Policy studies for educational leaders: An introduction.* (3rd ed.). Upper Saddle River, NJ: Prentice Hall.

I like the educational and practical focus of Fowler's (2009) text on policy making. Education leaders would find its discussion of the policy-making process a useful complement to the step-by-step method of analyzing policy presented in this text.

Patton, C. V., & Sawicki, D. S. (1993). *Basic methods of policy analysis and planning.* Englewood Cliffs, NJ: Prentice Hall.

Patton and Sawicki provide an excellent overview on the method of policy analysis. Their approach may be especially interesting to education leaders who have a background in economics. Like other methods texts in policy analysis, the authors indicate that the first step in the process is the definition of the problem.

3

Taking the First Step
Define the Problem

CHAPTER OBJECTIVES

After reading this chapter, you will be able to:

- Write a clear description of a negative condition
- Structure the negative condition to read like a policy problem
- Bound and clarify the scope of the policy problem identified
- Develop goals and objectives for solving the policy problem identified

EDUCATION VIGNETTE

Education leaders at all levels have been mulling over the condition of schools. Your state department of education has called a conference for leading education and business interests. At a working session, the conveners of the conference break you into small groups to discuss the condition of education in your state. They want a sense of the persistent problems that exist. You are appointed leader of your group and start to take notes. A heated argument ensues when some members of your group argue that education remains "a tide of mediocrity" awash with problems; others disagree and claim that the problems of schools are a "manufactured crisis" and have been overstated. You want to bring your own analysis of the education problem to the table and convince people to buy in.

What is the problem as you see it, and how do you get your colleagues and your constituency to see your point? Would you respond differently depending on your education context?

STRUCTURING THE PROBLEM

Writing a Clear Description of the Problem

The first step in defining a policy problem is being clear about what the problem is. As noted by Fowler (2009), Bardach (2009), and Dunn (2004), not all negative conditions rise to the level of a policy problem, and not all policy problems become policy issues that analysts need to examine. Booth, Colomb, and Williams (1995) argue that a clear description of a problem starts with the identification of a particular situation and with details of its undesirable consequences. Dunn (2004) adds that policy problems are un- realized needs or opportunities for improvement, and for analysts to structure policy problems appropriately, they will need to provide information about the *nature*, *scope*, and *severity* of the problem. Nature refers to the status of the problem. Is it stable, wors- ening, or getting better? Scope refers to those included in the problem definition. Are you looking at the problem from a community perspective, a national level, or through a global lens? The severity of the problem refers to the magnitude of the problem. Is it affecting a lot of people? Is the problem having a big effect on the community of inter- est? Is the rate at which the problem is changing high, low, or steady? Thus, to capture the essence of the condition, policy analysts will go through several structuring phases simply to define the problem.

DIFFERENT PHASES IN PROBLEM STRUCTURING.   Dunn notes that there are differences between simply trying to get a sense of the problem situation and structuring the prob- lem in a way that is meaningful for policymakers and practitioners. He argues that problem structuring is a "continuously recurring phase of policy inquiry in which ana- lysts search among competing problem formulations of different stakeholders" (Dunn, 2004, p. 72). In this way, sensing the problem is similar to the discussion on **issue rheto- ric** provided by Bardach (2009), where there is interest in defining a condition as bad and the language surrounding that discourse comes from the "ordinary language of debate and discussion" (p. 4). It also coincides with the "policy talk" described in Tyack and Cuban (1995) and cited in Heck (2004). **Policy talk** refers to the general discourse surrounding key elements of the policy problem.

In Dunn's discussion, structuring the problem is not the same as problem solving because the former requires complex, higher-order methods of dissecting a problematic condition. He argues that this step is iterative and should precede lower-order methods of problem solving, which he sees as a technical rather than analytical task. I consider that the primary purpose of the policy analytical process is a search for an appropriate solution and would not necessarily describe the problem-solving aspect of it as simply technical. Notwithstanding, I agree with Dunn that if the problem is made overly sim- plistic, analysts may be using limited resources inappropriately and may actually be spending their time solving the "wrong" problem.

Problematic Characteristics of Policy Problems

Policy problems are, at their heart, ill-structured problems (Dunn, 2004). **Ill-structured problems** are so-called because it is difficult to know where they begin and where they end. The very nature of a democratic policy process accentuates the challenges of prob- lem structuring because decision making in a democracy involves multiple decision makers, unknown values, and unlimited alternatives or at least options with uncertain

> - Do you have a clear statement of a condition that exists and that you would like to change?
>
> - Have you made sure that no solution is embedded in your description of that condition?
>
> - Have you provided research evidence of that condition? You should not force the reader to rely on your gut instinct.
>
> - Have you described fully the context in which the condition exists? (What is the nature and extent of the problem? What are the concrete steps taken to address it (if any)? Is there discussion of past attempts to solve the problem, people affected, and so on?)
>
> - Will readers be clear about the condition you are describing, the problem you want to change, and the end goal you have in mind? Readers should not be confused about the path that you would like to explore.
>
> If you answer no to any of these questions, you need to go back and rewrite the problem definition.

FIGURE 3.1   Guide to Structuring a Problem Statement

outcomes. In structuring policy problems and seeking their resolution, analysts must recognize their underlying complexity. That is, policy problems are a challenge to define because they are *interdependent*, the process of defining them is *subjective*, the choice of definition can seem *artificial*, and the nature of these problems is *ever changing*.

PERSONAL VERSUS POLICY PROBLEMS.   These attributes contrast with the relative simplicity of personal problems, which are often well structured because there is only one or a few decision makers, a small set of policy alternatives, and clearly ranked preferences regarding outcomes (Dunn, 2004). For example, if parents are concerned about the well-being of their child, they will have a clear idea of why they are concerned: Amy is not happy at school; Johnny cannot read; Mozart was not allowed to take band. Parents also have an implicit understanding of the values underlying their concern. Within typical constraints, parents do not have to persuade others that their values reflect the appropriate definition of well-being. They can simply pursue those strategies that allow them to alleviate the negative condition for their child. Granted, this may be oversimplifying the private decision-making process because, even in the raising of their own child, parents have to be mindful of the laws of the land, their resources, the rights of others, and so on. Notwithstanding, there is a limited number of decision makers in the personal context to argue about what *good* looks like. While everyone is connected to others, it is presumed that personal decisions will have an impact on the individual and the family, not the broad collective as a whole.

INTERDEPENDENCE OF PROBLEMS.   The world can be a messy place, with the symptoms of a problem, its causes, and its essence all interconnected. For example, if we find the condition of low student scores problematic, is that a symptom of poverty or a cause of it? As we try to structure the problem, should we start with conditions that affect poverty, or should we start with the factors that affect achievement? What should be our bottom line in that instance, and how do we know where to begin in a chain of factors that may all be less than ideal?

In many ways, the interdependency of policy problems is like that well-known nursery rhyme of the old lady who swallowed the fly, and then the spider, and the bird with the refrain being, "Who knows why she swallowed the fly. . . ." As education leaders, we may not always know why schools are not ideal, but the role of policy analysts is to identify those problems that can be fixed and should be fixed using collective resources.

Where do problems begin and end? Children get up in the morning and they go to school. Is it the responsibility of education leaders to ensure that they have had breakfast, transportation to school and back home again, a nutritious lunch, and so on? In the United States, our answer to that question has generally been in the affirmative, and there are lunch programs and busing offered by most school districts. More controversial is the question of providing for the mental health of children and whether it should be part of schooling and reflective of an education problem. Proponents of providing health and human services in schools often argue that if policymakers do not address the needs of the whole child, they will not be able to address the single metric of academic performance. Opponents of health and social services in schools argue that these services are beyond the purview of schooling and siphon scarce resources from academic studies. Others argue for partnerships among schools and health and human service agencies to balance both sides of the argument. For example, in 2008, Mississippi policymakers required students to take a one-half unit of comprehensive health to be eligible for graduation. To accomplish this, the state of Mississippi authorized and empowered the state board of health and the various county health departments to establish and provide for health education programs in the public schools of that state. To fulfill that function, these organizations could employ county health educators. Education leaders in that state used that framework to ensure that all students could access the information and skills necessary to make high-quality, age-appropriate health decisions. As another example, education and other policy leaders in Hawaii have adopted a partnership between schools and health services under their Healthy Children Healthy Communities Model. This model stresses the importance of using school–community partnerships to develop a systemic, comprehensive, multifaceted approach to ensuring high outcomes for children.

Problem structuring is often a difficult process because you must determine where the problem begins and where it ends. This is where your values and understanding of the world will determine how you choose to define the problem. Existing research also provides helpful guidance about how other people interested in improving the problem chose to tackle it and what made them successful or not in resolving it. For instance, education policies in the 1960s focused on addressing low student achievement among the poor by incorporating lunch programs in the Elementary and Secondary Education Act. Lunch programs were seen as a way to address low student achievement by improving the welfare of children. In that structuring of the problem, the focus was on equalizing opportunities for children, which in turn were supposed to increase overall scores. By the 1980s, policymakers tended to focus on the economic implications of low student achievement rather than tackle economic factors as the root cause of poor school performance (e.g., *A Nation at Risk*). Consequently, a strategy chosen by policymakers in improving schools targeted improving scores because of its implications for the economy rather than focusing on improving economic opportunities because of its impact on student achievement.

SUBJECTIVITY AND ARTIFICIALITY OF STRUCTURING POLICY PROBLEMS. The interdependence of policy problems can be frustrating because, in the end, the structuring of policy issues may seem subjective and artificial. The process is subjective, but subjectivity does not mean that those who are making the decision should not be informed and reflective. Education leaders have to decide on their main goals in making the world (or at least the school) a better place. While Dunn (2004) is right that policy problems are probably best tackled simultaneously, taking on all, or even many, of the ills of society may be an overwhelming and daunting endeavor. Doing so may lead to the case where "the best is the enemy of the good" and nothing gets done (e.g., Colander, 1991). My advice to education leaders would be to determine what the goal of a particular framing of a policy problem would entail, and if that goal is acceptable, then that should be the policy problem tackled. This approach is clearly subjective and the delineation of problems may be artificial, but that is the nature of the policy analytical process.

DYNAMIC NATURE OF POLICY PROBLEMS.   Even when education leaders are comfortable that they have discovered the problem that they would like to solve, the nature of that problem can change over time. Education leaders must be fully aware of the tangible and changing consequences of the problem that they have identified. Thus, they need to formulate arguments that make sense even in ever-changing and messy contexts. By clearly formulating the problem, they are better able to articulate the rationale for the courses of action they would like to take. Booth and his colleagues (1995) offer six questions that education leaders must be able to answer and thus provide clarity and grounding for their description of a condition that they would like to change:

1. What is your point?
2. What evidence do you have?
3. Why do you think the evidence supports your claim?
4. How would you respond to rebuttals?
5. Are you entirely sure about your response to concerns?
6. How strong is your claim? (That is, will it hold up in different contexts?)

Your responses to these questions essentially lay a strong foundation for defining a policy problem. Your responses include a clear statement regarding what you want readers to believe (claim), the reasons that you think that your audience should believe what you claim, the general principles that underlie your assertions, and the limitations that you make on your conclusions (Booth et al., 1995, pp. 89–90).

Building on Your Condition Statement

In structuring the condition to read like a policy problem, you need to provide a descriptive statement grounded in data. Bardach (2009) indicates that a helpful strategy in creating a problem statement is to write in terms of excesses and deficits. (I call this the Goldilocks syndrome: the chair is too small, the porridge is too hot, or the bed is too hard.) As education leaders we may find that achievement scores are too low, dropout rates are too high, or the achievement gap between student populations is too big. At its very essence then, the writing of a policy problem statement requires explicit, descriptive analysis with implicitly normative undertones.

You should be able to describe the essence of your problem in one statement. The presence of the word *too* in a statement ensures that the framer of the statement is not content with the extant condition. Because readers may not be clear why this lack of contentment exists, however, it is your responsibility to create a working definition of

1. Too many third-graders are not reading at grade level.

2. Too few students are proficient in math.

3. Too many schools are not making annual yearly progress.

4. Too few first-generation college students persist in college.

5. Too many low-income students do not complete high school.

6. Too few students earn their bachelor's degree in 4 years.

FIGURE 3.2   Examples of Descriptive Problem Statements Consistent with the Policy Literature, Especially Bardach (2009)

the problem statement. Using the educational examples from the previous paragraph, part of defining the problem statement requires that education leaders provide evidence of why student scores are too low, what data and arguments support their contention that the dropout rates are too high, or what facts indicate that the gap in achievement between student groups is too big.

To do that, establishing absolute standards of what would solve the problem or making unfavorable comparisons with relevant peer groups is important. For example, to use an absolute standard to justify seeing the condition of student scores as being too low may entail reference to the No Child Left Behind Act of 2001 that all children should be proficient, and if less than 100% of children are proficient, then a problem exists. You can also simply provide analogous statistics to an appropriate referent group and say that the condition is problematic because it causes "us" to be less "good" than "them." For example, in the now well-known 1983 *A Nation at Risk* report, the authors claim that the "tide of mediocrity" that washed over the education system was a great threat to the success of the United States on the global stage.

MAKING THE CONDITION A PROBLEM

Part of transforming the condition into a policy problem is to describe the consequences to society if the condition remains as is. You can do that by embedding "so what" in your expanded condition statement. Let's say that readers agreed that student performance is too low, but so what? Why should they care about that particular condition? Part of why readers and a broader audience will care is knowing something about the background of the condition. (1) Who is affected? (2) How many people are affected? (3) How are they affected? (4) Is the broader society affected? (5) How is it affected— economically; politically; morally? (6) Is the impact big or small? While we are answering these six questions, our discussion must always be clear that the world does not have to be the way it is and that we can do something about the condition being defined as problematic. Recall the discussion in the previous chapters where a condition does not transform into a policy problem unless there is an understanding that it *can* be solved and *should* be solved using government resources. Your responses to the six questions also tie into the reasons you think that the problem exists. We are ready for a more in-depth discussion on bounding the scope of the problem and an examination of the causal factors therein.

1. Who is affected?

2. How many people are affected?

3. In what ways are people affected?

4. Is the broader society affected?

5. In what ways is the broader society affected (economically, politically, morally)?

6. Is the impact big or small?

FIGURE 3.3 Summary of Questions That Must Be Answered to Address Consequences of Not Solving a Problem

SCOPE OF THE PROBLEM

Bounding the Problem

By structuring the problem in a particular way, you are leaving some things out and including others. It is important to make clear from the first step of the policy analysis process that at the end of the journey, actions generated from the process will not create a perfect world but will create a better one. As an education leader, you have to make choices about how to delineate the problem and where in the complex chain of cause and consequence you plan to start. Your choice will influence the consideration of certain phenomena as causes, consequences, or evidence of the problem at hand. Your choice may also influence whether actors consider themselves to be winners or losers under the change you propose.

WHO IS INCLUDED? A key aspect of bounding the scope of the problem is not only knowing where to start in the chain of factors but also knowing who the stakeholders are. **Stakeholders** comprise those individuals or groups who are affected by and who influence the choice of action taken to resolve the policy issue identified. Your discussion about the consequences of the problem will provide insight about the impact of policies chosen to address the problem and the groups affected by those policies. Reviewing the literature on policy making can reveal how you can prioritize among those actors. For example, Marshall and colleagues (1989), as cited in Heck (2004), offer a categorization of influence where actors may be grouped into five key categories: insiders, near circle participants, far circle participants, sometimes players, and forgotten players. **Insiders** include political actors who set the agenda and are instrumental in moving policy forward. This group of stakeholders includes the leaders of countries, their top appointments, and other leaders of policy-making communities. In democracies, they typically consist of elected officials and are analogous to the visible participants described by Kingdon (1995). **Near circle participants** are those individuals or groups who can play an influential role on the political decisions made by insiders. This group typically consists of legislative and executive staff members, who serve the official leaders. **Far circle participants** may not be influential in the formation and adoption of policy but may play an important role in its implementation. This group often includes teachers, district administrators, community liaisons, and so on. Those policy actors considered to be **sometimes players** do not have a consistent role to play in the policy-making process, although their level of participation and influence may vary with the issue. This group may include grassroots organizers, community representatives, and so on. Groups on the margin are **forgotten players** whose influence on the governmental agenda (and thus policies generated) is sporadic. Quite often, forgotten players belong to groups that are marginalized due to ethnicity, poverty, culture, and so on. As Spring (2005) and others have noted elsewhere, quite often those groups and individuals who have the most influence on the policy decisions being made are not the ones who will be affected the most directly by implementation of the policy.

Bardach (2009) groups stakeholders in the policy process differently and describes stakeholders in general as "interests." For any policy action examined, there are individuals and/or groups who support that action, oppose it, or are indifferent. Therefore, to optimize the political feasibility of certain policy options, Bardach asserts that one should formulate them so that supporters are converted into allies and opposition is neutralized or negated. However you choose to identify and group stakeholders, an analysis of them in the policy analytical process lays important groundwork for assessing the political feasibility of various actions later on. Knowing more about the underlying conditions affecting the existence of the problem will provide essential insight on who is affected as well as potential ways of resolving it.

Causes of the Problem

The reason we think a particular condition exists is tied to our values, worldviews, philosophy, priorities, disciplines, education, experience, and so on. Heck (2004) argues that we can examine policy through three main lenses. As noted in previous chapters, these three lens are largely from a rational framework, where we emphasize goals; a cultural framework, where the emphasis is on relationships; and an institutional framework, where structural factors are the focus. These disciplinary groupings are not exhaustive, but they are helpful in allowing us to organize the literature regarding a problem of interest. Let us revisit the example problem statement that we had in Chapter 2 where too many students in higher education do not earn a bachelor's degree in 4 years. From that statement, we can create a Venn diagram of the possible causes of the problem cited in the literature (see Figure 3.5). All three disciplinary perspectives overlap, but each perspective will likely delineate the problem differently, and thus education leaders relying on different perspectives may offer different approaches to solving the problem identified.

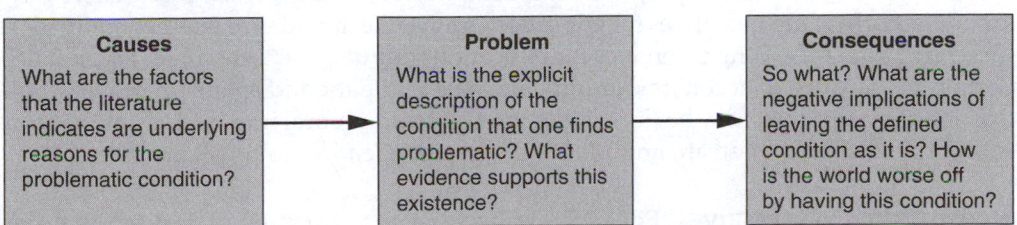

FIGURE 3.4 Structuring a Problem Statement by Deconstructing the Problematic Condition

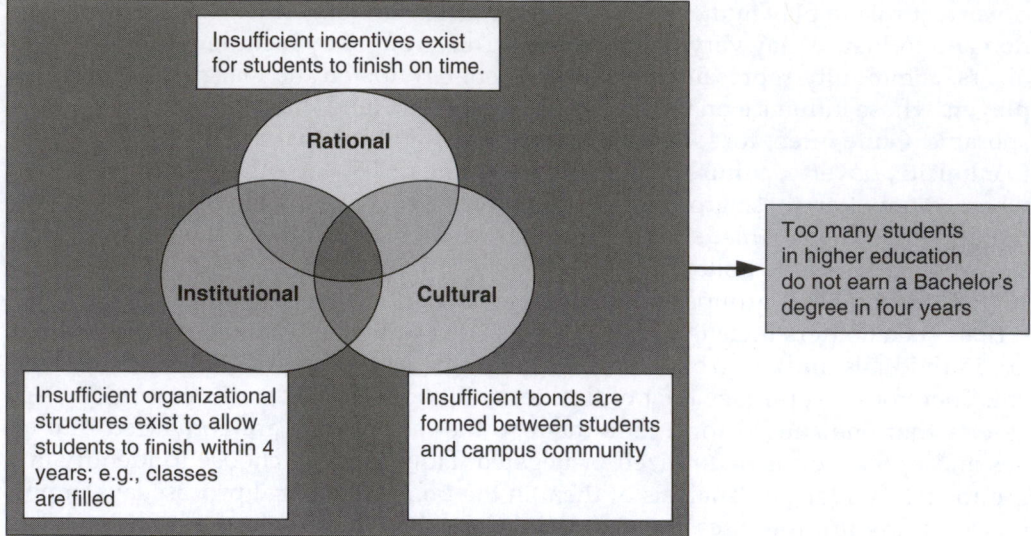

FIGURE 3.5 Example of Different Disciplinary Perspectives on the Possible Cause of a Policy Problem

RATIONAL PERSPECTIVE. Education leaders using a **rational perspective** may examine and conclude that students in higher education are not completing their bachelor's degree in 4 years because they have insufficient incentives to do so (e.g., Ehrenberg & Mavros, 1995; Gillingham, Seneca, & Taussig, 1991). If education leaders subscribe to that viewpoint, they may argue that there should be incentives built into the system that would allow students to change the benefit and cost structure currently being applied by students. This approach may include economic arguments to develop policies that force or facilitate the private costs and benefits to the individual student to be more reflective of the social costs and benefits to the university and the society at large. This may entail providing a discount on tuition to students who complete their education within 4 years and sharply increasing the costs of attending school if more than 4 years are taken to complete their studies. At the secondary level of education, if the problem is perceived as student performance being too low, one strategy would be to provide students with an incentive to achieve better grades by paying them for their academic performance or attendance. For example, education leaders in Chicago, Illinois, rewarded students with perfect attendance with trips to the circus. Leaders at a Massachusetts high school offered a cash incentive program to students to increase attendance (e.g., Wallace & McDermott, 2010). The success of these programs has been varied, and Harvard researchers have found that providing incentives for education inputs like attendance was generally more successful than providing incentives for education outputs, like test scores (Fryer, 2010). Certainly, there are noneconomic arguments to be made for and against particular policies. At this point, you may be thinking of the equity and moral implications of the strategies proposed, and these are important for education leaders to consider.

INSTITUTIONAL PERSPECTIVE. Education leaders using a structural or **institutional perspective** may formulate the lengthy completion of the bachelor's degree as a problem caused by institutional barriers. From this standpoint, education leaders may consider factors such as unavailability of classes, inappropriate planning of student schedules, and so on. Given the factors identified, education leaders will look for alternatives that address these structural challenges. Their favored strategies may include increasing class size (thus making more space available), improving advice offered by faculty advisers (e.g., Ferrer del Valero, 2001), and reviewing college admission decisions (e.g., Wang & Pilarzyk, 2007). An example of a structural approach to improving education contexts is the use or abandonment of tracking to promote improved performance and/or equity. For example, education leaders at an economically, ethnically, and culturally diverse secondary school in California eliminated ability grouping at the school level in order to balance the dual goals of excellence and equity (e.g., Cooper, 1996). By contrast, Gordon Brown, prime minister of Great Britain from June 2007 to May 2010, sought to have ability groupings in key subjects as the norm in schools (e.g., Grouping kids by ability harms education, 2007).

CULTURAL PERSPECTIVE.   The same problem (insufficient numbers of students completing a bachelor's degree in 4 years) may be delineated quite differently by education leaders relying on a cultural perspective. The emphasis offered by education leaders relying on a **cultural perspective** is the influence of relationships on the phenomenon. That is, they would likely regard the problem as being caused by creating insufficient ties between students and the broader college community, both inside and outside the classroom (e.g., Thomas, 2000; Tinto, 1997). For education leaders drawn to this perspective, resolution of a problem must be anchored in the development and building of relationships. Consequently, one strategy that may be offered to increase the timely completion of the first degree may be to improve the classroom experience of students by promoting a collaborative learning experience as well as the adoption of collaborative learning strategies, as was done by the Seattle Central Community College. Outside the classroom, the creation of Welcome Week at the University of Minnesota was an explicit effort on the part of university administrators to increase the time freshmen would be on campus before the official start of classes and to start early with the building of bonds between the university and the students.

In the education arena, the creation or strengthening of cultural bonds between students and the broader campus community is not unique to higher education; examples also abound in elementary (primary) and secondary schools. For example, the creation of schools within a school is an attempt on the part of policymakers and administrators to create greater school cohesion and connectedness. This approach is justified in part because of its perceived positive effect on student performance (e.g., Maroulis & Gomez, 2008).

Policymakers and analysts can rely on multiple lenses and perspectives to identify what they consider to be the heart of the problem and what needs to be done to resolve it. For example, the United States Department of Education indicates that the No Child Left Behind Act of 2001 (which was subsequently reauthorized in 2007) contains four pillars: (1) stronger accountability for results, (2) more freedom for states and communities, (3) proven education methods, and (4) more choices for parents (U.S. Department of Education, PowerPoint presentation available at http://www2.ed.gov/nclb/overview/intro/presentation/index.html). These four pillars are indicative of what policymakers have identified as the underlying causes of inadequate performance of students and among student groups. That is, if the policy calls for stronger accountability for results, the implication is that a lack of accountability was a key factor in the lack of proficiency among students and the perceived underperformance of the education community. The same analysis may be made for the remaining three pillars. The Race to the Top Fund, which is part of the American Recovery and Reinvestment Act of 2009 (ARRA), Section 14005-6, Title XIV, (Public Law 111-5), provides competitive grants to encourage and reward states that are creating the conditions for education innovation and reform. These grants presume that one reason students are not doing well is because of insufficient incentives in the system to support educational innovation and reform. While an understanding of the underlying factors of a policy problem is important in the creation of appropriate solutions, knowing where you want to go is crucial to resolving the issue. In essence, defining the problem is incomplete without an explicit statement of the goal of the analysis.

GOALS AND OBJECTIVES OF SOLVING THE PROBLEM IDENTIFIED

The Goal is the Obverse of the Problem

The goal of the analysis is to find an alternative that results in the obverse of the problem identified. Thus, if the problematic condition statement reads, "Too few students are performing proficiently," then the goal would be to have more students performing proficiently. Patton and Sawicki (1993) note that goals are "formally and broadly worded statements about what we desire to achieve in the long run" (p. 187). For instance, the goal of No Child Left Behind (NCLB) is to have 100% proficiency among the nation's children. An explicit statement of the goal or goals also acts as a check on whether the problem that you have identified really is the one on which you would like to focus your efforts and limited resources. If the goal identified is not where you ultimately would like to be, that is a red flag and you will have to revisit and redefine your problem statement.

Objectives are Working Definitions of Goals

Providing a general description of how the world should look after resolution of the problem identified is a necessary but not sufficient step in policy analysis. Equally important is providing a working definition of what it means to reach that goal. This specification is often characterized as objectives, indicators, or benchmarks (e.g., Patton & Sawicki, 1993; Garner, 2004). This specification must be focused on a specific end state, with concrete measures of how you will know when that goal has been achieved.

The goal is to have:

1. More third-graders who read at grade level.
2. More students who are proficient in math.
3. More schools who make annual yearly progress.
4. More first-generation college students who persist in college.
5. More low-income students who complete high school.
6. More students who earn their bachelor's degree in 4 years.

FIGURE 3.6   Examples of Goal Statements (Obverse of Statements in Figure 3.2)

Table 3.1 Examples of Education Policy Problem with Associated Goals and Objectives

Problems	Goals	Objectives
Too many third-graders are not reading at grade level.	More third-graders who read at grade level.	The percentage of third-graders who read at grade level, as measured by [test], will increase from 35% to 50% by 2014.
Too few students are proficient in math.	More students who are proficient in math.	The percentage of students in [specify system] who are proficient in math, as measured by [test] will increase from 50% to 75%.
Too many schools are not making annual yearly progress.	More schools that make annual yearly progress.	The number of schools that are making annual yearly progress as measured by the requirements of the NCLB will increase from [specify number] to [specify bigger number] by 2012.
Too few first-generation college students persist in college.	More first-generation college students who persist in college.	The percentage (or number) of first-generation college students who remain enrolled in college will increase from [specify number] to [specify bigger number] by 2015.
Too many low-income students do not complete high school.	More low-income students who complete high school.	The percentage of low-income students who complete high school will increase from the present rate of [specify percentage] to [specify bigger percentage] by 2014.
Too few students earn their bachelor's degree in 4 years.	More students who earn their bachelor's degree in 4 years	The number of undergraduate students who earn a bachelor's degree in 4 years will increase from its present level of 35% to 85% by 2015.

Source: Compiled by the author as an illustrative guide to distinguishing among problem, goals, and objectives.

OBJECTIVES VERSUS ALTERNATIVES.   At this point of the discussion, students often question the difference between objectives and alternatives. An objectives may be considered a "what": what will let us know that we have achieved the goal. These may include output data on graduation rates for specific populations, pass rates of student groups, and so on. An alternative is a "how": that is, the strategies that will be promoted to ensure that objectives are met. For example, if we wanted to get to Duluth, Minnesota, from Minneapolis, the goal would be Duluth. The objectives would be the signposts or markers that allow us to know what points we have reached on our trip. Alternatives would be the means by which we achieve the goal: We could drive, walk, take the bus, or fly. To use an example more directly relevant to education, if the goal is to have better educated students, we need a concrete measure of what "better educated" is. Under the guidelines required by the federal government, "better educated" is measured by pass rates on statewide tests given in the third through eighth grade. Those pass rates thus serve as the objectives associated with the goals of the policy.

Chapter Summary

A comprehensive statement of a policy problem has three components: (1) a descriptive statement of the condition with accompanying evidence; (2) a discussion of the consequences of not solving the condition, also with accompanying evidence; and (3) a discussion, grounded in the literature, of the factors that led to the existence of the problem. At the heart of the problem statement is a description of the condition and data organized into meaningful evidence to support the description. By organizing the discussion according to these three components, an education leader can go a long way in providing a clear definition of the problem. If you read through the narrative, you would find that sentences supporting the existence of the condition were part of the opening paragraphs. Sentences describing the factors resulting in the problematic condition and the consequences of not solving it would follow, and they would be grouped according to their categorization as a causal factor or as a consequence of the condition. By organizing the problem statement this way, the reader can follow the logic of the education leader in his or her definition of a policy problem.

You have now tackled one of the most challenging steps in policy analysis. It is time to move on to making your case.

Review Questions

1. What do you think are some of the challenges in developing a clear problem definition? How would you address these challenges?
2. Write a clear description of a problem that you would like to tackle in your role as education leader.
3. How does your description of the problem make it clear that this is a policy problem and not a personal one? How well did you address the nature, scope, and severity of the problem?
4. Given your description of the problem in Review Question 2, indicate the goals and likely objectives of solving it.
5. At the beginning of the chapter, you were introduced to different definitions of an education problem facing the United States. How would you define the problem? Would your definition be consistent or inconsistent with the definition offered by policymakers at various levels of government (including federal, state, district, and school)?

News Story for Analysis

"Faulty federal math hurts reserve schools." *National Post* (f/k/a *The Financial Post*) (Canada). October 30, 2008 Thursday. National Edition. BYLINE: John Ivison, *National Post*. SECTION: CANADA; John Ivison; Pg. A4. DATELINE: OTTAWA

OTTAWA—Prime Minister Stephen Harper said during the election campaign that the most serious problem this country [Canada] will face going forward is a shortage of skilled labor. As the global financial crisis bites, and thousands are thrown out of work, he might be reassessing that statement.

But while it may not be his most immediate headache, there's no doubt that the effect of so many Baby Boomers retiring, coupled with a low birth rate, is going to be an economic earthquake, the tremors of which were already being felt before the current crisis hit. The Bank of Canada released a survey recently, in which 40% of firms said labor shortages were restricting their ability to meet demand.

This should be good news for Canada's First Nations. Their people are young—the median age on reserves is 22, compared to 36 for all Canadians—and they have burgeoning population growth, with a rate three times the rest of Canada.

Yet, aboriginal Canadians are unlikely to be the source of solutions to the problem in years to come, unless there are some drastic changes to public policy, according to a new study for the CD Howe Institute by Simon Fraser University professor John Richards.

By looking at 2006 census data, Professor Richards discovered only two-thirds of aboriginal Canadians between the ages of 25 and 44 have a high school diploma, compared with nine out of 10 non-native Canadians.

The global figure masks some even more worrying statistics—less than 40% of First Nations adults who live on reserves graduated from high school, a gap of 50% with the rest of Canada. In Manitoba, only one in four males aged 20 to 24 on reserves is likely to have finished high school.

This matters because the employment rate nearly doubles for those with a high school diploma and continues to rise as you move up the education ladder. Only one in three aboriginal Canadians who did not graduate from high school had a job in 2006, according to the census.

Since there are currently 75,000 kids in schools on reserves, the findings suggest we are storing up trouble, as a small army of poor, unemployed natives looks for outlets for its discontent, instead of contributing to increasing the nation's store of wealth.

So, what to do? Outcomes for Indians living off-reserve and for Metis were much better (60% and 75% graduation rates, respectively) but, short of cutting off federal funding for the reserve system (an option with which many readers may feel sympathy, but which is politically toxic), the answer has to lie in improving the quality of reserve schools.

The problem here is that many of them are run by local bands that have neither the resources nor expertise to develop a curriculum, assess students and teachers, or manage facilities. They are further hindered by funding that does not match

provincial levels. In 1996, the federal government instituted a 2% cap on funding increases that, over time, has meant a 7% drop in real dollars, after adjustments for inflation and population growth.

As the *National Post* revealed in April, spending by the Department of Indian and Northern Affairs Canada (INAC) on the average native student was $6,916 in 2006–07, compared with a provincial average of $8,165 (INAC had never released that number before, saying comparisons are "difficult"—no wonder).

The inevitable result is that teachers get paid less on reserves, there are more students per teacher and there are fewer resources. When combined with the haphazard governance regimes, the grim graduation statistics should come as no surprise. There have been attempts made to arrest this decline, particularly in New Brunswick and British Columbia, where a tripartite agreement between Ottawa, the provincial government and aboriginal groups has produced a First Nations Education Steering Committee to run the reserve school system.

This is an approach advocated by Michael Mendelson, senior scholar at the Caledon Institute, who has noted that non-native rural schools were consolidated into larger boards many years ago, "sometimes over the strenuous objection of local committees."

Even though the B.C. initiative shows promise, there has been little real progress because it diverts funding from participating bands to the new aboriginal-run school authority. Local band councils, more anxious about preserving their autonomy and funding than the graduation rates of their young people, are resisting reform, according to the Richards report.

The way to break this logjam would seem to be the promise of increased reserve education funding to provincial levels, if bands participate—essentially making them an offer they can't refuse.

James Wilson, director of education at the Opaskwayak Education Authority in Manitoba, thinks this strategy would work. "My father, who's now retired, said that we fought so hard and for so many years to control education locally that it's now hard to let go. But we have to be willing to look at why we did it in the first place and ask whether we should give up control, if it is for the benefit of our students," he said.

The federal government has said it will increase native education funding by $268 million over five years—a move Mr. Wilson says is a step in the right direction, but one that is unlikely to bridge the gap between what on-reserve and provincial schools spend (the increase works out at around $700 per head, while the funding gap in such provinces as Alberta, Saskatchewan and Manitoba is close to $3,000).

For a government that has pitched a vision of self-governing, self-sufficient First Nations communities, funded by their own tax base, increased aboriginal education funding should be considered an essential investment, even at a time when the specter of deficit looms so large.

Material reprinted with the express permission of: "National Post Inc.".

Discussion Questions

1. What are the different definitions of the policy problem inferred in the article?
2. What are the causes of the problem that are implied by these different definitions?
3. For each definition identified, describe the implications for policy and the potential impact on stakeholders.
4. Indicate the dominant disciplinary lenses through which the various stakeholders see the problem of education. In what ways does the narrative used in this article reflect these lenses?
5. With which definition of the policy problem would you agree? Explain.

Selected Websites

Mississippi Department of Education. Office of Healthy Schools. Available at

http://www.healthyschoolsms.org/ohs_main/ resources/state_policies.htm

The official website of the Office of Healthy Schools of the Mississippi Department of Education. The office bills itself as having an understanding of the impact of the health of children and adolescents on Mississippi and America's future. The Mississippi Department of Education (MDE) restructured and consolidated its health and safety-related programs under the umbrella of the Office of Healthy Schools, which is a product of the state's Department of Education and The Bower Foundation. Through the efforts of the Office of Healthy Schools, the Mississippi Department of Education offers a system of coordinated school health services to 152 school districts to assist them in developing organizations that make the connection between good student health and high academic achievement. Education leaders may find this site helpful because it presents one example of how state policymakers tried to address the needs of children by using multiple partnerships.

U.S. Department of Health and Human Services and Center for Mental Health Services. *School-Community Partnerships: A Guide*. Available at

http://smhp.psych.ucla.edu/qf/Commout_tt/ School-Com2-8.pdf

This website presents an excerpt from a PDF document published jointly by the U.S. Department of Health and Human Services and the Center for Mental Health Services. Education leaders may find this site helpful because it documents various school–community partnerships across the United States. These partnerships reflect a variety of ways in which education leaders and others have defined the goals of education and the problem of schooling.

U.S. Department of Education. PowerPoint presentation of the No Child Left Behind Act of 2001.

http://www2.ed.gov/nclb/overview/intro/ presentation/index.html

This site offers a reader-friendly version of the 600+ page document of the No Child Left Behind Act of 2001. This website may be useful for education leaders because it highlights aspects of the report that current policy leaders emphasize in their definition of the problem. This site also allows education leaders to focus on the framing of problems from a rational perspective and the resultant goals that are established.

Selected References

Maroulis, S., & Gomez, L. M. (2008, September). Does "connectedness" matter? Evidence from a social network analysis within a small-school reform [part of a special issue entitled Small Secondary Schools]. *Teachers College Record, 110*(9), 1901–1929.

This article examines how school-within-a-school reform provided opportunities for high school students in a large secondary school to build stronger relationships with their peers. Education leaders may find this article helpful in viewing the definition of student achievement from a cultural perspective. It also details the impact of school-within-a-school reform on student performance and the importance of context on this impact.

Orfield, G. (2000). Policy and equity: Lessons of a third of a century of education reforms in the United States. In F. Reimers (Ed.), *Unequal schools, unequal chances: The challenges to equal opportunity in the Americas.* Harvard University Press: Cambridge, MA.

Orfield describes the major themes of two different policy eras in U.S. educational policy since the 1960s. He characterizes the decades from 1960 to 1980 as a time that emphasized equity, while the decades after 1980 have had a strong emphasis on competition and standards. He argues that the definitions offered in the earlier era resulted in policymakers achieving more success in narrowing educational gaps and increasing educational attainment levels. Education leaders may find this chapter interesting because of the historical framing it offers on the different problem definitions that have prevailed.

Thomas, S. L. (2000, September/October). Ties that bind. *Journal of Higher Education, 71*(5), 591–615.

This study offers yet another example of an education problem defined from a cultural perspective, this time for students at a 4-year liberal arts college. Thomas examined college student integration and persistence, and highlighted the differential effects of various network characteristics on persistence. Education leaders may find this article of interest because it shows how relationships can influence student integration and persistence within the higher education system.

Wang, Y., & Pilarzyk, T. (2007, Fall). Mapping the enrollment process: Implications of setting deadlines for student success and college management. *Journal of College Admission, 197*, 24–33.

This article looks at the problem of education through a structural lens. Wang and colleagues argue that management decisions should be informed by detailed enrollment data, especially on how the timing of student decisions affects their academic success. The authors look at the enrollment flow at a large, urban, community-based technical college to recommend and monitor enrollment decisions. They tried to find the optimal balance among honoring the college mission, easing admission processing, providing retention efforts, and maximizing fiscal support. Education leaders may find this article of interest because of its institutional perspective and the insight on problem definition and goals when viewed with institutional incentives in mind.

4

Make the Case by Assembling the Evidence

CHAPTER OBJECTIVES

After reading this chapter, you will be able to:

- Describe the purpose of assembling evidence
- Identify the evidence needed based on the purpose of analysis
- Determine the value of specific data
- Locate relevant sources
- Categorize types of data

EDUCATION VIGNETTE

You have been recently elected to the school board. You are anxious to make changes to the strategies previously adopted by the leaders of the community because you think that they were wrong. You have a gut feeling that if teacher contracts were revised to include more time for professional development and more incentives for student achievement, productivity would go up in the school district. You are surprised when you attend the first working meeting of the new board and many of your colleagues strongly disagree with you. They argue that focusing on tougher curriculum standards and investing in international baccalaureate programs at the early levels are the solutions to take. After 2 hours of arguing, the meeting closes with no resolution. The superintendent is charged with obtaining information on the validity of each approach.

What data do you think will be persuasive? Which data would you direct her to collect?

PURPOSE OF ASSEMBLING THE EVIDENCE

Functions of Research

Heck (2004) notes that policy-related research serves multiple purposes. He summarizes these functions as (1) identifying choices to lead to the optimal resolution of a problem, (2) examining processes by which public values are transformed into policy actions, and (3) identifying the outcomes resulting from policy action. Addressing each of these goals effectively requires the use of evidence.

All three functions are important for policy studies writ large, but the essence of policy analysis is identifying choices that lead to the optimal resolution of a problem. However, it is not enough to point out problems and to identify solutions if others are not persuaded by your analysis. Policymakers often disagree about the appropriate choices to be made regarding public policy. It is imperative that policy analysts demonstrate that the facts support their description of the world and, ultimately, their solution to what they find wrong with it. Consequently, policy analysis requires evidence-based strategies because, while decision makers may rely on their gut instincts, it is more convincing to point to the facts. This chapter is largely about the process of assembling evidence, including the gathering of data and their ultimate transformation into persuasive proof.

Transforming Data into Evidence

LAYING THE FOUNDATION.   McDonnell and Elmore (1987) note that "the search for causes and potential solutions contains both analytical and normative aspects" (p. 145). This is supported by Dunn (2004), who adds that "all policy choices are based on factual as well as value premises" (p. 7). Collecting data and assembling them into evidence is therefore an essential part of the policy analytical process. You will have to collect data to demonstrate the nature and extent of the problem. For example, when federal policymakers defined an education problem as too little time spent in school, they gathered data on the average number of hours spent in a U.S. school and compared those data with the number of hours spent in non-U.S. schools. This was the description of the problem underlying the Time for Innovation Matters in Education Act introduced in the U.S. Congress both in 2008 and 2009.

As an education leader, you will need to collect data to identify the particular features of the policy problem that you will try to ameliorate. For instance, education leaders may point out that a lack of high-quality teachers will be the focus of their attempts to address poor student achievement. Examples include the many state and federal policies that have focused on attracting and retaining good teachers through a variety of policy mechanisms, including investment in professional development programs and initiating compensation based on pay for performance.

To offer persuasive arguments, education leaders also need to collect data to illustrate the similarities or differences that this problem shares with past policies. For example, education leaders around the globe may look across their borders and throughout their nation to see how others addressed similar problems. Many Japanese policymakers have looked to the United States to determine which education policies could foster creativity among their students. Many U.S. leaders have looked to Japan for insights on how to address middling scores in math and science.

Whatever the reason driving your collection of data, you will have to assemble them as evidence to make your case for a particular course of action. Biddle (1996) asserts that the failure of many education reforms is rooted in the lack of evidence that underlay their adoption and implementation. He notes:

> For want of evidence, our schools often fail to accomplish the key tasks we expect of them. And for lack of research concerning their supposed problems and the actual effects of programs for their "reform," the policies we initiate in such schools are often misguided, wasteful, counterproductive, or destructive." (p. 12)

Many educators applaud the call for data and the requirement of evidence-based strategies to justify education policy decisions (e.g., Kowalksi, Lasley, & Mahoney, 2008). Many foundations increasingly tie funding to a track record that supports the likelihood of success or the ability of grant seekers to demonstrate proof of their accomplishments. A key provision in the No Child Left Behind Act of 2001 is that education practices have to be grounded in scientific research. Similarly, the Race to the Top federal grant also provides incentives for proposals that have empirical evidence underlying them. Notwithstanding the general agreement that we have to have policies grounded in evidence, there is still disagreement about the most appropriate way to provide support for one's conclusions.

ASSESSING THE NATURE AND EXTENT OF THE PROBLEM.   An integral part of all the steps in policy analysis is showing proof of your assertions. If your claims are not grounded in reality and in a basic set of facts on which most people can agree, your arguments are not likely to be persuasive (McDonnell & Elmore, 1987). Bardach (2009) suggests that data are the basic building blocks of developing evidence. He distinguishes among data, information, and evidence:

> *Data* are facts. . . . *Information* consists of data that have "meaning," in the sense that they can help you sort the world into different logical or empirical categories. . . . *Evidence* is information that affects the existing beliefs of important people (including yourself) about significant features of the problem you are studying and how it might be solved or mitigated (p.11).

Dunn (2004) distinguishes among data, information, knowledge, and wisdom. Like Bardach, he notes that data are the raw facts, and information is the systematic ordering of these facts in a particular way. He adds that knowledge is the result of organizing the information in a way that is meaningful. Wisdom comes when this knowledge offers profound insight.

Data do not always have to be quantitative and statistical in nature (e.g., Bardach 2009), but in establishing the existence of a policy issue, it is often important to use statistics. For instance, if you argue that student achievement is low, it is important to demonstrate the basis on which you make that claim. Even if your audience does not agree with your assessment, at least they will be clear what *you* mean by low student achievement. Consequently, policy analysis begins with a descriptive statement of the condition grounded in empirical evidence. It would likely include "statistics that describe the state of the policy system and provide a benchmark for comparing current conditions with those of earlier times or different places" (McDonnell & Elmore, 1987,

p. 145). Lidman and Sommers (2005) state that the "compleat policy analyst will love numbers, even if he or she finds them hard to love" (p. 629).

While I consider the use of numbers important in establishing policy problems, I am aware that numbers are not necessarily an impartial, accurate depiction of reality. Statistics may be invalid, entered incorrectly, misinterpreted, or misused. My sister tells me the story of getting a 91 in Regents math at her high school in New York State and having it show up as a one on her report card. Her subsequent grades illustrated her exemplary performance, but if we took a snapshot look at her performance at the time that the error was made, we would have considered her a failing student. If this happens systematically to a group of students and remains undetected, we would be seeing an inaccurate picture of reality. Numbers by themselves do not necessarily tell you about power relationships and why a problem exists; they do not necessarily reveal hidden biases or differential interpretation and implementation of policy (e.g., Coburn, 2001; Louis, Febey, & Schroeder, 2005). However, similar concerns may be voiced regarding non-numeric data: People forget; memories are faulty; individuals may want to reshape history. It is good to check your facts from a variety of sources, whatever type of data are being used.

ASSESSING THE PARTICULAR FEATURES OF AN IDENTIFIED POLICY SITUATION.   The world is a complex place with interrelated policy problems. Data are not only necessary to establish and illustrate the existence of a phenomenon but also for determining the levers by which change can occur. An extensive review of the literature can help in the exploration and examination of relationships between and among key variables. Assembling evidence in this way can help you assess the particular features of an identified problem. It also allows you to determine more credibly which conditions are malleable to intervention and which are not.

ASSESSING PAST POLICIES.   In gathering evidence on past policies, you will be able to get a better sense of the links between particular activities and the outcomes that they are likely to yield. The data assembled should increase your understanding of the similarities and differences between the present policy problem and the one from which you plan to draw inspiration and make inference. Several key questions must be addressed to make an assessment of the past useful for the present: How different or similar is the problem addressed by past policies to the present phenomenon that you wish to mitigate? In what ways is the present problem different from the one that past policies addressed? How are they similar? How many people were targeted by the past policy? Did the policy achieve its intended goal? Did it achieve its goal, fully, partially, or not at all? What are the indicators that support that assessment?

USING THE PURPOSE OF THE EVIDENCE TO DETERMINE WHAT IS NEEDED

Dunn (2004) characterizes policy analysis as having five key policy-analytic methods: (1) monitoring, (2) forecasting, (3) evaluating, (4) recommending, and (5) problem structuring. He indicates that each of these methods produces and requires different types of information. The discussion in the previous chapter addressed problem structuring. The remainder of this section briefly addresses the information provided by the other

- How are the problems addressed by past policies different from or similar to the present phenomenon that you wish to address? In what ways are the problems different? In what ways are they similar?
- How are the circumstances surrounding the cited policy similar or different from the conditions that you presently describe?
- Are the major stakeholders the same?
- Did the policy achieve its intended goal? Did it achieve its goal fully, partially, or not at all? What are the indicators that support your assessment?

FIGURE 4.1 Sample Questions to Ask in Assembling Evidence to Assess Past Policies

policy-analytic methods of monitoring, prescribing, evaluating, and forecasting. More complete discussion of these policy analytical processes will be addressed in subsequent chapters.

Evidence for Monitoring

A key function of data collection in public policy analysis is simply to gain an understanding of what happened. That is, one may simply want to monitor the outputs associated with policy intervention. *Merriam-Webster's Collegiate Dictionary*, 11th Edition, defines *monitoring* as ". . . watch[ing], keep[ing] track of, or check[ing] usu[ally] for a special purpose." Dunn (2004) asserts that to "monitor public policies in any given issue area we require information that is relevant, reliable, and valid" (p. 278). In assembling data for monitoring, you must be clear about the indicators that will allow you to know if and how the phenomenon that you describe has changed over time. For example, if you are concerned about the number of students who complete high school, that number would be an important statistic to track. Did that number go up, go down, or stay the same over a specified time period? If a change occurred, did it go in the direction expected or desired? Did that change correspond to the intervention that you put in place? As noted by Dunn (2004) and others, the result of assembling evidence for monitoring is being able to observe policy outcomes. These observations can ultimately be measured against some normative standard of what presently exists and what you would like to see in the future.

Evidence for Prescription

While monitoring requires simply the tracking of output, prescription carries with it the added task of making recommendations. Consequently, assembling evidence for prescriptions would not only require regular documentation of specified outputs, it would

- Did the selected indicators go up, down or stay the same over a specified time period?
- If a change occurred, did it go in the direction expected or desired?
- Did that change correspond to the intervention that you put in place?

FIGURE 4.2 Sample Questions to Ask in Assembling Evidence to Monitor Outputs

- Do you have data that demonstrate patterns?
- Are the patterns that you can identify linked to particular outcomes? How sure are you of these connections?
- Do you want these outcomes? If yes, recommend actions tied to them. If no, recommend doing something different.

FIGURE 4.3   Sample Questions to Ask in Assembling Evidence for Prescription

also require an understanding of patterns, associations, and causation. For example, if increasing curriculum standards is systematically associated with higher student achievement, then you may recommend increasing curriculum standards if the goal sought is higher student achievement. The research may suggest, however, that other strategies have stronger associations with increased student productivity, and you may choose to prescribe alternate approaches. The evidence you gather and present for prescriptions should be comprehensive enough that it allows you to assess which key patterns of relationships will most likely lead to effective resolution of the policy problem identified. For example, education policymakers in New York State have long relied on increasingly rigorous curriculum standards as a means of improving student achievement (e.g., Alexander, 1998; Bishop, 1996; Roellke, 1996).

Evidence for Evaluation

Evaluation requires the comparison of data of *what is* against a normative standard of *what should be*. When assembling data to act as evidence for evaluation, the outputs tracked must provide information required by the goals and objectives of solving the problem. Evaluation is a normative process where the data has to address notions of bad and good in some way. Consequently, providing information only on compliance is not sufficient in completing a comprehensive evaluation of a policy action. There must be an understanding of how outputs associated with the policy have changed and if those changes have an impact on outcomes in the way predicted and sought by the analysts. For example, if policymakers increased the number of rigorous courses required to earn a high school diploma, at the end of a specified period, they will expect students to perform better based on a predetermined standard. The data that will be necessary to make the case for evaluating the success (or lack thereof) of a policy intervention would have to satisfy policy opponents, not only that the condition improved, but also that that improvement can be tied to the policy implemented. To do this, we could provide data before and after the policy intervention. This approach allows observers to know if a change in the policy problem took place and in the way desired. However, because changes in output could have occurred anyway, you would also want to have data for schools that did not implement the intervention of increasing the number of rigorous courses required to earn a high school diploma. This comparison would allow you to assess more accurately if the pattern of change were substantially different between those schools that had implemented the recommended policy action and those schools that did not. To the extent that changes after the policy are in the desired direction and can be tied to your policy actions, you can feel comfortable that you have made the case that your policy worked. These documented associations contribute to the extant literature so that they can be used for forecasting.

- Do you have a list of indicators for outputs you would like to examine?
- Do you have data on the outputs of interest for your school setting before and after the policy intervention?
- Do you have data on the outputs of interest for school settings that did not implement the policy intervention?
- Do you have data on the outputs of interest for other school settings that implemented the policy intervention?

FIGURE 4.4   Example of a Data Checklist That Will Help in Evaluating

Evidence for Forecasting

As indicated elsewhere, public policy analysis is largely about making recommendations for the future. Because of that, policy analysts must have some idea of what the future holds. To inject some degree of certainty in the analytical process, you may rely on past trends continuing into the future. When you use data to forecast, you may be able to persuade others by using data to show the continuation of patterns. For example, Oakes (1990) has argued that if present trends continue, the United States will be at a disadvantage on the world stage when it comes to math and science: Minority populations continue to grow but they are not represented proportionally in science, technology, engineering, and math.

Another way of forecasting is to use theoretical relationships rather than data for evidence about what the future holds. Less persuasive for many policymakers who may not agree with your assessment is conjecture because the evidence that you rely on is purely personal.

DETERMINING THE VALUE OF SPECIFIC DATA

Patton and Sawicki (1993) highlight five basic strategies of gathering data: an investigative approach, historical data, basic facts, political information, and forecasts and projection. Investigative approaches entail asking people questions or analyzing documents. Historical data requires you to gather data that have been collected over time and reflect key elements of time periods important to your analysis. Basic facts are data commonly collected or known. Political information covers data that address relationships, power, and values. Data from forecasts and projections are based on predictive theory or projection techniques that reflect estimates of future values. The value of each strategy depends on the data sought, with the use of investigative approaches being the most expensive, and the employment of basic facts the least expensive. Bardach (2009) argues that, because obtaining data is costly, you need to assess the costs of assembling evidence against simply guessing. He suggests that making an educated guess is appro-

- Do the data show patterns? Do you expect those patterns to continue? Why?
- Are you relying on theory to know what will likely happen next? How credible is that theory?
- Are you relying on expertise? Who are these experts? Who is likely to believe their scenario of the future?

FIGURE 4.5   Example of a Data Checklist That Will Help in Forecasting

priate in some instances, but he emphasizes that an educated guess must be informed by previous knowledge of the issue.

How Do You Make Good Use of Data?

BUILDING YOUR ARGUMENT.   Government and other sources produce many statistics that will allow you to provide grounded indicators of the assertions you are making. My advice would be that assembling basic indicators to illustrate the existence of a problematic phenomenon is essential for building your argument regarding the importance of alleviating a specified problem. This approach requires you to document what you know and how you know it. Whether you should collect more facts depends on your assessment of whether more precise data will lead to substantially different results from what you expect with the data you presently have (Bardach, 2009).

ASSESSING DATA CONTEXTS.   As noted elsewhere, not all data and research are created equal (e.g., Haller & Kleine, 2001; Kaplan, 1998; Kowalski, Laskey, & Mahoney, 2008). Kowalski, Laskey, and Mahoney (2008) offer four guiding questions in helping administrators and teachers become critical consumers of research:

1. Are the research findings the result of conceptual exploration regarding pedagogy?
2. Are the research findings the result of rigorous research utilizing experimental designs?
3. Have the research findings emerged from multiple contexts?
4. Are the research conclusions idiosyncratic to one setting? (p. 158)

The value of the evidence gleaned from research depends partly on your responses to these questions. If you want to adopt a new pedagogical strategy in the classroom, simply doing what a neighboring school or state does may not be effective if the approach is not yet tried and true. Relying on cooperative learning to do a writing assignment in a class where children do not know how to read is not likely to be an effective approach.

If the innovation is merely a conceptual exploration regarding pedagogy, perhaps it would be better to implement it on a small scale. If the innovation is based on a rigorous experimental design, you may be more confident of the causal relationship presumed, and you may be more willing to invest more resources in its trial. The impact of context also influences the confidence you should place in certain research findings and its relevance to your particular context. On the one hand, if an innovation works in multiple settings, chances are good that it may also work in yours. If none of those contexts are parallel to your situation, however, the data may not be helpful. Let's say that the results are based on the conditions of one setting. The more that setting is different from your particular context, the less applicable are the findings. However, even if the findings are based on one setting, you may still be more willing to rely on them than on results tried in many contexts. That is, if that one setting shares several characteristics with yours, you may be willing to trust that you will obtain similar results trying the innovation in your context.

HOW TO LOCATE RELEVANT SOURCES

People and Documents are Key

Data come from two principal sources: people and documents (Bardach, 2009). These two categories are comprehensive but are not mutually exclusive. People can inform the data contained in documents, and documents contain information that contributes to the expert knowledge of people. While educators may prefer and rely on one type of data source to get answers to their unanswered questions, both are important. Heck (2004) observes that, regardless of the source, "the collection of data is not neutral. Data collection represents political decisions about what types of information are useful in determining how the schools are doing" (p. 14). The questions posed by policymakers and others should determine the appropriate source and method of data collection used (Heck, 2004; Kowalski et al., 2008). Note, however, that the process of collecting data is different from that of analysis and decision making.

COLLECTION STRATEGIES.   Common strategies for obtaining data from people include interviews, participant observation, surveys, and questionnaires. Methods for gathering data from documents include archival analysis, content analysis, and secondary data analysis. What we obtain from these sources is data that informs our understanding of the essence of a problem, the nature of relationships between and among key variables, and a foundation for our claims.

DATA FROM PEOPLE WITHIN AND OUTSIDE YOUR ORGANIZATION.   As a policymaker, administrator, or teacher, you may have several questions regarding the effectiveness of education. You will often need to find a balance between internal and external sources to get a comprehensive and accurate picture of the education condition you are facing. You will be able to make more informed decisions by gathering data from individuals both within and outside your organization.

Knowing the internal workings of your organization is helpful for ensuring that it is functioning efficiently and effectively. While it is true that constant measuring does not necessarily lead to better outputs, research suggests that using data to inform your decisions can lead to more reflective decision making. Being more thoughtful in making decisions is helpful, but it is also necessary to assess the impact of those decisions. If you are a policymaker at the state or national level, you may already have a bird's-eye view of the potential implications of policy. What you need is a close-up of districts, schools, and classrooms to know the actual effects of policy on any one institution in your state or nation. One way to do that is to ask questions of individuals within your organization and of those who are directly affected by the policy. You may take one spot in your state or country and ask the relevant leaders and members of institutions that are randomly selected about their understanding of the policy and their perception of its impact. Another approach would be to identify sites that seem to be doing particularly well in implementing a particular state or federal policy and then ask individuals associated with those sites for their sense of that policy, what works and what does not.

This purposive approach was the strategy adopted by Louis, Thomas, Gordon, and Febey (2008). They examine the impact of political culture on a state's policy-making mechanism, and they focus on the policy-making mechanisms in Indiana, Nebraska, and Oregon. They chose those three states because of their similarities in size but differences in education policy histories. Within each state, these research-ers interviewed between 8 and 11 education policymakers who represented a diverse range of positions and organizations. The authors conducted 1-hour interviews in a semistructured format, and the questions asked revolved around states' accountability and school leadership policies, key education stakeholders, and levels of collaboration among those stakeholders. The researchers found that political culture matters in how a state responds to leadership and accountability initiatives. This information is im-portant for federal policymakers as they design policies to have an impact on student achievement.

On the other hand, leaders within schools may already have a variety of strategies to collect information on what is happening within their institutions. These strategies may include classroom observations, "learning walks" (Wallace Foundation, 2006), and individual meetings with children and parents. Just as leadership at upper levels of the education organizational hierarchy need to get a closer snapshot of the condition of education on the ground, educators nearer to the point of delivery also need to get a more panoramic view in order to place their observations in context. Kowalski and colleagues (2008) note, for example, that the timing of observations may present very different pictures of teacher efficacy. To address that problem, the authors argue that administrators should use multiple sources and different methods.

DATA FROM DOCUMENTS WITHIN AND OUTSIDE YOUR ORGANIZATION. In addition to observing people's behavior and documenting their perception, data also exist within a variety of documents. Kowalski and colleagues (2008) note that the National Center for Education Statistics and the websites of the different education departments across the country are the document sources for much of education policy research. Minutes from meetings, agendas, and other archival data can also provide important insight into the workings of an organization. Fowler (2009) suggests, for example, that because of the importance of language in school leadership, getting access to that "talk" can yield im-portant insights.

Not to be overlooked are the data provided by other researchers. For example, Leithwood and colleagues (2004), in an examination of how leadership influences stu-dent learning, conducted an extensive review of the literature to compile evidence on the impact of leadership on student performance. They conclude that leadership is second only to teaching among school-related factors that affect student performance. They write that it is the conscious linking of leadership practices to student learning that highlights the importance of leaders to organizations. The direct connections that leaders can make to the core function of teaching and learning become more difficult as organizations become bigger and leaders become more removed from the classrooms.

HOW TO CATEGORIZE TYPES OF DATA

Quantitative or Qualitative Debate

Much research relies on both quantitative and qualitative data. As the labels suggest, quantitative data refer to those data that are grounded in numbers, while qualitative data refer to those that are grounded in words. Ultimately, the data collected and the analysis used should be guided by the questions posed. Grady (1998) distinguishes be-tween the two types of data by defining quantitative data as "impersonal but consistent, number driven," while qualitative data are "personal but inconsistent, people driven" (p. 6). He goes on to highlight nine key differences between quantitative and qualitative analyses based on their purpose, focus, data, instrumentation, reality, values, orientation, conditions, and results. *Purpose* refers to the goal of the analysis. *Focus* refers to the unit of analysis that you are targeting for change. *Data* refers to the nature of facts that you assess, primarily numbers or primarily words. *Instrumentation* refers to the method used to collect the data. *Reality* denotes the nature of the environment that you would like to describe. *Values* refer to the methodological and philosophical concerns that drive your analysis. *Conditions* indicate the limitation in which your findings hold true. *Results* refer to the actual findings and their implication for the field and practice. In general, Grady argues that quantitative analysis strives for predictability and neutrality, while qualitative analysis strives for dynamic, rich, and value-explicit results.

Heck (2004) offers a useful summary of the type of research questions that are more appropriately addressed using quantitative versus qualitative analysis. Questions regarding how many, how often, and causal relationships are especially appropriate for quantitative methods. Questions pursuing how, why, and processes lend themselves to qualitative approaches. Heck (2004) also indicates that quantitative analysis is particularly suited for nonexperimental, experimental, and quasi-experimental research designs. For case studies and historical analyses, he suggests that both approaches are appropriate depending on the research questions being explored. Grady (1998) argues, however, that case studies anchored only in quantitative analysis would likely produce flat and thin data, with little substantive and practical implications for policymakers and practitioners. In the end, education leaders must decide how best to make their case with the data at hand.

Chapter Summary

This chapter reviewed the basic details of the tasks associated with getting the appropriate data to conduct your analysis. The discussion offered ways to think about data so that you are prepared, not only to point out problems and to identify solutions, but to ground your analysis in reality in order to be more persuasive. The chapter also considered the variety of data that can serve as evidence and the utility of each type depending on the purpose of the analysis. Evidence may be assembled to buttress problem structuring, monitoring, prescribing, evaluating, and forecasting. In assembling data for monitoring, explicit indicators must be present to allow you to know if and how the phenomenon that you describe has changed over time. Assembling evidence for prescriptions would not only require regular documentation of specified outputs, it would also require an understanding of patterns, associations, and causation. For evaluating, you need to document the changes associated with the policy. To the extent that changes occur in the desired direction and can be tied to your policy actions, you can feel comfortable that you have made the case that the policy worked. If changes cannot be tied to policy actions or do not occur in the direction sought by policy proponents, you can make the case that the policy did not work. Assembling evidence for forecasting may lead you to presume that past trends will continue into the future.

Data primarily come from people and documents, and we often classify them as qualitative or quantitative. By now, you should be familiar with the different sources of policy-relevant information and should be ready to transform data into knowledge. As you go from data to knowledge and from legwork to analysis, you should be ready for the next step in the process: establishing the values that will drive your analysis.

Review Questions

1. As an education leader, why would you gather data? How does your rationale tie in with the various purposes of policy analytic research?

2. What is your preferred strategy or strategies for gathering data? Why?

3. What is your favored approach for data analysis? Why? Is this approach particularly suited to a specific policy analytical function?

4. Do you agree that there is a difference between data and evidence? Explain your re-

sponse. Provide examples from your professional context in your response.

5. How do you transform data into evidence? Give an example.

6. Reread the chapter-opening education vignette. Which data do you think are needed? Is this response different from the one you gave when you started the chapter?

News Story for Analysis

"More teaching, less money." *National Post* (f/k/a *The Financial Post*) (Canada). November 3, 2008 Monday. National Edition. BYLINE: Lorne Gunter, *National Post*. SECTION: EDITORIAL; Lorne Gunter; Pg. A14.

Those who are hoping that our aboriginal citizens [in Canada] will be lifted out of poverty and dependence by the billions of federal dollars currently being pumped each year into aboriginal communities and programs—nearly $11,000 per man, woman and child for First Nations, Inuit and Metis—should stop holding their breath. Money is neither the problem nor the solution.

The problem is a lack [of] education. And until Canada corrects the education gap between its aboriginal and non-aboriginal citizens, there will be little improvement in conditions, no matter how much money is slathered on aboriginal communities with the very best of intentions.

Last week, the C. D. Howe Institute released a fascinating, yet ultimately disheartening study on the "education gap."

Author John Richards, a public policy professor at Simon Fraser University, first offers what should be considered very hopeful statistics: According to his calculations based on the 2006 census, employment rates for aboriginals and non-aboriginals are nearly the same at comparable levels of education.

Meanwhile, aboriginal Canadians with a high school diploma have an almost identical employment rate (just over 60%) [compared] to non-aboriginals with a diploma. Those with a trade or

a college certificate have up to 75% success, similar to that of non-aboriginal journeyman and college grads. And, compared with non-aboriginals with degrees, aboriginal Canadians who have completed university even have a slightly better shot at employment in their field.

In other words, where they possess the required training and skills, aboriginal Canadians do not face barriers to finding work.

The trouble comes when looking at what percentage of both groups achieve each level of secondary and postsecondary learning. Obtaining a high school diploma has become "nearly universal" among non-aboriginals. "Nearly 90% have done so," says Prof. Richards. However, even among non-aboriginals aged 20–24 "about 40% lack high school certification," according to Richards.

More troubling still, this youngest group of working-age aboriginals may be regressing. Among those 25–44, the proportion without a diploma is just 32%, meaning that after falling for nearly three decades, the dropout rate may be rising among aboriginals, even as it continues to fall in the rest of the population.

Similarly, 68% of non-aboriginals aged 25–34 have some form of postsecondary training, compared to 50% among those 45 and older—showing a growing commitment to education beyond high school. Yet among aboriginals, "the proportion with a university degree among those under 45 has increased very little relative to those over 45."

Also distressing is the news that while the generation of aboriginals aged 35–44 outperformed those over 45 in obtaining some type of postsecondary training, the generation aged 25–34 seems to have fallen back to the older generation's levels: About 40% of aboriginals over 45 have some education beyond high school vs. 47% of those aged 35–44, but just 42% of those aged 25–34.

Prof. Richards contends this may indicate that aboriginal Canadians wait until they are in their 30s to go to college, trade school or university, or it may "signify a more disturbing phenomenon; stagnation in intentions to undertake postsecondary training among young aboriginals."

Given that the four westernmost provinces have far and away the largest First Nations populations, and that in those provinces one-in-eight children four years old or younger (one-in-four in Saskatchewan and Manitoba) is aboriginal, the social and fiscal implications will be staggering on the Prairies, in B. C. and in the territories if aboriginal Canadians start turning away from education.

Prof. Richards suggests turning over on-reserve schooling to boards independent of band politics, and that off-reserve public schools (where most aboriginal kids are taught) should increase the involvement of aboriginal leaders and parents, "set measurable targets for improvement" and use data to identify aboriginal students who are not achieving.

That's probably sound advice. But here's an additional idea: The decrease in aboriginal education attainment corresponds to the recent increases in what was already hearty federal funding for aboriginals. Perhaps we are subsidizing the decline.

While it is not possible to live lavishly on federal handouts, it is possible to do more than survive. Concurrent with adopting Prof. Richards' recommendation, we might want to remove the disincentives to education inherent in the current funding structure.

Source: Material reprinted with the express permission of: "National Post Inc."

Discussion Questions

1. Given the data cited, do you think that an education problem exists for Canada's aboriginal citizens? Explain.
2. Using the discussion in the chapter, what are the types of data used to support assertions in this article?
3. Do you agree with the conclusions drawn by the author of the article? Explain your response.
4. What additional data would you like to see in order to buttress or rebut the assertions and conclusions of this author?

Selected Websites

Minnesota Department of Education (Mn DoE). Available at

http://education.state.mn.us/mde/index.html.

The official website of the Minnesota Department of Education. The department's mission is to "[i]mprove *educational achievement by establishing clear standards, measuring performance, assisting educators and increasing opportunities for lifelong learning.*" These are all strategies that require the use of data. Education leaders may find this website helpful to see how data are collected and made available for a variety of purposes. The site also contains direct links to data files that education leaders can use to document a variety of education problems.

The Wallace Foundation. Available at

www.wallacefoundation.org/Pages/default.aspx.

The official website of The Wallace Foundation, a nonprofit foundation that supports and shares ideas and practices to improve learning and enrichment opportunities for children. The site contains national surveys, summaries of field knowledge, and practical guides on a variety of policy issues affecting children. Education leaders may find this website interesting because of the ready availability of data. They can click on the knowledge center tab for access to a variety of articles, reports, and tools.

U.S. Department of Education. Institute of Education Sciences. National Center for Education Statistics (NCES). Available at

www.nces.ed.gov/.

The official website of the National Center for Education Statisitcs, located in the Institute of

Education Sciences. The National Center for Education Statistics (NCES) is the primary federal entity for collecting and analyzing data related to education in the United States and other nations. Education leaders would find this website helpful because of its wealth of data on numerous education issues.

Selected References

Biddle, B. J. (1996, December). Better ideas: Expanded funding for educational research. *Educational Researcher, 25,* 12–14.

Biddle argues that there is an urgent need to fund, review, and disseminate the knowledge generated by educational research. Education leaders may find this article interesting for the viewpoint it presents on the use of data (or lack thereof) in education.

Coburn, C. E. (2001, Summer). Collective sense-making about reading: How teachers mediate reading policy in their professional communities. *Educational Evaluation & Policy Analysis, (23)*2, 145–170.

Coburn researches the relationship between instructional policy and classroom practice. This paper uses an in-depth case study of one California elementary school to examine the processes by which teachers construct and reconstruct multiple policy messages. Education leaders may find this article interesting because the author highlights how building leaders can help shape how teachers use data and make sense of policy.

Grady, M. P. (1998). *Qualitative and action research: A practitioner handbook.* **Bloomington, IN: Phi Delta Kappa Educational Foundation.**

Grady provides a good overview of research using qualitative methods and design. Education leaders may find this handbook useful because it provides a quick way to learn or refresh their knowledge of data collection and analysis in a way that will help them do research in the field.

Haller, E., & Kleine, P. F. (2001). *Using educational research: A school administrator's guide.* **New York: Addison Wesley Longman.**

The authors offer a practical guide for school administrators about how to understand and use educational research. Education leaders may find this a useful resource for guiding how they use data to inform their decision-making process.

Kaplan, A. (1998). *The conduct of inquiry: Methodology for behavioral science.* **New Brunswick, NJ: Transaction Publishers.**

Kaplan provides an excellent overview of social science research methodology. Education leaders may find this book helpful if they would like a more detailed assessment of the standards and strategies used for social inquiry.

Kowalski, T., Lasley, T. J., & Mahoney, J. W. (2008). *Data-driven decisions and school leadership: Best practices for school improvement.* **New York: Pearson Education.**

Kowalski and his colleagues offer a practical guide for using data to evaluate education programs. They argue for increased reliance on data to make sound decisions on what policies work well for children. Education leaders may find this book helpful for the information it provides on conducting sound evaluations in school environments.

Lidman, R., and Sommers, P. (2005, September/ October). The "compleat" policy analyst: A top 10 list. *Public Administration Review, (65)*5, 628–634.

This article provides a quick and enjoyable read on the use of data in policy analysis. It touches on the role of uncertainty in the policy analytical process. Education leaders may find this article useful because it serves as a reminder that, while you want to make the best use of data, the process of transforming data into evidence is not perfect.

Louis, K. S., Febey, K., & Schroeder, R. (2005, Summer). State-mandated accountability in high schools: Teachers' interpretations of a new era. *Educational Evaluation & Policy Analysis, (27)*2, 177–204.

The authors collect data on the perspectives of implementers of policy to assess the effectiveness of that policy in changing practice. Their findings, using qualitative analysis, suggest that teachers' interpretation of accountability policies were associated with their efforts to change classroom practice. Education leaders may find this article interesting because of the insight it provides on the connection between the perception of implementers and the likely effectiveness of policy. These kinds of links can help education leaders identify patterns, make credible forecasts, and make informed recommendations on related policy.

Louis, K. S., Thomas, E., Gordon, M., & Febey, K. (2008, October). State leadership for school improvement: An analysis of three states [Part of the special issue entitled Linking Leadership to Student Learning]. *Educational Administration Quarterly, (44)4, 562-592.*

Louis and her colleagues examine the effect of policy culture on states' policy-making mechanisms. This article provides another example of how education leaders can use the information provided in extant literature to inform their decision-making process. In this case, for example, education leaders would note the mediating effect of political culture and take that into account in their identification of patterns, forecasts, and policy recommendations.

5

Establish Your Driving Values

CHAPTER OBJECTIVES

After reading this chapter, you will be able to:

- Identify explicitly the values that you care about
- Establish evaluative criteria
- Write a description of what success looks like
- Identify the specific criteria that frame policy discussions
- Describe basic economic concepts as they apply to policy analysis

EDUCATION VIGNETTE

You are the chief state school officer in your state and have recently pored through the literature on class size reduction, alienation, peer effects, and academic achievement. You sit and ponder the readings and what their findings mean for children, the values that you hold, and the policies you should recommend. You wonder if you should increase busing or simply give parents more flexibility in choosing a school for their child. You wonder if you should reduce class size or rely more on technology and teacher aides.

As you think of ways to make schools serve their students better, what values will you bring to help you in making your choices? If this process leads to conflicting results, which value will ultimately drive your policy decision?

WHAT DO YOU CARE ABOUT?

Chapter 5 focuses on establishing and reflecting on the values that will help you to choose among the various policy options available. As a policy leader, and even as a student, your path is full of choices that must be made. Examples of making choices abound, as the next three paragraphs illustrate.

In an era of cutbacks, leaders of local governments, including school districts, may wonder if they should require all their employees to take leave without pay in order to balance their budget. Maybe leave without pay is an effective way to balance the budget, but would this approach be fair?

School board members may have to choose among a group of superintendent candidates to determine who should lead their district. How can they be sure they are making the right choice given the multiple hats that superintendents wear as leaders of the education community? What are the appropriate criteria that they should use to help them make their choice?

Increasing numbers of high-achieving students are considering different higher education options. Students are increasingly weighing the prestige of an institution against its costs. With the recession, more students are choosing to go to community colleges rather than attend more highly ranked public and private universities in an attempt to save money.

The fact is, when there is no ideal solution, we often have to make the best decision within the constraints that we face. Each of our decisions varies according to our values. In Chapter 1, I briefly discussed the worldviews and priorities that shape our decisions. Being aware of and reflecting on these values will allow you to be transparent in the decision process and in the evaluative criteria that you establish.

ESTABLISH EVALUATIVE CRITERIA

Relationship Between Values and Criteria

The groups and individuals involved in the decision process influence the values that one ultimately uses to select among different policy alternatives. Criteria are simply a concrete, working definition of these ideals. For example, if we value equity, we may ask whether a particular policy will lead to a fair distribution of benefits and costs. To the extent that we care about the answer to this question, equity is a criterion that will help us choose among alternatives. Perhaps we value efficiency and favor those policies that will lead to greater bang for the buck; that is, we may be particularly concerned about the ability of a policy option to deliver more of a specified impact for relatively little input.

With this type of reflection, you can define and establish useful criteria. The criteria may be derived from your analysis of documents or from interviews in which the values that stakeholders consider important are discussed and explored. As you consider your choices, you may be able to determine the broader ideological position with which your choices are consistent. You may also be able to tell if there are any inherent contradictions in the values that will surface as a result of your choice. In essence, the criteria selected say something about your assumptions regarding the role of society, government, and the economy (e.g., Fowler, 2009).

In some instances, policymakers will be purposefully vague in letting you know what considerations or criteria influence their decision. This ambiguity may allow them to obtain the broadest base of support possible; however, it is not helpful in narrowing down policy options. Thus, as policy analysts, it would be better to have explicit criteria in order to make the decision-making process transparent and to be clear about what trade-offs must be made.

In establishing evaluative criteria, three big questions will guide your analysis:

1. Will the policy resolve the problem being defined? Is it an effective policy? Does it seem like it will work at least in theory?
2. What are the consequences of implementing that approach? What are its impacts and on whom? Are these impacts different for different constituencies?
3. Is the policy workable given the constraints that exist? Is it feasible? (Policies that look good on paper may not be workable given the particular constraints of one's specific context.)

The answers to these questions will be influenced by the stakeholders in the process.

WHAT DOES SUCCESS LOOK LIKE?

Let us start with the four broad concepts for setting up evaluative criteria: goals, objectives, criteria, and measures (Patton & Sawicki, 1993). *Goals* are the obverse of the problem and serve as the idealized ends. *Objectives* are the specified targets associated with the identified goals. *Criteria* are the working definitions of the values that both constrain and drive your decision. *Measures* are the specific observations or calculations that put idealized concepts in concrete, quantitative terms. Addressing each of these concepts helps you to clarify the problem and to determine what its resolution will look like. For instance, if the problem is that too few students are graduating from high school within 4 years, the goal for resolving that problem would be a higher number of students graduating from high school within 4 years. If your problem definition and your goal seem unrelated, you need to redefine your problem, restate your goal, or both.

From the goal or goals described, you will be able to develop objectives. As noted, objectives are more focused and concretely worded statements about end states. In other words, like goals, objectives are future-oriented. Unlike goals, they address a definite population and timeframe. Objectives move us away from the more lofty ideals described in the goals and toward specific, concrete, and reachable ends. It is essential to define objectives once the goals of a program or policy have been identified. This approach allows evaluative criteria to be developed for each objective, and multiple measures of each criterion to be devised.

Criteria are even more specific than objectives. Bardach (2009) describes criteria as "mental standards for evaluating the results of action" (p. 37). They are explicit statements about the dimensions that will be considered to evaluate alternative policies and outcomes. In other words, they are the working definitions of the values that will determine in turn which option you choose to resolve the problem being described.

Measures are the most specific of the above concepts and are tangible operational definitions of criteria. In other words, the measure gives readers a real understanding of what good results for each criterion look like. It is not enough to state that you will know them when you see them. Policy analysis is a collective enterprise and requires explicit guidance for those interested in your decisions. By using measures, you allow your audience to know what you consider to be a better state of affairs. For example, if the criterion is effectiveness, what results would we have to see for us to consider that the policy is effective? In the case of ex ante analysis, what would you have to expect for you to consider that the policy is likely to work? If past policies are associated with high levels of proficiency on the National Assessment of Educational Progress exams, it would be reasonable to presume that similar policies would have similarly high rates of effectiveness. If the criterion considered is equity, we want to be able to measure the distributional implications of policy actions. For example, Alexander (1998; 2002; 2003) finds that, while mandating a rigorous curriculum is associated with increased overall exam scores in New York State, they are also associated with wider achievement gaps between the top- and bottom-achieving students. These findings suggest that standards-based policies, sine qua non, will not lead to more equitable distributions of student performance for those pupils who are the least well served by the present system. The rest of this section discusses more fully the conceptual underpinnings of specific criteria.

WHAT ARE THE SPECIFIC CRITERIA THAT FRAME POLICY DECISIONS?

The types of criteria used to frame policy decisions depend on the values of key stakeholders, the nature of the problem, the objectives sought, and the alternative policies or programs under review. While criteria may vary from problem to problem, they often must address what matters to policymakers, target groups, taxpayers, and other stakeholders. In the end, what often matters are the answers to these five questions: (1) Does it work? (2) Is it fair? (3) Can we afford it? (4) Will people support it? and (5) Who will implement it?

Does It Work?

When we ask if a policy is likely to work, we are essentially making an argument for considering effectiveness, or what Patton and Sawicki (1993) call technical feasibility. This criterion gauges whether particular policy options can resolve the problem at hand. Technical feasibility is important to include in all policy analyses because if our actions do not improve society, what is the purpose of conducting the analysis in the first place?

Effectiveness measures whether the policy or program achieves its purpose. Because we are focusing on ex ante analysis, our ability to answer the question Does it work? depends on our ability to make connections between the proposed course of action and extant research on the likelihood of its success.

HOW WILL YOU KNOW? Using knowledge gained from research on similar programs, you can assess to what degree the proposed action is likely to accomplish the stated objectives. As part of that analysis, you should be able to discern if you can trace changes in the real world back to the program proposed. In documenting your response, you should also be aware if the effects of the program are likely to be direct or indirect, long-term or short-term, quantifiable or not, and adequate or inadequate. Patton and Sawicki (1993) indicate that impacts are direct if they address a stated objective of the program and indirect if they create an impact not associated with a stated objective. For example, many supporters of charter schools cite high levels of parental satisfaction as one of the benefits of this reform (e.g., Vanourek, Manno, & Finn, 1998). If the stated aim of

- Are you able to trace the changes in the real world to the proposed program?
- Are the changes documented directly or indirectly related to the proposed program?
- Are the changes documented likely to be evident in the short-term or long-term (more than 5 years)?
- Are you able to document these changes in numbers or do you have to use words?
- Are the changes that you see or expect to see likely to result in a full resolution of the problem identified?

FIGURE 5.1   Does It Work? Template to Gauge Impact (Effectiveness) of Policy Options

the reform is to improve student achievement, then improved parental satisfaction may be considered an indirect impact.

Long-term impacts are experienced some time in the future. The lack of immediacy of their impact may influence the perceived effectiveness of the program. For example, efforts to improve teacher quality by restructuring teacher education programs are not likely to have an immediate effect. New teacher candidates who experience the reform will be affected initially, but a time lag exists between the time when teacher candidates are in education programs and the moment they enter the teaching force. Consequently, we may presume that changes in schools that are linked to changes in teacher education programs will not happen immediately. The evolution of the workforce and changes in socialization and pedagogical practices may not become evident until teachers who were trained before the reforms in the teacher preparation programs took place have retired.

Adequacy refers to the ability of the program to resolve fully the stated problem or fulfill the stated objective. It measures how far toward a solution we can proceed with the resources available. Capturing adequacy is a growing concern among many educators, and it has been the center of education discourse in reference to the appropriateness of school finance mechanisms. Currently, four key strategies have emerged from leaders in education finance on the appropriate working definition of adequacy. Guthrie and others have argued that professional judgment should be used to determine the appropriate funding for schools (e.g., Guthrie, 1983). Odden (2000) favors looking at successful schools as benchmarks for determining adequate funding. Reschovsky and Imazeki (2001) advocate a cost function approach, which is essentially the inverse of the traditional production function methods. There is also a state-of-the-art methodology that is deeply entrenched in the use of existing evidence and statistical procedures. More recently, Alexander and Schapiro (2009) have argued for the creation of an adequacy condition index in the same way that we have indicators of fiscal conditions. The search for adequacy is not only a quest for greater effectiveness but also a pursuit for greater equity.

Is It Fair?

Fairness is closely related to equity. When education leaders think about equity, they are often considering how the benefits and costs of policy are distributed. That is, both the impact of policy and the cost of its implementation are important. Equity is about the distribution of goods or services among individual members or subgroups. The focus is both on the consumption side (who benefits?) and on the production side (who pays?). Standard indicators of dispersion are important, and measures such as range, standard deviation, and coefficient of variation are commonly accepted in the field (e.g., Berne & Steifel, 1984; A Decade of Standards Based Education, 2006; Odden & Picus, 2009).

Equity is significant when the differential impact of a policy change is important. Because policy changes are often intended to modify existing discrepancies, the issue becomes one about whether certain groups or individuals will experience a disproportionate share of the burden or will receive windfall benefits. We want fairness both in terms of who has to pay for a policy and those who enjoy (or suffer from) the impact of a policy.

Five basic principles are often discussed in the literature regarding equity: horizontal equity, vertical equity, transitional equity, ability to pay, and benefits principle. All these concepts relate to equal and nondiscriminatory treatment; that is, people should be treated similarly unless there is good reason for the differentiation. It is often difficult to tell what constitutes a good reason, and there is still wide disagreement on the appropriate role of states, districts, and schools in the matter of achieving social equity.

HORIZONTAL EQUITY.   This definition of fairness calls for the equal treatment of equals but does not go beyond the basic concept to provide a working definition of what that means for the practitioner. It may be applied both to the impact and the cost of policy options. For example, policymakers disagree about the fairness of establishing gifted and talented programs: Some argue that it is unfair because children are not being given the same opportunities, and others argue about the appropriate grouping of students (Kelly, 1991). Crace (2006) highlights the varying definitions of gifted and talented offered by multiple organizations, ranging from the top 2% to the top 10% of students. One of the problems with the simple application of horizontal equity is knowing what makes for equally situated entities. Because each child is unique, it is difficult to tell which characteristic is a legitimate distinction vis à vis policy options.

VERTICAL EQUITY.   This conceptualization of fairness refers to the distribution of goods and services to those in unequal circumstances. But what constitutes unequal circumstances? For example, should the population be subdivided by region, city, or neighborhood? Should subgroups be categorized by their ethnicity, income level, IQ, achievement score, or socialization skills? It assumes that differential treatment would result in those who need more resources getting that support and in those who need less getting less.

- Is your policy likely to promote horizontal equity? Will there be a consistent impact on members of groups affected by the policy?

- Is your policy likely to promote vertical equity? Will the policy have a differential impact on targeted groups? Will more vulnerable groups get more support?

- Does your policy address transitional equity? Does your policy include provisions for easing the transition for groups adversely affected by any change in rules that your policy caused?

- Who will bear the brunt of paying for this policy? Will the payment for this option be tied to income or to those who receive a benefit from the proposed program?

FIGURE 5.2   Is It Fair? Questions That Gauge the Equity Implications of Policy Options

As seen from the example about gifted and talented programs, the appropriate distinction of unequal circumstances is difficult to capture. Making this distinction becomes even more problematic when the screening process used to identify beneficiaries of a program seems to produce uneven results. For example, African Americans, Latinos, English language learners, and students eligible for free or reduced lunch have long been underrepresented in gifted and talented programs. Members of the Equity in Education Coalition have argued that policymakers should eliminate the practice of labeling children as gifted and talented and simply provide all students a similarly accelerated program. Vertical equity not only requires appropriate grouping but also appropriate differentiation in the distribution of resources among groups. Consequently, achieving vertical equity is even more challenging than achieving horizontal equity because, if we treat everyone the same, we are at least accomplishing the equal treatment of equals on some level.

Considerations of vertical equity are not only relevant in a domestic context but also on the global stage. In many countries, girls have lower participation in formal education than boys do, students in rural schools have fewer opportunities for higher education than students in urban areas, low-income students achieve at lower levels than their wealthy peers do, and students with disabilities have few opportunities for integrated schooling. When groups or individuals have been treated unfairly in the past, vertical equity often requires the reallocation of resources to ensure more equitable outcomes in the future. For example, the third Regional Conference on Secondary Education in Africa (SEIA) held in Ghana in 2007 focused on the development of a report for the World Bank Institute. This document was a comprehensive report on how participating nations could enhance equity in gender, regions, abilities, and wealth for the good of their country. For example, to address gender equity concerns, policymakers in some participating countries may have to update their facilities as they change from single-sex to co-educational settings (e.g., New Vision, 2007). More recently, in 2011, members of the Forum for African Women Educationists Uganda (FAWEU) held a fundraiser to pay the university school fees for bright girls from poor families (New Vision, 2011).

To address the inequities in access to secondary education in rural regions, many of the SEIA conference participants called for universal secondary education to accompany past policy efforts at universal primary education. In Uganda, for example, the government implemented universal secondary education in 2007. Also in 2007, the president of Ghana, John Agyekum Kufuor, indicated that the government of Ghana would initiate education policies that focus on improving secondary education in that country. The proposed reform included enhanced access to technology, vocational and agricultural training, and partnerships with the private sector (e.g., Public Agenda, 2007).

In Central and Eastern Europe, policymakers grapple with policies on how to achieve vertical equity vis-à-vis children with disabilities. Large numbers of children with disabilities do not have access to mainstream schooling in the region, Instead they are often institutionalized or hidden away in their homes. United Nations Children's Fund (UNICEF) Senior Advisor of Children with Disabilities, Rosangela Berman-Bieler, urged governments to ratify the Convention on the Rights of Persons with Disabilities held in Russia in 2011. Ratification of the convention would signal the support of signatories for policies of inclusive education for children with special needs. This would include access to free primary as well as secondary schools (United Nations Children's Fund, 2011). To facilitate this access, education leaders may have to build access ramps to buildings, reconstruct buildings so that they have elevators, hire reading specialists for those who may need that accommodation, and so on.

In addressing how children from different backgrounds and abilities are educated, education leaders may have to reconsider how they presently allocate resources. Some communities are better situated than others to respond to the changes brought about by education reform. Consequently, policymakers may have to facilitate how communities make the transition from the status quo to greater equity among its population with different needs.

TRANSITIONAL EQUITY.   Fairness in this context means that we hold people harmless for the changes that we make in policy. We note if the rules of the game changed to the detriment of certain classes. We also consider the possibility of compensating the losers for the change in rules. For example, in Minnesota, policymakers created a funding stream in the 1990s where school districts would be partly compensated for the extra money that they had to expend on having more experienced teachers. That policy was changed, however, where there would be no offsetting resources based on the experience level of teachers. To help school districts deal with that loss of revenue, a transition clause stated that school districts would continue to be compensated for those teachers hired in the years when the law was in effect, but that revenue stream would eventually disappear for new hires.

When the Australian government adopted a new school funding formula in 2001, many schools with older, more experienced staff members received transition payments to ensure continuity. Previously, schools were funded for the actual cost of their teacher payroll, regardless of how many junior or experienced teachers they had. Under the new model, schools in Australia were funded on an "averages in, actuals out model." That model meant schools would be funded for teacher salaries at the state average for each position regardless of the actual payment made by schools (Jones, 2000). Thus, schools with higher proportions of experienced teachers would lose funding, while those with lower proportions of experienced teachers would gain.

Many so-called hold harmless clauses that exist in present law are attempts to ensure that groups can transition smoothly when the rules of the game have been changed. However, they often mean that the costs of implementing the policy are increased. Increased costs turn our attention to the question of who pays.

ABILITY TO PAY.   While the concepts of fairness discussed here may be applied both to the impact and costs of policies, ability to pay focuses on the equitable distribution of costs. Under this definition, it is essential to consider the ability of individuals to make the payments. Using this definition of fairness, one's ability to pay is linked to income. The literature offers three descriptive categories of distribution of payments: regressive, proportional, and progressive. A **regressive system** is one in which the proportion of income collected increases, on average, as income levels decrease. A **proportional system** describes one where the proportion of income collected is the same, on average, regardless of income levels. A **progressive system** of revenue collection is one where the proportion of income collected increases, on average, as income levels increase. Note that these are descriptive statements in which the values of the policymakers direct the appropriate distribution. In an education setting, tying payment for services to the ability to pay of individual constituents may result in, for example, a sliding technology fee being charged to all higher education students whether or not they use technology facilities on campus. At the elementary and secondary school levels, many schools now charge fees for extracurricular activities, where children from families with higher incomes pay more for these activities than their less privileged peers. Another illustrative example of the ability to pay principle in action is the federal and state subsidized lunch programs offered in P–12 schools. With this program, children who are from families below an established level of income are eligible to receive lunch at a discounted cost or for free.

BENEFITS PRINCIPLE. This concept of fairness is predicated on the existence of a link between those who pay for a particular policy option and those who receive its benefits. Because of the nature of many publicly provided services, establishing this link may be difficult. For schools, this may mean charging those students who participate in extracurricular activities for the cost of those programs. Because this expense may inhibit students with less means from participating, a potential cause for concern in terms of vertical equity crops up. Many school leaders grapple with the appropriate funding for noncore programs, especially in an era of shrinking budgets. Many policymakers have chosen to balance both the benefits and ability-to-pay principles. They have a sliding scale for participation in after-school activities, where only those who participate have to pay, but the school subsidizes students who need the financial support.

CAN WE AFFORD IT?

What Is the Role of Economics?

Economics is fundamentally about the allocation of resources, which serves as a good foundation for making decisions in policy analysis. You should be able to inform your thinking about the affordability of the options that you are considering. Where more precise information is unavailable, you should still be able to rank the likely cost of each option as being more or less costly than the other. When thinking about costs, equity considerations may come into play because the dollar or other resource impact on one group is often not the same as that on another.

Common checks of the fairness of the distribution of costs and benefits are done by looking at differential impact based on residential location, income class, race and ethnicity, age, sex, family status, homeownership status, as well as current versus future generations (e.g., Bardach, 2009; Dunn, 2004; Patton & Sawicki, 1993).The economic literature discusses who should be considered in costs and benefits. As cited in Patton and Sawicki (1993), Trumball identifies five principles in determining standing: (1) willingness to pay by affected parties, (2) ex ante perspective, (3) cost-benefit analysis viewed within the context of the big picture, (4) evaluation consistent with physical and social constraints, and (5) preferences of all who are affected taken into account.

Policymakers and analysts alike often borrow economic concepts to establish criteria from which a recommendation is made. A full-fledged discussion on economics is beyond the scope of this text, but it is useful to be familiar with key economic concepts. The economic concepts highlighted in this discussion include opportunity costs, private versus public benefits, provision versus production, counting costs, and decision tools. The importance of this discussion is to understand and to make clear to your audience why one policy option is better than another based on fiscal considerations.

OPPORTUNITY COSTS.   In an economic framework, costs are more than just the out-of-pocket expenses of purchasing certain goods and services. Costs also include the opportunity lost by choosing one option rather than another. In technical terms, opportunity cost includes the loss of both tangible and intangible resources devoted to alternatives (Patton & Sawicki, 1993). Opportunity costs are at the heart of the policy analysis recommendation: an explicit recognition that, by choosing a particular way of resolving the problem, you may be closing off other avenues of resolution. Because resources are scarce, you will not be able to do everything that you would like to do, and policy choices have to be made. For example, education leaders may find that they have to choose between having more classrooms with fewer children or fewer classrooms with more children. Having smaller class sizes is associated with higher student achievement in the early grades, but this strategy has implications for the number of teachers hired and the building space needed. However, having larger class sizes may have a negative impact on student achievement and the need for bigger classroom space to hold more children. In 1996, education leaders in California opted to reduce class size across the state, resulting in an acute shortage of space and certified teachers. The additional need for teachers prompted by the new policy is associated with an increase in the portion of uncertified teachers among staff (Class Size, 2004).

PRIVATE VERSUS PUBLIC BENEFITS.   Many policymakers argue that public intervention is appropriate only when the market does not do certain activities well. When individual activities are limited to private impact, there may be no need for government action. Understanding the distinction between public and private benefits is often the foundation for providing justification for government action in addressing a problem rather than leaving its solution to private entities (Bardach, 2009). Many economists argue that a good rationale for public action is when market failures exist.

   Market failures occur when the market is unable to allocate resources efficiently because of a gap between conditions that are best for society and the aggregate of the conditions that are best for individuals who make up that collective. That is, the whole is bigger (or at least different) from the sum of its parts. This disconnect occurs when the net costs faced by individuals are different from those of society, perhaps because a single supplier or buyer has distorted the price, impairing the ability of the market to allocate resources appropriately. The market is able to allocate resources efficiently when there are no transaction costs, but there are few collective actions that will have no transaction costs associated with them. **Transaction costs** are costs associated with the exchange of goods or services for money or kind or in the implementation of policy. For example, the cost of busing inner-city youth to the suburbs goes beyond the explicit money spent on transportation. The children incur costs in terms of time spent on the bus and the more intangible costs of alienation from leaving one's community.

   Individuals may not be willing to pay for a good or service that they can enjoy without payment if they can get a free ride. A **free ride** occurs if an individual enjoys the benefit of a good or service without incurring the costs of providing that good or service. If every person chose a free ride, eventually, society would not be able to afford sufficient quantities of the good or service, even if its provision would improve the community as a whole. For example, in Minnesota, open-enrollment plans allow students to attend public school outside their residential school district as long as there is sufficient space in that school. The state of Minnesota still covers the costs of the nonresident student, and the state aid follows the child. The open enrollment policy thus offers opportunities for children in some families to attend public schools in districts outside their local residential and taxing jurisdiction. Because children can attend school outside their local school district and taxing jurisdiction, connections are weakened between the public school that they attend and the local school taxes that their families must pay. If a child attends school outside the residential district, his or her family has little incentive to agree to pay higher property taxes when asked to do so in local school funding referenda. Whether a local referendum is passed in the residential school district, the school that the child attends outside the district would not be financially affected. However, if a child attended a school in a district for which the local school funding referendum was successful, that child would benefit from the additional funds raised to support that district's schools. In an economic sense, the most positive financial outcome for families is for their district to have a failed referendum (thus not increasing their school tax) and for the nonresidential school district to which they send their child to have a successful referendum (thus having more resources for its schools). As long as there is space available in neighboring districts with good schools, families have an economic incentive to have referenda fail in their district and pass in others. This is the educational equivalent of a free ride, where families can benefit from more resources being spent on schools without paying the additional costs. If every family chose that outcome, however, eventually no school district would pass local school referenda and no additional resources would be raised. Alexander (2002) documents instances where families in Minnesota oppose referenda in their school district with the intention of sending their child to a higher-spending, higher-tax neighboring community under open-enrollment plans.

The presence of externalities also creates a gap between aggregate net benefits of individuals and that of society as a whole. **Externalities** are the effects to which the market assigns no value but still have an impact on society. Patton and Sawicki (1993) assert that the goal of public policy is often to add the value of externalities into the market decision.

PROVISION VERSUS PRODUCTION.   Policy options come with provision and production considerations. Provision refers to who will pay for the program; production refers to the technical delivery of the good or service. It is important to distinguish between the two processes. For instance, there is general agreement in the United States about public provision of elementary and secondary schooling. However, debate about public delivery of these education services is increasing (Carnoy, Jacobsen, Mishel, & Rothstein, 2005; Finn, Manno, & Vanourek, 2000). The typical student in the United States attends a traditional public school, which is financially supported by the use of local, state, and national revenues. The education services received are usually delivered by governmental organizations that are under the jurisdiction of local school boards. In 1992, charter schools were born. These organizations are labeled public schools because the bulk of their funding comes from public dollars, but their services are typically delivered under the management of private entities. While proponents of vouchers may argue that dollars should follow students to whatever schools they choose, the dollars to which they are referring often include public dollars. For example, in Florida, more than 25,000 low-income students use vouchers at over 1,000 private schools (e.g., Lim, 2010).

COUNTING THE COSTS.   Costs are an obvious constraint that must be acknowledged in making realistic policy choices. In economic parlance, costs are synonymous with resources used rather than simple expenditures itemized in budgets. Much of the cost-benefit analyses that we use to inform our decisions on the affordability and viability of policy options focus on the *additional* benefits and costs of implementing a program. Three economic considerations dominate these analyses: tangibility of costs, monetarizabiliy of costs, and direct nature of costs. Tangible impacts can be counted. Monetarizable impacts can be counted in monetary terms. Direct costs can be directly ascribed to the selected program. Legislative intent can determine if impact is direct or indirect. While direct costs must be counted in the final cost analysis, Patton and Sawicki (1993) indicate that the decision to include indirect costs is a matter of public policy.

Policy analysts often take a broad view of costs and consider both the monetary and nonmonetary aspects of the decisions made. Where possible, it may be easier to compare policy options if costs are measured on the same scale, with a dollar value placed on even those items that do not have specific dollar costs associated with them. For example, King (1994) adopted a comprehensive cost approach in her evaluation of three education reforms. When costs were not available in monetary terms, she monetized the value of the extra time that teachers would have to spend working in order to implement a particular school reform successfully. When there was no consistent way to capture the intangible costs and benefits associated with particular programs, she described these intangibles so that readers could understand the cost as best as possible.

COSTS VERSUS BENEFITS.   Just like goals seem to be the mirror image of problem definitions, benefits are the flip side of costs. As Patton and Sawicki (1993) note, benefits can be direct or indirect, tangible or intangible, short- or long-term. While costs may have more measurable dimensions, quite often benefits may be harder to pin down in terms of actual numbers. Patton and Sawicki thus suggest the use of comparable marketplace prices to get an idea of what one is likely to gain or lose from the impact of particular alternatives. Important considerations also include an understanding of the effect of scaling up or down of programs and whether a change in scale will fundamentally change its average costs. Such a change introduces economies or diseconomies of scale. **Economies of scale** exist when increasing the size or scale of the program leads to a reduction in its average cost. **Diseconomies of scale** occur when increasing the size of the program causes its average cost to increase. For example, if increasing the number of students participating in an online course did not lead to increases in the total costs of providing the course, expanding this program would lead to economies of scale. That is, as the costs are distributed among more students, average costs decrease. By contrast, if rising numbers of students lead to a strain on the system and increased technical difficulties, ultimately raising the average cost of delivery, then the program would experience diseconomies of scale.

When considering the costs and benefits of adopting and implementing a program, we still want to address whether the program has a differential impact on different groups. By addressing this issue, we are incorporating equity considerations into the financial possibilities that exist. To the extent that we are not counting everybody when costs and benefits are being considered, political dynamics are at play.

- Is this policy within our budget?

- What other options are being excluded if we choose this policy?

- Will the benefits of this policy accrue primarily to individuals or to the collective?

- Are the benefits of this policy greater than what it costs?

- How does the cost of this policy compare to other options that could be used to solve the problem? Is it higher, lower, or about the same?

FIGURE 5.3   Factors Affecting Affordability

DECISION TOOLS.   You can use standard economic tools of analysis to help in choosing among policy options. You can evaluate the affordability of individual projects by conducting a simple cost analysis, or you can compare their economic feasibility with other options by employing cost effectiveness or cost-benefit analysis. Because you may be working under tight deadlines, it may be helpful to look at the literature for existing evaluations of programs to get a sense of the relative cost of the options that you are considering.

HOW CAN YOU TELL?   When you bring an economic perspective to decision making, you pay more attention to the efficiency and affordability implications of policy choices. Generally speaking, efficiency occurs where there is an absence of waste. Economists often adopt the more technical economic definition of **Pareto efficiency**, where the existing allocation of resources are such that no one could be made better off without making someone else worse off. That is, there is no slack in the system.

While **efficiency** requires a ratio and describes a relationship between inputs and outputs, simple cost analysis (**affordability**) focuses on the inputs used to produce a particular output. Economic efficiency requires that the benefits to be gained in the use of resources be maximized; affordability requires that you have sufficient resources to implement the policy option considered. Efficiency can be considered a continuous variable, with different degrees of efficiency being demonstrated by variations in the return on investment associated with different policy options. This return represents a balance between the cost of inputs and the benefits received. Because different policy approaches may yield different outputs, it is helpful to use cost-benefit analysis as a means of standardizing the net benefits expected from each project. While cost, cost-effectiveness, and cost-benefit analysis can yield useful information on the resources required by a policy option, they are only tools; you (or your boss) are the decision maker.

USING THE ECONOMIC TOOLS.   **Cost analysis** seeks to identify the costs associated with conducting a particular alternative. **Cost effectiveness** measures the relationship between inputs and outputs but does so by keeping either the costs or the objectives consistent across policy options. When the objectives of policy are held constant, the goal of this analysis is to accomplish a certain objective at minimum cost. When the costs are held constant, the goal of this analysis is to achieve as much of the stated objectives as possible within the cost constraints. For both simple cost and cost effectiveness analysis, only costs need to be monetized. With simple cost analysis, there is no assumption regarding the profitability, feasibility, or economic efficiency of a program.

COST-BENEFIT ANALYSIS   A **cost-benefit analysis** provides a framework by which the total costs may be compared to the total benefits of a program. That is, both costs and benefits need to have dollar values attached to them. Projects are evaluated against other totally monetized policies using net present values or benefit cost ratios as analytical tools. **Present values** capture the value of costs and benefits as expressed in the value of dollars used today. Present value conveys the notion that enjoying a good or service now is better than waiting to enjoy it in the future. Consequently, the value of future payments and future benefits have to be discounted to reflect the notion that paying a dollar a year from now is not as painful as having to pay it now. Similarly, getting a dollar a year from now is not as helpful as enjoying the use of the dollar today. In other words, when you calculate the present value of costs and benefits, these dollar values are discounted (i.e., standardized) to reflect the same timeframe.

Feasibility is achieved whenever the present value of the benefits exceeds the present value of the costs. **Net present value** is the difference between the discounted dollar value of benefits and the discounted dollar value of costs. If the net present value is greater than 0, the project is financially feasible. The **benefit cost ratio** is the ratio of the discounted value of benefits over the discounted value of costs. If this ratio is greater than 1, then the project is financially feasible.

WILL PEOPLE SUPPORT IT?

When making decisions in a collective, it is important to have the support of key stakeholders. By asking yourself if people will support a particular option, you are essentially getting at its political viability. Some stakeholders are more influential than others. You will have to consider the potential impact of your policy option on relevant power groups such as legislators, administrators, citizen coalitions, neighborhood groups, unions, public officials, influential citizens, and other sources of power and political alliances. Citing Marshall, Mitchell, and Wirt (1989), Heck (2004) suggests that, in state educational policy making, there are five rings of influence: insiders, near circle, far circle, sometimes players, and forgotten players. These five terms were defined in Chapter 3. It may be crucial to have the support of insiders, but it is also important to give voice to all the stakeholders, including the forgotten players.

- Who supports this policy option?
- Are the people who support this policy option insiders, forgotten players, or at other levels of influence?
- Are the people who oppose this policy alternative insiders, forgotten players, or at other levels of influence?
- What is the priority of this policy for those who support it? Are supporters in favor of any change or are they wedded to this approach?
- What is the priority of this policy for those who oppose it? Are opponents against all change, or do they just dislike this strategy?
- What are supporters of this policy willing to give up to ensure that this policy option is passed?
- What are opponents of this policy willing to trade to make sure that this policy option dies?

FIGURE 5.4   Questions Regarding Political Acceptability

How Acceptable Is the Alternative to Different Groups?

To assess the acceptability of different alternatives to different groups, we must examine what the various actors believe about the problem and what they need or want. As part of that initial political analysis, you must document the base positions of key groups and note their nonnegotiable points. By addressing these points, you can determine whether a policy is acceptable to actors in the political process and if clients and other actors are receptive to any change in the status quo.

What Factors Influence the Political Acceptability of Policy?

Heck (2004) identifies seven factors that can have an impact on what he calls the action situation: (1) participants, (2) their positions, (3) the set of allowable actions and their links to outcomes, (4) potential outcomes that are linked to an individual sequence of actions, (5) level of control that participants can exercise, (6) information available to actors about the structure of the action situation, and (7) the costs and benefits that they assign to outcomes (p. 143). Participants are those who can influence the policy process; their positions are the stances they take in support of or opposition to particular policies. The set of allowable actions consist of the strategies that are within the legal, fiscal, and social parameters of the community that you lead. Potential outcomes are the strategies and practices that education leaders deem effective from their knowledge of practice and the literature. The level of control refers to the flexibility afforded to stakeholders to make the decision on what gets done. For example, many federal judges have ruled that challenges to state school funding models are outside their purview and that they are a matter for state judges and policymakers (e.g., *San Antonio Independent School District v. Rodriguez*, 1973). The costs and benefits assigned to options will influence the decisions education leaders make. The presumption is that individuals want those outcomes in which their benefits exceed their costs. Because participants face different constraints, have different costs, and employ different power rationales, their individual assessments of what is beneficial may be different from what the collective decides.

The acceptability of a policy is also based on the perceptions of relevant stakeholders that the policy chosen will mesh with the values of their community. If decision makers perceive that the policy or program will meet community needs, it is generally more acceptable. No matter how responsive stakeholders consider an option to be, however, the policy action must be consistent with existing laws, rules, and regulations.

How Can You Measure the Acceptability of a Policy?

Fowler (2009) makes similar points in her summary of power relationships and the use of a modified PRINCE (**pr**obe, **in**teract, **c**alculate **e**xecute) analysis taken from Coplin and O'Leary (1998). The framework requires an ordering of key stakeholders in groups opposed to or in support of a particular policy action. For each of these groups, you document their stance on the issue, indicate their relative power to influence the issue at hand, and consider the priority that they place in supporting or opposing a particular policy option. By multiplying the values placed on each factor for each group, you can get a sense of the strength of support or opposition that each group assigns to a particular policy. By summing all those in favor and comparing that sum to the sum of all those against, you have a rough estimation of the political viability of any policy option considered. The values that you assign to each group are subjective, but they should be grounded in the literature.

How Can You Change the Acceptability of a Policy Intervention?

By conducting a PRINCE analysis, you can pinpoint the greatest support and the greatest challenge to a particular policy approach. For example, if you estimate that a policy does not have sufficient support, it could be because of the relatively low priority given to it by its supporters, the relative lack of power of its supporters, or the lukewarm nature of the support given. Once you have identified where the weakness lies, you can devise a course of action that could lead to a change in the dynamics of support, thus altering the viability of the option. You may also decide that the political costs of making this option more acceptable are not worth it.

WHO WILL IMPLEMENT IT?

No matter how good a policy seems to be in theory, if it does not get implemented, it does not work. What would allow a policy to be more than words on paper and reflect change in real life? This type of thinking underlies considerations of administrative operability. Will the people who are in charge of implementing the change be willing or able to do so?

Is There Sufficient Administrative Capacity?

The answer to this question addresses whether it is possible to implement the proposed policy or program within the political, social, and administrative context. It is important to raise questions of implementation authority early in the analytic process, both to avoid settling on an alternative that no one can implement and to identify changes that will be needed in order to establish implementation authority for potentially superior alternatives.

WHAT ARE THE MAJOR ORGANIZATIONAL LIMITATIONS? When considering organizational limitations, it may be helpful to consider Bryson (1988), who highlights four key problems that can affect the implementation of a strategic plan: **human problems** in the management of attention, **process problems** in terms of the management of strategic ideas, **structural problems** in the management of part–whole relations, and **institutional problems** in terms of the appropriate exercise of transformative leadership. The **political culture** of the broader environment may also influence administrative culture and the willingness of implementers to accept change.

HOW CAN YOU TELL? You can follow some general guidelines that address whether your policy options can be implemented. These guidelines may be summarized as (1) difference from the status quo, (2) policy instrument, (3) support of personnel, and (4) available resources. You can create a template using these key categories and then score each policy based on how well it did on each dimension of its ability to be implemented. The higher the overall score, the policy would be considered more likely to be implemented, other things being equal.

- Will the proposed policy lead to organizational changes, power dynamics, and outcomes that are different from the status quo? Are these differences small or large?
- What policy instrument does this option require?
- Do the people who have to implement programmatic changes support this policy?
- Will this policy require reallocation of existing resources (including time)?
- Will this policy require additional resources?

FIGURE 5.5 Questions to Ask for Assessing Likely Ease or Difficulty of Policy Implementation

Difference from Status Quo.   The more different a policy is from the status quo, the more time and other resources will be needed for it to be fully implemented. This situation may be the result of practitioners lacking sufficient authority, or perhaps the learning curve of fulfilling new responsibilities is steep. Simple reform presents fewer implementation challenges than radical restructuring. For example, if you are thinking about going from a junior high school format to a middle school format, this may be a difficult transition if your current system is structured to house primarily elementary programs, from kindergarten to grade 8; junior high schools, grades 9 and 10; and senior high schools, grades 11 and 12. For some countries, a major restructuring effort may include the transformation of single-sex high schools into coeducational institutions.

Policy Instrument.   The type of policy instrument chosen also influences the ability of policy options to be implemented. McDonnell and Elmore (1987) note that mandates require the highest level of capacity on the part of implementers while capacity-building policy instruments require the least. The opposite is true for policymakers, whose responsibility it is to fund those policies. **Mandates** are rules that lay out what needs to be done; those who do not follow the rules face specific consequences. **Capacity-building policies** are strategies where policymakers invest in expanding the capabilities of the community or organization by enhancing or developing the learning, knowledge, and skills of those targeted by the policy. More details on policy instruments are provided in Chapter 6 and will be revisited in discussions of implementation in Chapter 10.

Personnel Support.   Another factor that affects the likely implementation of a policy option is if the field staff and personnel support it. Fowler (2009) notes that policy implementers "usually want to run a good program that benefits children, [but] they also have personal interests at stake" (p. 322). Consequently, those policies likely to enhance the professional reputations of implementers and improve their chances of career advancement may be better supported than those that seem to diminish their reputations or limit their authority.

Available Resources.   The existing capability of the groups expected to fulfill the responsibilities proposed in the policy also influences the ability of the policy to be implemented. You may use research and ask questions of implementers to determine if the proposed resources are sufficient for fulfilling the objectives of the policy. The greater the gap between the resources called for and the resources on hand, the less likely that the policy will be implemented successfully. Key areas to look at are the equipment, physical facilities, and other support services that are in place. As noted by McDonnell and Elmore (1987), ". . . identifying resources and constraints is how policymakers assess what is feasible . . ." (p. 146). The importance of providing sufficient resources for the successful implementation of policy is underlined by a policy statement by the Council of Chief State School Officers (CCSSO). It urges policymakers to provide the necessary funding to schools to ensure that schools offer all students sound education opportunities (e.g., CCSSO, 2010 p. 5).

WHAT IF THE CRITERIA CONFLICT?

Values sometimes conflict. Actions that are theoretically the most effective may face the biggest political and administrative challenges. Radical action may lead to dramatic change, but dramatic change can ruffle feathers *and* be costly. The seminal work by Okun (1975) discusses the trade-off between the values of efficiency and equality. He suggests that policies that are the most equitable are not the most efficient, and vice versa. Should you choose the option that maximizes the opportunity to achieve more equity or the one that maximizes the chance of greater efficiency? This question does not have one right answer because the answer varies with the context. The key point is that by establishing criteria, you identify your driving values, which allows you to reflect on your own choices and to be informed about what people would be willing to give up if values conflict with each other.

Reflecting on what you really care about and the driving values of all decision makers involved in the process pays dividends, which we discussed earlier in this chapter as well as in Chapter 1. The priorities you or other decision makers bring determine the choices that are available should the criteria conflict. If there is disagreement on priorities, a decision rule may be needed, which may lead to an ordering of criteria through consensus building, majority vote, unanimity, or unilateral decision making on the part of the person in charge. Bardach (2009) suggests that you should also categorize criteria in a hierarchy of "must haves" and wants. In this way, you will weigh the "must have" criteria more heavily than those that are simply desired.

Chapter Summary

You have now learned about the third step of the policy analysis process: establishing your driving values. This chapter focused on establishing and reflecting on the values that will help you choose among the various policy options available. The groups and individuals involved in the decision process influence the values that you ultimately use to select among different policy alternatives. The political process and community mores help to determine whose values count and who provides input into the discussion. Once the desired vision for society has been established, criteria provide concrete, working definitions of these ideals. In selecting appropriate policy options, you will likely ask yourself these five questions: (1) Does it work? (2) Is it fair? (3) Can we afford it? (4) Will people support it? and (5) Who will implement it? Your chosen criteria will thus address the effectiveness of policy, its equity, its costs, its political viability, and its ability to be implemented.

Now that you know *how* you are going to choose, it is time to discuss how to create the alternatives *from* which you will choose, which is the subject of Chapter 6.

Review Questions

1. What would be your top concern in making education policy? How does this concern reflect your driving values?
2. What do you think is the role of public schools in promoting social equity? What rationale underlies your response? What policies would you support? What policies do you oppose? Why?
3. Do you agree with the notion that ethical deliberations do not enter into the analysis of costs and benefits? Explain your response.
4. Given the discussion of costs, how would key concepts influence the discourse on vouchers and open enrollment programs for elementary and secondary schools?
5. Is an equal distribution of resources the same as a fair distribution of resources? Give a rationale for your response.

News Story for Analysis

"A class of their own; Schools hope single-sex education will help boys excel." *National Post* (f/k/a *The Financial Post*) (Canada). October 16, 2010 Saturday. National Edition. BYLINE: Kenyon Wallace, *National Post*. SECTION: CANADA; Pg. A12.

When the Edmonton Catholic School Board begins holding seminars next month on the creation of an all-boys academy, it will become the latest educational body to take up what is becoming an increasingly popular idea.

Another Alberta school board, the Calgary Catholic School District, has just started its first school year offering segregated classrooms from Kindergarten to Grade 6. Last November, Chris Spence, the Toronto District School Board's director of education, announced his intention to establish an all-boys academy next fall and introduce 300 "boy-friendly" classrooms across the city. The board, like many others across the country, already offers single-gender classrooms in some schools, and there are similar experiments being run at schools throughout Canada.

While many education experts applaud the idea as a way to "let boys be boys," some academics question the need for separate classes or schools, saying boys don't actually learn differently than girls. Some blame the public system for neglecting to encourage boys to excel, particularly in literacy skills. Others lay the blame on a culture where academic achievement is frowned upon.

In today's pop music landscape, dominated by the likes of Eminem, 50 Cent and Justin Timberlake, chart-topping songs do not extol the virtues of working hard at school.

It's been a long time since songs like Sam Cooke's 1960 hit, Wonderful World, in which the protagonist sings about how he "Don't know much about history," or most other academic subjects, but vows to win the heart of his baby by working hard to become an A student, dominated the charts.

"We've gone from a culture where young men wanted you to think they were smart to one where they want you to think they're gangsters," said Dr. Leonard Sax, a psychologist and author of the book *Boys Adrift*.

"The culture in which we live—North American Anglophone culture—is a culture that today disrespects academic achievement for boys."

Statistics show boys underachieve in comparison to girls, are increasingly disengaged, and exhibit more disruptive and violent behavior in school.

There is little dispute that boys have for years been underperforming girls on standardized testing, particularly in literacy, but opinion among researchers and experts is mixed over whether the solution lies in single-gender education.

A recent study by researchers at the American Association of University Women Educational Foundation found that over the past decade, improvements in academic performance by girls have not been made at the expense of boys, who, on the whole, have also made scholastic gains.

"Single-sex schools do not confer an advantage in terms of student achievement for boys or for girls," said Charles Ungerleider, a sociology professor at the University of British Columbia and former B.C. deputy minister of education, who has studied the performance of students in single-gender versus co-educational schools.

He says the evidence is clear: "When you have carefully controlled comparisons of single-sex and mixed-sex schooling, we find that girls and boys perform about the same."

But educators in schools experimenting with single-gender classes say, at least anecdotally, that boys' attention spans are improved when they are segregated, partly because teachers can tailor programming to cater to similar interests that may exist between boys, and because there are fewer distractions, i.e., girls.

Leanne Timko, principal of Calgary's Sacred Heart School, which began offering single-sex classes this September in Kindergarten to Grade 6, says while it's too early to tell whether grades will improve in boys-only classes, teachers have noticed improved behavior.

Citing research that suggests male students respond better to auditory instructions, she said the school has introduced sound systems in boys' classrooms, where teachers wear microphones and their voices are amplified through speakers. Some classrooms have also been rearranged to allow more space for boys to move around.

"It's been quite dramatic to see how their attention has shifted," Ms. Timko said, noting that parents have been enthusiastic about the changes.

She adds, however, that single-gender education isn't the best option for every student.

"It's a program of choice," she said. "We're continuously learning about the differences between boys and girls. The goal of the segregated classroom is the same goal as the coeducational classroom, and that is to provide the best education for every kid."

Cecil B. Sterling Elementary School in the Hamilton-Wentworth District School Board has been offering single-sex classrooms from Grades 6 through 8 for eight years. Superintendent Manny Figueiredo says boys' engagement in classroom activities has improved, but it's unclear if segregation has led to better academic performance.

"Isolating the classrooms alone doesn't yield results," he said. "What yields results is the classroom instruction. By putting boys together, we've got a group of learners who have similar interests and similar learning styles . . . that allows teachers to program for boys and their needs."

Catering specifically to boys' interests and needs is something that seems to have been lost in many classrooms across the country, says University of Alberta professor Heather Blair, a specialist in elementary education.

In an age when schools have become hypersensitive to all things remotely violent or potentially offensive to anyone, boys, she says, lack the encouragement to explore their interests—which often surround action-adventure, war, and fantasy—particularly when it comes to reading and writing.

"If boys are watching and reading fantasy, and that's what they're interested in, that's what they will want to write about," said Prof. Blair.

"But we have [t]his questioning in teachers' minds, because there tends to be a lot of violence in that stuff. There's a whole bunch of censorship going on and we need to learn how to give boys the opportunity to write about what they want."

She also says she doesn't believe a cognitive difference in learning processes exists for boys and girls, nor does she think there is a crisis for boys in education.

One problem with standardized tests is that they don't measure literacy outside the traditional subjects of reading and writing, she says.

"Boys are multiply-literate," said Prof. Blair, citing the results of a six-year study she recently completed that followed a group of Alberta boys from Grade 4 through . . . Grade 10.

"These boys took up all kinds of digital literacies way before girls. In the long run, I actually think they're way ahead of the game. What we're getting in these standardized test scores is only part of the picture."

While talk within school boards of creating single-gender options is newsmaking stuff in this country, Canada is actually a latecomer to the discussion, says Brad Adams, executive director of the International Boys' School Coalition and former head of the senior school at Upper Canada College.

The United States, New Zealand, Australia, United Kingdom and South Africa all have successful boys-only school models.

But many Canadian faculties of education, school boards and ministries tend to be dogmatically opposed to single-gender education on the basis of its apparent inequity and a belief that the system should use differentiated teaching and learning.

"The argument is that if every child is unique, why would we segregate by something as socially constructed as gender?" Mr. Adams said.

He debates the common belief that co-ed schools provide a greater opportunity for boys and girls to interact, and therefore more "well rounded" students.

"There are exceptions, but many co-ed schools are already and sometimes not so subtly divided by gender," Mr. Adams said. "Girls tend to dominate arts programs, take on more leadership positions, do more service, and populate the honor roles. For too many boys, it's too easy to opt out, to be too cool for school, to fall back on rigid stereotypes."

Dr. Sax, who is also the founder of the National Association for Single Sex Public Education in the U.S., says critics of all-boys schools miss the point.

"Single-sex education is not the objective, it's a means," he said. "The objective is to help every child to achieve their full potential academically and intellectually."

Part of the rationale for public boards offering single-sex education where teachers can create an alternative culture where "it's cool to be smart," he says, is that private all-boys or all-girls schools are too expensive for the average family.

"The argument isn't about which option is better. That's the wrong question," Dr. Sax said. "Children are diverse and parents ought to have a choice. Why not offer single-sex education as a choice? It's about social justice."

Source: Material reprinted with the express permission of: "National Post Inc."

Discussion Questions

1. What do you think are the essential programs for schools? Why?
2. What are the values expressed in this news story? Which criteria would you derive from these values? How would you know if you had more or less of these values reflected in policy?
3. As an education leader, would you support single-sex schools? Explain your response.

Selected Websites

Council of Chief State School Officers. Available at *http://www.ccsso.org/*.

The official website of the Council of Chief State School Officers (CCSSO). The council is a nonpartisan, nationwide, nonprofit organization of public officials who head departments of elementary and secondary education in the states, the District of Columbia, the Department of Defense Education Activity, and five U.S. extra-state jurisdictions. The site contains a rich array of information on educational issues across the United States. The CCSSO is committed to providing information to state education leaders that address their ability to improve the performance of their education system. Because the council seeks consensus on major education issues, education leaders will find the site particularly useful in terms of how this organization balances the plethora of values and stances held by its members in the recommendations that they provide.

National Association for Gifted Children. Available at *http://www.nagc.org/*.

The official website of the National Association for Gifted Children (NAGC). Members include parents, teachers, educators, other professionals, and community leaders. They provide strong advocacy for the establishment and support of gifted and talented programs in schools. Education leaders may find this site helpful for the information it provides about gifted and talented education across the country and summarized in its annual report: *State of the States in Gifted Education*. Leaders of this organization express a definite viewpoint on the value of gifted and talented programs in schools and often hold contrasting views from that held by members of the National Coalition for Equity in Education (listed next).

National Coalition for Equity in Education. Available at *http://ncee.education.ucsb.edu/aboutus.htm*. The official website of the National Coalition for Equity in Education (NCEE). The coalition consists of early childhood through university educators and supports the achievement of equity in education.

The NCEE is strongly committed to providing emotional and intellectual support to educators as they work for the transformation of educational settings. Members of this group often offer strong criticism of gifted and talented programs because of their potential to discriminate against students from less privileged communities. Equity is a strongly held value and underlies many of the policy recommendations made by members of this group. Education leaders may find this site interesting for the information and perspective it provides on what a successful education system looks like.

Selected References

Alexander, N. A. (2002). **Race, poverty, and the student curriculum: Implications for standards policy.** *American Educational Research Journal, 39*(3), 675–694.

This article examines the links between the minority and poverty status of public secondary schools and course-taking patterns within those schools. The findings have mixed implications for the effectiveness and equity of standards-based policies. Curriculum standards were associated with higher student participation in core and advanced courses. However, links between course-taking patterns and the minority and poverty status of schools persisted in big-city school districts but were somewhat weaker for schools in the rest of New York State. School size played an increasingly important role on course taking for schools in all locations. Education leaders may find this article interesting for the information it presents on the trade-offs that sometimes exist between pursuing more effective versus more equitable policies.

King, J. A. (1994). **Meeting the educational needs of at-risk students: A cost analysis of three models.** *Educational Evaluation and Policy Analysis, 16*, 1–19.

This article provides cost comparisons of three comprehensive models for bringing at-risk students to grade level during their elementary school years. Education leaders may find this article valuable for the insight it provides on conducting a comprehensive cost analysis of education programs and the specific information it offers on the relative costs of Robert Slavin's Success for All Schools, Henry Levin's Accelerated Schools, and James Comer's School Development Program.

Odden, A., & Picus, L. (2008). *School finance: A policy perspective* **(4th ed.). Madison, WI: McGraw Hill.**

Odden and Picus provide an excellent roadmap of the issues that underlie school finance in the United States. Their text offers a strong theoretical underpinning for many of the values that shape education finance discussions, including equity, efficiency, and adequacy. Education leaders may find Chapters 1 through 4 especially helpful for the overview provided on school finance, legal parameters, and equity considerations as they apply to the financing of schools.

Okun, A. M. (1975). *Equality and efficiency, the big tradeoff.* **Washington, DC: The Brookings Institution.**

This is a classical treatise of the presumed trade-offs between having policies that result in greater efficiencies and policies that result in greater equity. Education leaders may find this book interesting because of the excellent overview it provides regarding these values that often undergird policy discourse.

6

Develop Alternatives

CHAPTER OBJECTIVES

After reading this chapter, you will be able to:

- Identify generic strategies of policy intervention
- Modify existing solutions to broaden the alternatives available
- Identify major policy types
- Distinguish among policy mechanisms and describe best-practice contexts

EDUCATION VIGNETTE

You are the superintendent of a struggling school district. Overall enrollment is declining, but the proportions of students who are eligible for free and reduced lunch and those who speak English as a second language are increasing. The state in which you are located is experiencing a fiscal crisis and has cut its budget drastically, including the amounts expended on schools and for special programs. You are faced with a large budget deficit, and you are examining different policy options to increase the budget without adversely affecting community morale and student achievement. The prospect of closing schools, cutting specialist classes like music, consolidating programs, or undergoing a state takeover of some schools are unpalatable, but you know that you cannot continue as you have. You brace yourself to face the school board and members of the community as they clamor to hear your ideas.

What do you say?

WHAT ARE ALTERNATIVES?

Alternatives are the policy options that you are considering to resolve a problem. They describe the interventions you are taking into account to resolve or alleviate the negative condition that you identified. The process of developing alternatives parallels what Duke (2004) characterizes as the design phase of the educational change process, which "involves what needs to change in order to address identified educational needs" (p. 91). More specifically, Duke, Bradley, Butin, Grogan, and Gillespie (1998) define educational design as "the process of creating the means by which educational intentions can be achieved within a specified context" (p. 159).

Alternatives Are Not Outcomes

Alternatives are not to be confused with the outcomes sought and are always a *means* to an end; they are not an end in and of themselves. Alternatives are the "hows" of the analytical process; they detail *how* you plan to mitigate the negative condition that you have identified as a policy issue. When creating alternatives, you are developing a particular action or package of actions that will help to address the problem. The literature observes that we are often wedded to a particular way of doing things and too often lose sight of what we would like to accomplish with our efforts (e.g., Dunn, 2004; Bardach, 2009).

Alternatives Are Not Implementation Plans

Creating alternatives are not the same as developing an implementation plan (the subject of Chapter 10). Rather, you are creating a grounded wish list of strategies that you would like to pursue to change the status quo. As noted by Duke (2004), while you must be aware of the factors that may constrain implementation of a policy, those factors are not the essence of policy design. The essence of constructing an alternative is determining *how* it addresses key links in the causal chain of factors leading to the problem.

Basic Alternatives and Their Variants

Bardach (2009) suggests that it is important to tell the difference between a basic alternative and its variants. Basic alternatives may differ from each other because of differences in the items that they address. For example, several factors have an impact on student achievement, including teacher quality, governance, peer groupings, curricula, and student ability. When developing alternatives, you may decide that you will focus on teacher quality or time spent in school. The actions chosen to mitigate the negative impact or accentuate positive effects of various underlying factors are the basic alternatives.

Variants of a particular option emerge because of the different methods of implementation and financing that they require. For example, if you create alternatives that address teacher quality, you may decide to provide incentives for school districts to have highly qualified teachers, or you may mandate that they have qualified teachers. You may choose to finance the proposed policy by reallocating current resources, investing additional amounts, or a combination of both.

Duke (2004) notes four bases for differentiating alternatives: purpose, the unit of change, the nature of change, and the magnitude of change. *Purpose* refers to the goal of intervention. For example, is the intervention primarily meant to increase accountability, improve children outcomes, or reduce costs? *The unit of change* refers to the individual, group, or organization that you will target to effect change. For example, will the proposed action target the behavior of students, teachers, the school community as a whole, or the state? *The nature of change* refers to the type of change that you propose. That is, is the alternative going to alter the production process, change the outputs produced by the system, change the governance structure, or change the attitudes and behavior of individuals? *The magnitude of change* indicates whether the alternative is designed to modify the entire system, as in systemic reform, or to affect a small part of it, as in a pilot program.

DEVELOPING ALTERNATIVES BY MODELING THE SYSTEM

Bardach (2009) suggests that in creating alternatives, you should consider the appropriate metaphor for modeling the system that you would like to change. He offers three important metaphors: market models, production processes, and evolutionary systems. **Market models** replicate relationships in a market. **Production models** replicate the creation of outputs. **Evolutionary models** replicate the gradual changes that occur over time in a system. Each of these three metaphors is discussed more completely in the next section of this chapter. The utility of models is the insight that they provide about the nature of the relationships among key variables within the system. By discerning the nature of relationships, you can change them in a way that produces outcomes you find more favorable than the present condition.

The Metaphor of the Market

The metaphor of the market presumes that individuals are self-interested and that outcomes can be improved through competition. Leading policymakers have used it frequently since the 1980s. Because of the nature of the competitive relationship presumed by this metaphor, policymakers who share this viewpoint rely heavily on alternatives that use market mechanisms, including the increased use of alternatives that increase choice (e.g., charter schools, vouchers) and affect price (e.g., incentives). Diane Ravitch, a noted researcher, educator, and former proponent of this perspective, has increasingly criticized the validity of the parallels made between school systems and markets (Ravitch, 2010).

The Production Metaphor

The production metaphor equates school systems with a production process where inputs, throughputs, and outputs are related. Many scholars in school finance have adopted this approach (e.g., Monk, 1989) and have developed various education production functions. They view alternatives in terms of how they influence the production process of schooling. They identify the various ingredients that go into the "production" of an educated child, often measured as student achievement. Researchers conduct analyses of the impact on outcomes of changing the nature of one or more key schooling ingredients through policy actions. An example of a question answered by this type of analysis is, What are the implications of mandating higher curriculum standards, thereby increasing the "quality" of an important input (Alexander, 2004)?

Evolutionary Models

Evolutionary models recognize the changes that occur over time within a system. Policymakers who use this metaphor tend to create alternatives that address common processes within a system that in turn affect "variation among competitors, selection and retention" (Bardach, 2009, p. 19). For example, if an educational system produced too many low-performing graduates, policymakers may decide to influence the "natural" results produced by the system by educating actors within the system of the type of outcomes preferred. The use of rating systems, where schools that make yearly progress are considered to be better than schools that do not, are reflective of this approach. Bardach refers to this as a change in the pool of competitors. You may also choose to influence the processes that result in the production of these graduates so that there is better selection between the types of graduates sought and the schooling processes that are rewarded. The Investing in Innovation (i3) federal grant, which targets innovative and effective practices within schools, is reflective of this approach. Bardach refers to this as a change in the "selection mechanism." You may also choose to change the nature of the system so that you reduce the propensity of institutions to produce low-performing graduates. The transformative models embedded in recent federal rules that call for the closing of underperforming schools are reflective of this approach. Bardach refers to this as changing the "retention mechanism."

Doing Nothing Different

When developing a list of alternatives, many researchers advocate including the option of doing nothing different from before (e.g., Bardach, 2009; Patton & Sawicki, 1993). However, doing nothing different is unlikely to lead to change unless the environment is changing around you. Given environmental constraints, more effective options may not be immediately viable. For example, tying teacher pay to values added in student achievement is increasingly popular in inner policy circles. Research suggests, however, that because of potentially large measurement errors in student data, student achievement should not be the sole criterion for determining teacher pay. The rest of this section discusses the source of alternatives and closes with the various policy types and mechanisms that may be employed to implement a particular strategy.

HOW DO YOU GENERATE ALTERNATIVES?

When developing alternatives, you must start first with the problem and the goal of addressing it. By this stage, you should have an understanding of the values, goals, and objectives of key stakeholders. Second, create a conceptual graph that illustrates the underlying interaction of factors that have led to the creation of the problem that you describe. As noted by Duke (2004), "[s]uccessful designs [of alternatives] for educational change result from systematic thinking—from an appreciation of the interrelationships between and among design elements and those who work and learn in schools" (p. 117).

- Do you have a clear statement of the problem?
- Do you have an understanding of the values, goals, and objectives of key stakeholders?
- Have you created a conceptual graph detailing relationships between the problem and associated variables?
- Do your alternatives reflect the underlying factors of your problem?

FIGURE 6.1 Guiding Questions for Generating Alternatives

Sources of Alternatives

Alternatives are the specific tasks undertaken to address the identified causes of the problem. To get an idea of the appropriate tasks that you should consider, you can go to several sources. First, you can review the literature to examine and explore research findings that present a similar context to your own. Examining the literature may give you ideas about what you can change realistically and what is out of your hands. Second, you can examine the experiences of others with related problems. For example, the Minneapolis public schools sent a contingency of its leaders to Chicago and other cities to examine key reform initiatives. This led to the recommendations by the superintendent to (1) create a portfolio of autonomous school models, (2) create an Office of New Schools to seek out and manage the authorization of such schools, and (3) collaborate with high-quality third-party school providers.

Additional sources of alternatives include the insight of experts and your legal obligations (e.g., Patton & Sawicki, 1993). When relying on the expertise of others, you can modify general guidelines, or you can customize alternatives to fit your localized problem. Because of the difficulties stemming from the creation of new solutions, Duke (2004, p. 93) notes that "many educators prefer to *adopt* or *adapt* existing designs rather than to *create* a new design" (emphasis in original).

GENERIC ALTERNATIVES. As you think about the variety of issues that are faced by policymakers and administrators, you will find that many of the changes discussed are often reworkings of an old solution. Weimer and Vining (1992) indicate that your search for alternatives may lead you to existing policy proposals. For example, Promise Neighborhoods is a federal program that is modeled on the Harlem Children's Zone (HCZ). The HCZ was developed by a community-based organization and offers students comprehensive services, such as preschool and college counseling, to foster high student achievement.

You may also recognize a solution in generic policy strategies. For example, if you want to increase the quantity demanded of a good or service, economic analysis suggests

- Look to the literature.
- Look to the experience of others with related problems (professional judgment).
- Look to the insight of experts.
- Look to your legal obligations.

FIGURE 6.2 Sources of Alternatives

that you must find a way to reduce its price. Governmental units can generally alter the price of a good or service through the use of taxes or subsidies. Other generic strategies include changing the standards required (e.g., through the use of regulation or provision of information) and changing power structures (e.g., through the structuring of private rights) (e.g., Bardach, 2009).

CUSTOMIZING POLICY INTERVENTIONS. According to Osborn (as cited in Patton & Sawicki, 1993), you can create the new out of the old in several ways. You can adapt the design of an existing policy so that it will have a bigger impact by increasing its scale (magnify). For example, many antibullying programs were implemented initially at the school level and expanded into statewide and national zero-tolerance policies.

You can modify a policy design so that it operates on a smaller scale (minify). For example, the 1997 federal Comprehensive School Reform Demonstration shared the same purpose as transforming school programs of the 2009 American Recovery and Reinvestment Act (ARRA). The 2009 program calls for four reform models to improve failing schools: (1) turnaround, (2) restart, (3) school closures, and (4) transformation. The earlier policy spread its resources across 7,000 low-performing schools, while the AARA targets the 5,000 lowest performing schools.

You can transform a policy by substituting one level of decision making with another. Some district leaders have transformed the relationship between management and teachers since gaining the authority to "transform" schools under provisions of the No Child Left Behind Act. For example, a Central Falls, Rhode Island, superintendent's proposal to fire all the teachers in a failing high school after contract talks broke down was approved by the board members of that district (Zezima, 2010). The dismissal of the faculty members represents a transformation of the relationship between management and teachers for two key reasons. First, the firing of teachers would normally fall on building leaders, not district leaders. Second, the firing of the entire faculty and the imposition of mandatory professional development according to federal guidelines reflect more state and federal involvement in district governance than is typical for school districts in the United States.

You could also adjust the initial policy design to combine decision-making authority as well as rearrange the responsibilities of selected implementers. In Tennessee, for example, districts, along with other educational organizations (e.g., Teach for America), can license teachers. Teacher licensing used to be the sole purview of the state. Another example is Illinois, where state officials approved a policy that outside organizations must partner with districts in efforts to turn around low-performing schools.

To determine the appropriate modifications, you must focus on the location in which you would like the change to occur. Consider how you would finance that change and be aware of the current financing of policies supporting the condition that you would like to change. To generate reasonable policy options, you must be clear about the decision sites and points of influence, and be mindful of how to manage risks. There is abundant research to help ground your approach (e.g., Weimer & Vining, 1992). The remaining discussion relies extensively on Lowi's (1964) seminal article on policy types and McDonnell and Elmore's (1987) and McDonnell's (1994) discussion on policy mechanisms.

- Where do you want the change to occur? Are there existing policies that addresses similar conditions? What modifications will cause existing proposals to be better aligned with the current context?
- How do you plan to finance the change that you propose?
- How are current policies dealing with similar problems financed?
- Who gets to make key decisions under your new plan? Are these the same individuals who were key decision makers under the old policy? Will the modifications you propose make the plan more or less popular with influential stakeholders?

FIGURE 6.3   Guiding Questions to Consider When Modifying Alternatives

POLICY TYPES

Lowi (1964) argues that policy options can be categorized into three main policy types: distributive, redistributive, and regulatory. **Distributive policies** entail presenting additional resources to a community or group for whom the problem is being solved. **Redistributive policies** entail taking from one subgroup within the community and giving it to another subgroup. **Regulatory policies** require specified actions or results that may or may not involve the explicit allocation of resources.

Distributive policies are the least likely to face political opposition and tend to be the most costly kinds of actions, other things being equal. Redistributive policies are the most likely to face political opposition. However, they may not require additional resources and thus may not incur as much additional costs as distributive policies. Regulatory policies fall somewhere between distributive and redistributive policies in terms of their expected implications for adoption, implementation, and costs. These policy types may be broken down further into policy mechanisms, which are the specific levers that policymakers and practitioners employ to get things done.

POLICY MECHANISMS AND BEST-PRACTICE CONTEXT

McDonnell and Elmore (1987) and McDonnell (1994) indicate five key policy instruments or mechanisms: inducements, capacity-building policy, system change, mandates, and hortatory policy.

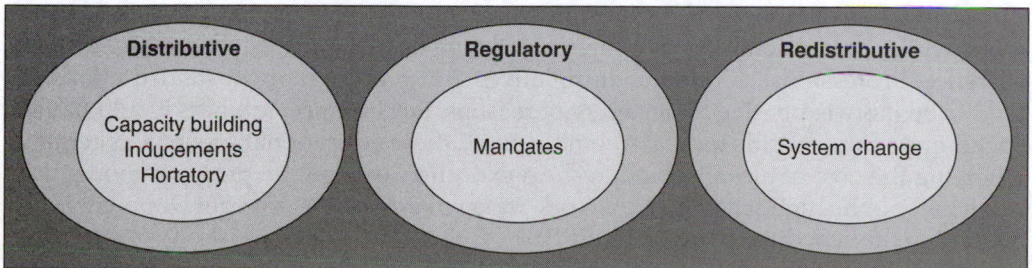

FIGURE 6.4   Relationship Among Policy Types and Instruments

Inducements

Inducements are short-term transfers of resources and are best used when diverse behavior is acceptable. Because these instruments are distributive in nature, they are less likely to meet political resistance, and policymakers may use this approach to introduce new programs. A concern with reliance on inducements stems from the fact that communities that have relatively more resources are often in a better position to respond to the demands of this policy instrument. While inducements are not necessarily competitive, educational units do not automatically receive funding with this mechanism, as they would through traditional school funding formulas. That is, with inducements, dollars follow behavior and output rather than being automatically awarded to all governmental units based on enrollment, poverty levels, and so on. Thus, communities that are already doing well on the measure sought (e.g., higher student achievement) are more likely to be rewarded than those communities that are not doing well. However, many leaders of programs that have low student performance argue that they need more, not less, resources to turn around the poor results in their setting. They assert that giving more resources to education units that are already doing well, and holding back funding from those that are not, serves to accentuate inequities among groups. For example, leaders of rural districts and urban programs with tight budgets and relatively low student performance often express concern that they are disadvantaged by funding programs that distribute dollars through inducements rather than through formulas.

Examples of inducements include the federal Race to the Top grant where financial incentives are provided to states if they pursue particular educational programs and innovative ideas encouraged by the U.S. Department of Education. An example of inducements at the state level is Q-Comp, a teacher-pay incentive program funded by the state of Minnesota. The program rewards school districts that include student achievement in their criteria determining pay for teachers.

Capacity-Building Policies

Capacity-building policies are long-term investments in the material, intellectual, or human resources of an organization. Capacity building is best used when existing institutions are *unable* to produce a desired policy outcome. These policies are distributive in nature and are unlikely to have strong resistance to their implementation. However, they tend to be expensive and the returns on that investment are not evident in the short term. Capacity building may be an especially difficult instrument for policymakers to employ when budgets are tight because more obvious and immediate needs may take precedence. An example of capacity-building policies include investment in the professional development of teachers. Research suggests that, for this investment to be worthwhile, professional development should be ongoing rather than a one-time occurrence. Professional development initiatives that require more sustained effort also tend to be more expensive for a variety of reasons. For instance, teachers would have to spend more time outside the classroom to attend these educational sessions, potentially incurring the cost of hiring substitutes. An exception is a unique program model used in a small public high school in New York State where professional development is embedded in the scheduling (Sawchuk, 2010a).

Many professional development programs are designed as an inducement for individual teachers in the form of continuing education units. It is possible that these programs could be mandated, and thus teachers would be required to attend specific sessions. This type of mandate is similar to the requirement in many states that teachers have a Master's degree in order to be tenured.

System Change Policies

System change policies lead to a transfer of decision-making power and authority to different elements in the system. They are best adopted when existing institutions or other agents are *unwilling* to respond to demands for change. Because these instruments result in redistributing resources (including power), they are often politically difficult to adopt and implement. This approach presumes that, by simply shifting responsibility for carrying out change to someone else, change will occur. Portions of the No Child Left Behind Act of 2001 reflect this strategy, where families are given the option to attend another public school (at the previous school's expense) if the school their child currently attends is consistently deemed a failing school. The underlying notion is that this transfer of authority acts as an incentive to educators to do better if they face the possibility of losing students and the revenue that they bring.

Mandates

Mandates are policies with language requiring compliance and meting out punishment if that compliance is not met. This strategy is best utilized if there is strong societal support for the policy, and its goals and uniform behaviors are desirable to the broader population. Mandates are favored by policymakers because the costs of this strategy fall largely on implementers. In fact, cost may not be fully considered in the creation and adoption of alternatives. A consistent complaint by many educational leaders is that policymakers on higher rungs of the organizational ladder require them to complete tasks but do not provide funding to cover the costs. Providing a free and appropriate public education for students with disabilities, as required by the Individuals with Disabilities Education Act, is often cited as an example of an unfunded mandate. Nonetheless, the United States District Court in *Mills v. Board of Education* has asserted that excluding children with disabilities while providing able-bodied children with public education denies equal protection. The court has long ruled that cost is not a justifiable reason for denying an education to children with disabilities.

Hortatory Policies

Hortatory policies are comprised of information and symbols that appeal to the values of members of the system. These types of policy options are best employed when the populations targeted are most likely to act on the information received. Common examples of hortatory policies at the elementary and secondary school levels are the posters in school hallways extolling the virtue of school pride and detailing the behavior that is expected of students. Another popular hortatory campaign is in response to the rising credit card debt owed by college students. On the University of Minnesota, Twin Cities campus, for example, posters tell students that they should live like students now so that they will not have to do so later.

Ideally, policy packages should contain policy actions that employ diverse mechanisms. Fowler (2009) suggests that an alternative is more likely to be effective if it mixes

1. How do the options identified coexist or conflict with your notions of schooling?
2. How do the options identified address the underlying causes of the policy issue?
3. What are the implications for the options identified on the success of children?
4. Are you considering a policy change simply to keep up with the rest of the educational community?
5. Will the changes have an impact on the production process, governance structure, educational outputs, or individual behaviors?
6. Who will be responsible for overseeing the change in action in your proposed alternative?
7. How does the proposed funding differ from the status quo?
8. Will the options you consider standardize outcomes?
9. Will the options you consider promote flexibility for implementers?

FIGURE 6.5 Questions to Consider As You Develop Policy Alternatives

and matches different policy levers so that there is a diverse portfolio. Diversity helps to balance the strengths and weaknesses of the policy instruments being considered.

As you generate and contemplate various policy options, think about how they coexist or conflict with your notions of schooling and their implications for the success of children. Are you considering change simply to keep up with the rest of the educational community? Will the changes you propose generate reform or policy churn? (Policy churn occurs when there is more symbolic activity than there is substantive change.) Will the changes have an impact on institutions or families, or both? What influence is the policy designed to have on governance, production, outputs, or individuals? Who will be responsible for overseeing this change? Will the options you consider balance the need to have established outcomes with the flexibility of reaching them? These are key questions to consider as you generate various alternatives.

Chapter Summary

This chapter covered the different strategies that you can employ to create change. You can start from scratch or reinvent the old, making it something new. When developing alternatives, you are identifying tasks that you think will change the status quo. Change can be difficult, however, and it will cost you time, money, goodwill, and so on. Change can create a sense of instability, lack of reliability, and vulnerability among stakeholders. As part of that change, you need to consider the merits of doing something different and ensure that it is compatible with the context that you face. From the onset, you should think about the impact on key populations if the policy you propose does not work in the way that you imagine.

Resources are scarce, so you will not be able to do everything that you want. Once you have found a reasonable set of options, you must choose among them so that you can recommend which action or package of actions will allow you to balance the criteria that you care about. Weighing and choosing among the alternatives is the next step in the process and is the focus of Chapter 7.

Review Questions

1. What are some of the difficulties involved in changing the status quo?

2. As you consider the variety of issues faced by policymakers and administrators, you will find that many of the changes discussed are often reworkings of an old solution. Identify key policy alternatives recently proposed by state, district, or local policymakers. Using the discussion in this chapter on refining policy alternatives, identify an older policy option that spawned the more recent proposal. Indicate what modifications were done in the most recent enactment.

3. Create a conceptual graph of a problematic condition. Based on the relationships that you identify, generate a short list of alternatives. Indicate the policy mechanism that you would choose in your policy design. Provide a rationale for your response.

4. Reread the chapter-opening education vignette. Has your response changed after reading this chapter? If yes, how has it changed? If no, how does your initial response reflect the chapter themes?

News Story for Analysis

"How do you put a price on learning? Paying students for performance is a controversial idea." *National Post* (f/k/a *The Financial Post*) (Canada). November 20, 2010 Saturday. Toronto Edition. BYLINE: Kenyon Wallace and Vincent McDermott, *National Post*. SECTION: TORONTO; Pg. A19. LENGTH: 1367 words

As arguments between teenage girls and their fathers go, this one is unusual.

Fifteen-year-old Samantha Ivory, a Grade 10 student at Cass Technical High School in Detroit, Mich., thinks she should be paid to go to school and get good grades.

She already does well but says cash rewards for good attendance and better test scores—currently the subject of a new statewide "pay-for-performance" bill—would improve her motivation and that of her peers to stay in school. Besides, she could use the money for college.

"If students get paid, dropout rates will be lower. It would make others do better in school by giving them a reward," Samantha said from the east-side Detroit home she shares with her parents and four siblings.

But for Samuel Ivory, Samantha's father, the idea of his daughter making money for doing what every North American child should be doing anyway doesn't sit well.

"It's kinda like a Catch-22," he said. "When I went to school, it was something I had a desire to do, school work, and . . . I knew school was going to benefit me later on in life. If the school has the money, they should use it to fix up the schools or get another teacher in there."

Judging from the public outcry, it's a sentiment shared by many north of the border, where this week Toronto District School Board education director Chris Spence suggested via Twitter that the board's new anti-poverty task force consider a similar program.

"Should we pay kids in our more disadvantaged communities to do well in school? Perhaps, as part of a poverty-reduction scheme?" he wrote.

The proposal initiated a flurry of media coverage, lit up talk-radio phone lines, and even rattled the higher echelons of government when Ontario Education Minister Leona Dombrowsky told the legislature her government doesn't support the idea.

"The problem we're trying to solve is we have more of our marginalized students who are not performing well in school," Mr. Spence said in an interview with the *National Post*. "Let's think about this a little differently: What might help these kids ensure that they do their homework, ensure that they come to school and be more engaged in their school? Let's think outside the box for a moment. . . . Maybe some kind of incentive system is going to help them."

While Mr. Spence's idea might have offended some Canadian sensibilities, school boards across the United States have been experimenting with the idea for years, offering students anything from cars, DVD players, iPods and trips to Disneyland for perfect attendance records and improved test scores.

In Chicago, students with perfect attendance are rewarded with trips to the circus. One high school won a concert by Kanye West for showing the greatest attendance improvement.

A few years ago, a student at Oldham County High School in Buckner, Ky., was reportedly given a yellow Ford Mustang for good attendance and behavior.

One school in Washington, D.C., paid a student more than $1,000 for the same thing.

The incentives look good on paper, but they have had varying degrees of success.

In 2004, Chelsea High School in Chelsea, Mass., introduced a cash incentive program to students to combat poor attendance. The school promised to deposit $25 into the bank account of every student who had perfect attendance during each school term. A student would get an extra $25 bonus by achieving perfect attendance for an entire year, meaning one could potentially walk away with $400.

About 80% of students at Chelsea High School live below the poverty line.

"Some students thought it was patronizing. They actually took offence to the money," said superintendent Thomas Kingston. "Those students who were already doing all right anyways, thought, 'Hey! This is OK. I can pick up some change on my way out.'"

After four years, officials saw no improvement and cancelled the program. "We thought that maybe the money might make a difference, but it doesn't."

The experience at Stone Creek Elementary School in Rossville, Ga., however, was markedly different.

Principal Mike Culberson didn't pay students, but offered prizes ranging from ice cream to Xbox video game consoles. It worked.

Between 2003 and 2004 the number of students missing more than 15 days during the year dropped to 4.7%, down from 15%. Mr. Culberson says test scores improved as a result.

"We tell kids, 'We can't force you to come to school, but we can encourage you with these rewards to want to come to school,'" he said. "If we don't show them something they want, they won't work hard to get it."

Researchers at Harvard University recently completed a two-year study in which they paid $6.3 million to 38,000 students in 261 schools across four cities to see if monetary incentives had any impact on performance.

What they found was intriguing. When students were rewarded for better attendance, behavior and for reading more books—elements characterized as educational "inputs" by the researchers—academic performance improved. But when a $50 incentive was offered simply for better exam or test scores—educational "outputs"—students did not perform better.

Researchers suggested this was because students, as much as they wanted to get better grades and therefore more money, didn't know what it would take to improve their performance.

"In order to improve the output, you have to make the assumption that children already know how to learn. They don't," said Thelma Morris-Lindsey, executive director of the Dallas, Tex.-based foundation Earning by Learning, which commissioned the Harvard study.

For the past 15 years, Earning by Learning has been encouraging elementary and high school students to read by paying them between $1 and $2 for every book read, up to a maximum of 20 books in a school year. Using a combination of private and corporate donations, the program has helped more than 75,000 students read nearly 730,000 books. After finishing each book, students take a comprehension test that they must pass with a score of 80% or higher in order to get paid.

Ms. Morris-Lindsey says the findings of the Harvard study show the importance of providing incentives during a student's learning process instead of simply rewarding good test scores.

"You have to provide incentives for the prerequisites," she said. "You cannot alone incent a child for a good grade because children have to learn the process they have to go through to get that good grade. As children read, they comprehend more. As they comprehend more, you get a byproduct of good grades. You get a thinker."

Encouraging students to improve their academic performance is a laudable practice, but many school boards are motivated to do so for slightly less altruistic reasons. Under the No Child

Left Behind Act of 2001, schools are ranked partly for attendance records. And much of how states distribute federal money is determined by average daily attendance. For schools in poor districts, this can mean millions.

But some educators warn students are being sent the wrong message about learning if they are taught to view it as an economic transaction, an outcome one professor characterizes as the "hidden curriculum."

"If students are in a math lesson and they're paid to be there, what's really going on here? Kids are being taught that it's only worth learning something if you're going to receive some sort of monetary compensation," said Trevor Norris, a professor at the University of Toronto's Ontario Institute for Studies in Education. He has studied the growing trend of schools providing students with commercial compensation, such as iPods and free lunches.

"The idea of directly tying learning to monetary compensation seems to run very deeply against the whole idea of learning. If in the end we end up promoting consumer values more than educational values, we should be concerned about that."

The Toronto District School Board's anti-poverty task force has identified 110 schools out of 600 that are negatively affected by poverty, and will hold public hearings early next year before making any decisions on the proposal.

"For some kids, maybe some kind of incentive system is going to help," said Mr. Spence. "But I don't know. I don't know the answer."

Source: Material reprinted with the express permission of: "National Post Inc."

Discussion Questions

1. What are some of the alternatives identified in the article? Which group of stakeholders favors each one? Why?
2. How would you characterize the policy type and mechanisms that dominate the alternatives proposed? How do you know?
3. Which of the alternatives described in the article would you most support? Which ones would you most oppose? Explain your response.
4. How would you choose alternatives that balance the different interests of stakeholders?
5. What are some of the alternatives that you would consider if you were an education policy-maker trying to improve education outcomes? Why?

Selected Websites

American Enterprise Institute for Public Policy Research. Available at

http://www.aei.org/.

The official website of the American Enterprise Institute for Public Policy Research (AEI). AEI is a private, nonpartisan, nonprofit institution dedicated to research and education on issues of government, politics, economics, and social welfare. The institute sponsors research and conferences on a variety of public policy issues. Education leaders may find this site interesting in terms of the education alternatives presented under its research tab. The variants of policy solutions tend to be consistent with a more conservative political orientation. Contrast the solutions offered here with those offered by the Canadian Centre for Policy Alternatives, whose website is also provided in this list.

Canadian Centre for Policy Alternatives. Available at

http://www.policyalternatives.ca/.

The official website of the Canadian Centre for Policy Alternatives (CCPA). The CCPA is an independent, nonpartisan research institute concerned with issues of social, economic, and environmental justice. The website contains information on a variety of research endeavors addressing children and youth. Education leaders can go to the publications tab on this site and select articles dealing with issues affecting children. They can also click on the tab on projects and initiatives and look for the CCPA's education project for more information on the education alternatives that they support. The organization also publishes a quarterly journal on education, *Our Schools / Our Selves*, and a selection of articles is available online. While the material offered is generally geared to a Canadian audience, all education leaders may find this a helpful place to review policy options and their potential impact as viewed from a progressive standpoint.

Center on Educational Governance at the University of Southern California. Available at *http://www.usc.edu/dept/education/cegov/about.html*.

The official website of Center on Educational Governance (CEG) located in the University of Southern California's Rossier School of Education. The center relies on an interdisciplinary approach in its policy solutions to educational problems. Education leaders may find this site helpful because of the research-based alternatives it offers on a variety of educational topics, including assessment, governance, education reform, and leadership.

Council of the Great City Schools. Available at *http://www.cgcs.org/*.

The official website of the Council of the Great City Schools (CGCS). The council is the only national U.S. organization exclusively representing the needs of urban public schools. Education leaders in both urban and nonurban settings may find this site useful because they can see what topics and proposals make it to the organization's legislative agenda. The site also contains useful information on differentiating strategies to ensure the success of special populations based on schooling context. Of particular interest to education leaders are the reports and information accessed under the site's publication, research, and legislative services tabs.

National Rural Education Association. Available at *http://www.nrea.net/*.

The official website of the National Rural Education Association (NREA). The NREA is a national U.S. organization representing the needs of rural schools. Its membership comprises rural school administrators, teachers, board members, and other stakeholders interested in supporting rural schools. Education leaders in both rural and nonrural settings may find this site useful because they can see what topics and proposals make it to the organization's legislative agenda.

United States Equal Employment Opportunity Commission. Available at *http://www.eeoc.gov/*.

The official website of the United States Equal Employment Opportunity Commission. U.S. education leaders may find this site helpful because it outlines legal considerations that they must consider when developing a variety of alternatives. The site also allows leaders to see how the commission develops its own alternatives to perceived policy problems, as seen by the initiatives that they promote.

Selected References

Duke, D. (2004). *The challenges of educational change.* **New York: Pearson Education, Inc.**

This text describes the challenges of changing key aspects of the educational process. Education leaders may find this text helpful for its explanation of education change and the information it provides about how one can develop alternatives to effect change.

Lowi, T. J. (1964, July). American business, public policy, case studies, and political theory. *World Politics, 16*(4), 677–715.

Lowi wrote a seminal article on policy types that is often cited and quoted in the field. Education leaders may find a reading of the original material interesting to see for themselves how it has shaped much of our thinking of the general costs, political ramifications, and likely effectiveness of generic policy groupings.

McDonnell, L. M., & Elmore, R. F. (1987, Summer). Getting the job done: Alternative policy instruments. *Educational Evaluation & Policy Analysis, 9,* 133–152.

This article is a classic by McDonnell and Elmore. It does an excellent job in creating a framework for assessing the fit between policy mechanisms and particular policy contexts. Education leaders may find this piece especially helpful for the insight it provides on the best practice associated with various generic policy instruments.

7

Weigh the Options
Evaluating Alternatives

CHAPTER OBJECTIVES

After reading this chapter, you will be able to:

- Develop analytical strategies to evaluate alternatives
- Describe the potential benefits and costs of alternatives
- Describe key criteria and measures that will help weigh options
- Package alternatives for quick comparisons

EDUCATION VIGNETTE

You are the principal of a small, close-knit public high school in the Midwest of the United States. There has been a rash of school violence nationwide, both at the secondary and higher education levels, but you are not particularly worried about your school. Notwithstanding, the district superintendent has charged all principals to think of policies that balance individual freedoms, academic accountability, and school safety. Thus far, three options are on the table: (1) create a strict zero-tolerance policy, including the monitoring of student Internet activity; (2) implement a peace-maker program where nonviolent strategies are taught to the students; and (3) hire an additional counselor to reduce the number of students in each counselor's current load. As you try to balance the concerns of the community, you wonder what would be the best way to find working definitions of the criteria that are important. As you think about the board of directors, superintendent, parents, teachers, and other stakeholder groups, you realize that they may have different objectives. You are not sure how you will proceed, but you want to make sure that you can weigh the different options.

What do you do?

HOW DO YOU WEIGH YOUR OPTIONS?

In conducting policy analysis, you will have to weigh options even if the political or legal process will be the final arbiter of what is done. Cooksey and Freebody (1986) recognize that if you are deliberating, you need information. This chapter highlights the kind of analytical information that you should seek when weighing alternatives. This is not to say that the policy analytical process is not itself political. However, reflecting on the role of politics and normative considerations in the act of recommending policy action will be covered more fully in Chapter 8.

The explicit evaluation of alternatives is an important policy analytical step because if the decision-making process is covert and intuitive, it is more likely to reduce accountability. For example, Peterson and Rothstein (2010) indicate that there was skepticism on the part of many education leaders regarding the selection of Delaware and Tennessee as winners of the first round of the federal Race to the Top grant. The authors indicate that this skepticism was a result of the perceived arbitrariness of the selection process. Federal policymakers have subsequently revised the program since its first phase to ensure greater transparency on how states rise to the top. Consequently, one of the primary tasks in weighing your options is to be explicit and grounded about the rationale underlying your evaluation.

This chapter offers guidelines on how to consider and articulate the rationale used to weigh policy options. This process is closely tied to that described in Chapter 5, where we discussed driving values, but it has some key differences. The focus of the process used to establish driving values is to examine the cost of various alternatives, the net benefits associated with the outcomes associated with them, the administrative ease associated with implementing that alternative, and so on. Once you have established the broad concerns that you have, it is important to offer a rationale on how you will choose among these broad and sometimes conflicting concerns. This entails a discussion of not only the values of the analysis but also of the values of the system that will define how choices are to be made. That is, establishing your driving values and constructing alternatives will result in a set of alternatives from which you will choose based on the criteria deemed to be important. Weighing your alternatives will outline the process by which alternatives rise to the top. Consequently, this chapter offers guidelines on how to articulate the rationale used to weigh policy options. It is less about what the driving values of the analysis will look like (the subject of Chapter 5) and more about the technical skills and analytical information that will help you choose among them.

This discussion has three major sections. The first section focuses on discussing the future and assessing the potential net benefits of alternatives. This discussion is important because education leaders often have to anticipate what the future holds and act accordingly. Once you have established the parameters that will frame your decision, it is important to forecast what set of activities will likely lead to the desired outcomes on the values being considered. The second part of the discussion on weighing options indicates how you would frame the rationale for including key criteria. This part is important because it addresses explicitly the decision rule that will be used not only to choose among competing alternatives but also to rank the competing values that will drive the decision. The third section discusses how to package the alternatives and the use of quick analysis for systematic comparisons. This discussion is important for education leaders because no clear winner is likely among the alternatives being considered. Being able to provide a systematic comparison to your constituents and readers makes it easier for them to understand why certain packages of options rose to the top. The chapter closes with a summary of its key points.

Anticipating the Future

In weighing your options in ex ante analysis, you need to be able to say something about the future. That is, in evaluating alternatives, you are making an assertion about how well you think a particular option will do in achieving the objectives of the criteria chosen. Because you are projecting, conjecturing, or predicting, your assessment about how well each option will really do is uncertain. You need to state the probable intended consequences of the decision, identify the negative consequences, and explain how you plan to mitigate the negative effects (e.g., Willower & Licata, 1997).

SAFEGUARDS IN FORECASTING. Patton and Sawicki (1993) offer technical and political safeguards that you can use to avoid the inevitable errors in forecasting. They argue that a good rule of thumb entails being accurate but not unreasonable in your expectations of the data. For example, if you have information about school districts, this does not mean that you will be able to speak meaningfully about individual schools. Even when you make forecasts about the appropriate unit of analysis, you should understand the likely costs and benefits of the method chosen. Generally, simple forecast strategies may be less costly, but they may also yield less precise results.

In weighing the relative benefits of the policy options, it is important to check if more complex forecasting methods can yield more useful results than simple methods. For example, maybe the literature does not offer specific information on the net benefits for the alternatives that you are considering. You may be unable to tell the exact cost of implementing a new program without doing additional analysis. However, if greater accuracy will not lead you to rank the alternatives differently, it will not be a good use of resources to get more precise information. Instead, it may be better for you to compare alternatives using ordinal data that ranks alternatives (e.g., this program is more or less expensive than another) rather than spend more resources to generate a precise measure of the criterion.

The purpose of policy analysis is to offer a process where leaders can make the world a better place. To safeguard against making faulty prescriptions, education leaders can create scenarios for each strategy recommended for an uncertain future. **Scenarios** are descriptions you create to describe the future based on different assumptions of contexts and outcomes. In their creation of these descriptions, education leaders should anticipate how well the status quo can respond to the consequences of each alternative not working out as planned.

To clear political hurdles, it is useful to have a transparent process and to err on the side of caution. Describe for readers what the likely impact on outcomes are if your predictions are wrong. If you are unsure of the political and administrative support that particular options will garner, you should indicate how reliable your current political analysis is and what factors would cause your recommendations to change.

Discussing Relevant Criteria

Appropriately anticipating the future is an important aspect of weighing your options. As an education leader, you also need to make clear the basis on which the future is being forecasted. That is, the act of forecasting outcomes needs to be supplemented with the task of selecting criteria and their appropriate measures. You need to explain the importance of each criterion to the analysis. As part of your discussion, indicate which stakeholder group is affected by that criterion and detail the objectives associated with its inclusion. You must be clear regarding the dimensions and measures of each criterion. You will forecast these measures into the future. You should provide enough detail to the readers so that when you assert that one option is likely to be more effective (or fair, or feasible, etc.) than the other, readers will be able to look at the data and come to the same conclusion. Readers should be clear what you mean by *effective*, *fair*, or *feasible*.

MEASURING EFFECTIVENESS. When you are considering effectiveness, the focus is on expected outcomes. You need to look at the evidence to determine how likely a particular approach will attain the outcomes that you seek. The more closely the expected outcomes reflect your goals and objectives in your approach to solving the problem, the more effective you would consider that approach.

Patton and Sawicki (1993) identify four major methods of forecasting the effectiveness of a policy: opinion, sampling, time-series analysis, and associative techniques (e.g., regression). Forecasts generated from **opinions** rely on multiple time horizons and are often the least accurate, but they are also the least costly way to obtain data on the probable effects of an alternative. **Sampling** relies on examining the behavior or outcomes of a portion of the population and generalizing from those results. This method may generate highly accurate estimates, depending on the data available, the stability of trends, and the representativeness of the sample drawn. It also tends to be more costly than opinions but tends to be less expensive than time series or associative techniques. **Time series analysis** requires the collection of opinion or sample data over multiple periods. If the time period from which you are projecting is stable, this technique generally provides accurate projections. Because of the added complexities of this method, it is often more costly than simple opinion or sampling. **Associated techniques** examine systematically the relationships among variables. They tend to be the most costly forecasting methods, and the accuracy of their predictions is closely tied to the specified model on which they are based and the variables therein.

- What are the criteria that will undergird my choice?

- Why is it important to include these criteria?

  - Provide a rationale for each criterion. Which stakeholder group favors inclusion of this criterion? What are the objectives of its inclusion?

- How will I know if I have more or less of a particular criterion?

  - What will more effectiveness look like? What measures allow me to know?

  - What will more equity look like? What measures allow me to know?

  - What will more economical look like? What measures allow me to know?

  - What will more political feasibility look like? What measures allow me to know?

  - What will more of an ability to be implemented look like? What measures allow me to know?

FIGURE 7.1 Overarching Questions for Discussing Criteria in Weighing of Options

Rather than use any of the primary forecasting techniques identified, you may simply choose to go to the literature for guidance. By doing a comprehensive literature review, you may be able to provide sufficient grounding for the expectations that you describe and the policies you prescribe. For example, policy analysts for Growth and Justice, a progressive think tank, weighed a variety of education policy options based on information garnered from extensive reviews of the literature. Relying on extant research is helpful even if you are uncomfortable ranking the alternatives with the quality of information possessed. From previous research, you should be able to address whether the option you are considering is likely to be effective. For example, if the literature consistently indicates that more school time is associated with higher student achievement, then you may rate strategies to increase school time as effective in improving student achievement, citing the literature as evidence (e.g., Gandara & Fish, 1994).

MEASURING EQUITY. Considerations of fairness may lead you to focus on outcomes as well as on the policy mechanisms employed. The guiding questions for providing a working definition of equity focus on whether the outcomes associated with a particular strategy will lead to a distribution of benefits that mirror your notions of fairness. It also involves looking at how the costs (in terms of money, effort, time, etc.) are distributed across those who have to implement the strategy. You need to be clear about what dimensions of equity are important, and you need to detail what characteristics are associated with more equity. For example, is a policy considered more fair if more of its benefits accrue to those who were previously ill served by the system, or is fairness based on equal benefits accruing to all members of society? What measures will you employ to illustrate whether either definition is realized? For example, will you use standard statistical measures of distribution presented in school finance literature, such as coefficient of variation, the McLoone Index, and so on (e.g., Berne & Steifel, 1984; Odden & Picus, 2009)? Is there evidence in practice or in the literature that supports your expectations?

MEASURING COSTS. Economic considerations are often tied to the resources used to implement a particular option. Such considerations may include the affordability of a project or the efficiency of using resources in a particular way. Affordability may be determined by estimating the cost of implementing specified strategies and determining if those costs are within the likely budget of the implementing organization. The greater the portion of the budget that is needed to fulfill the objectives of the strategies outlined, the less affordable is the project, other things being equal. You can also determine

---

- Is a policy considered more fair if more of its benefits accrue to those who were previously ill served by the system, or is fairness based on equal benefits accruing to all members of society?
- Is there evidence in practice or in the literature that supports your expectations?
- What measures will you employ to illustrate your working definition of equity?
- Will you use standard statistical measures of distribution presented in the school finance literature, such as the coefficient of variation, the McLoone Index, and so on?

FIGURE 7.2 Guiding Questions in Measuring Equity

- Does the proposed project fit within current budget constraints?
- Does the proposed project fit within the amounts normally expended on similar programs?
- Is the proposed policy likely to be efficient, using standard economic measures employed in the literature?

FIGURE 7.3 Guiding Questions for Measuring Economic Viability

the relative efficiency of the alternatives by using standard economic measures such as net present value, cost-benefit ratio, or the internal rate of return (e.g., Patton & Sawicki, 1993). A project is economically feasible only if the net present value exceeds 0, the cost-benefit ratio is greater than 1, or the rate of return is more than the interest paid. Other things being equal, a project yields a more efficient use of resources the higher the levels of these ratios.

MEASURING POLITICAL FEASIBILITY. Political considerations are often wedded to stakeholder acceptance of the definition of the problem and buy-in regarding the strategies proposed. The more the political support outweighs its opposition, the more you can consider an option to be politically feasible. You would use the knowledge gleaned from stakeholder analysis (e.g., Coplin & O'Leary,1998) and general guidance provided in the literature to assess the level of political feasibility. For example, you may determine that a higher positive score on the power analysis will be considered more politically feasible. You will need to detail for the reader why an option got a higher score than did other alternatives. Is it because stakeholder groups who supported that option made it a priority? Was opposition to that alternative muted? How so? Being explicit about why you came to the conclusions that you did is important. Note that this is a subjective process, and political analysis is nuanced, but you should still have a clear, grounded rationale for the conclusions that you draw regarding the net political support for a particular alternative.

MEASURING THE ABILITY OF AN ALTERNATIVE TO BE IMPLEMENTED. Administrative operability is associated with the difficulty or ease of implementing a particular policy alternative. Your knowledge of the context in which options will be implemented allows you to asses whether a particular approach is more or less difficult to administer. The literature or professional knowledge will guide you in that assessment. Again, you must be clear about why you came to your conclusion. For example, you may be considering a variety of options to compensate teachers, including using individual teacher

- Does likely overall support of the policy exceed its likely opposition?
- Have stakeholder groups who support or oppose this policy made it a priority?
- How do the stakeholder groups stack up? Do powerful groups tend to support or to oppose the policy?
- Was opposition (support) to that alternative muted? How so?

FIGURE 7.4 Guiding Questions for Measuring Political Feasibility

- Is your plan very different from the status quo?
- Will those who have to implement your plan have less power than before?
- Do the proposed beneficiaries of your plan support it?
- Is the policy mechanism that you chose typically easy to administer?

FIGURE 7.5   Guiding Questions for Measuring the Ability of the Policy to Be Implemented

pay-for-performance programs, implementing schoolwide incentives, or rewarding faculty members based solely on their education and experience. You may decide that individual teacher pay-for-performance programs have the most challenges to implementation. You need to detail the basis for that conclusion and to provide the evidence that supports it. Is it because individual reward plans are the most different from the status quo? Will implementers have less power than before the policy is implemented? Is it because the beneficiaries of the policy do not support it? Are incentives hard to administer in general?

Packaging Your Alternatives

When packaging your alternatives, you may decide to group activities that are (1) geared toward implementers at different levels of the organization or system, (2) targeted at different beneficiaries, (3) focused on different underlying causes, (4) a modification of previous policies, or (5) an amalgamation of a hodgepodge set of activities. You must review each package on the set of criteria chosen for the analysis. Repackaging your strategies creates a different alternative that can affect the likely effectiveness of that proposal *and* its feasibility in terms of costs, political acceptability, and administrative operability. Consequently, in weighing options, you need to subject a repackaged alternative to the same review as its component parts.

Distinguishing Among Alternatives

Policy options are not mutually exclusive, but they must be distinguishable. To compare the alternatives, you need a systematic way of distinguishing among them and weighing their benefits (or limitations) against each criterion. The essence of an alternative is its ability to address the underlying factor resulting in a policy problem; variants include the implementation and financing mechanisms proposed. Whether you use

Alternative policy packages grouped separately based on:

- Implementers at different levels of the organization or system who will be responsible for its implementation
- Beneficiaries at whom the policy is targeted
- Underlying factors that drive policy strategy
- Previous policies
- Hodgepodge set of activities

FIGURE 7.6   Packaging of Alternatives So That They Can Be Evaluated and Weighed

quantitative or qualitative analysis, you need to compare all proposed alternatives on all relevant criteria. By the end of the analysis, readers should be clear about the distinctions among the options and why they rank the way they do on each criterion; that is, readers must be clear why select alternatives rose to the top.

USING QUICK QUANTITAVE ANALYSIS

Patton and Sawicki (1993) provide a good overview of quick methods of comparing alternatives. They include paired comparisons, satisficing, lexicographic ordering, the nondominated alternatives method, the equivalent alternatives method, the standard alternatives method, and the matrix display system (scorecard). These methods vary in their ability to deal clearly with multiple criteria and options in a parsimonious way. **Paired comparisons** are set up like the games in a National Collegiate Athletic Association (NCAA) basketball tournament, where one team (alternative) is pitted against another until the winner is the last team (alternative) standing.

Satisficing is choosing the first acceptable option. **Lexiographic ordering** is a modified version of satisficing, where decision makers do not weigh the criteria equally, and the first alternative that meets the most important criterion is the one that is preferred. The **nondominated alternative, equivalent alternative,** and **standards alternative methods** all try to standardize the different criteria so that the benefits and limitations of each option may be compared more easily. The process can be a bit cumbersome and may presume more agreement among stakeholders regarding the ranking of criteria than actually exists.

Using a **matrix** or a **scorecard** allows a simple illustration of key criteria and how the alternatives fare on each. Because this approach provides a relatively simple way to display multiple criteria and alternatives, it is emphasized in the remainder of this chapter discussion. Note that, regardless of the approach used, you must consider the potential consequences of the alternatives and deal with trade-offs. That is, an option may be technically effective but politically infeasible, politically feasible but too costly, theoretically effective but problematic to administer, and so on.

Creating a Scorecard

A scorecard is an outcomes matrix that has alternatives summarized down the rows and criteria summarized across the columns (Bardach, 2009; Patton & Sawicki, 1993). To compare each package of alternatives, start with a brief description of the key

	Criterion 1 • Needed or preferred? • More (less) is better?	Criterion 2 • Needed or preferred? • More (less) is better?	Criterion 3 • Needed or preferred? • More (less) is better?
Alternative A			
Alternative B			
Alternative C			

FIGURE 7.7 Example of Template for Creating an Outcomes Matrix (Scorecard)

components of each policy option. Identify and describe the policy types and mechanisms contained within the policy package. Those descriptions enable you to highlight how the choice of instrument, as well as its forecasted outcomes, can influence the feasibility of the policy alternative.

Evaluating Alternatives: The Single-Step, Norm-Based Approach

You can compare the alternatives as a group and rank them along each criterion. That is, for each criterion, rank how well an alternative is likely to do on this measure relative to other options considered. This process is analogous to comparisons made in standard normed tests, where students' performance is rated based on whether they outperformed or underperformed their peers on a particular exam. An example of how this evaluative approach works is illustrated by comparing three proposals for increasing the participation of women in college science programs: (1) providing incentives to female faculty members in the sciences, (2) providing incentives to female students entering the sciences, or (3) providing information to change perception of the sciences.

In weighing those alternatives, for each criterion, indicate which option is most likely to fulfill its objectives. The option that is most likely to produce the outcomes sought for a particular criterion is rated most highly on that criterion. The option that is least likely to produce the outcome sought for a specific criterion is rated the lowest on that criterion. Options that produce results in the middle are ranked appropriately. Thus, if providing incentives to female faculty members is considered the most effective of the three options, it would be ranked the highest on the effectiveness measure. However, providing incentives to female faculty members may also be the most costly, thus it is ranked lowest on the cost measure. Continue to compare and rank the alternatives on all the measures until you have considered all the criteria.

Once you have completed those initial rankings, leave the rankings as is and again let the political process determine which option is preferred given the rankings. You could also provide more guidance to policymakers given your knowledge and insight by

Alternatives	Effectiveness (More Leads to Higher Rankings)	Costs (More Leads to Lower Rankings)	Political Feasibility (More Leads to Higher Rankings
Provide incentives to female faculty members in the sciences	Highest	Lowest	Lowest
Provide incentives to female students entering the sciences	Medium	Medium	Medium
Providing information to change perception of the sciences.	Lowest	Highest	Highest

FIGURE 7.8 Example of Evaluative Process Using Single-Step Scorecard Rankings

Note: Information based on literature (e.g., Marschke Laursen, Nielsen, & Rankin, 2007 and modification of student papers.

indicating which option you recommend and why. For example, you may decide that the option that has the most number of top rankings on the criteria considered is the most appropriate choice. You may decide to designate one criterion as primary and then choose the alternative that is ranked most highly on that criterion. The key point is that you have to make it clear to the audience why a particular option rose to the top. The rationale offered should be consistent with the data and explicative narrative that you provide.

Evaluating Alternatives: The Two-Step, Criterion-Based Approach

Rather than conduct the comparison and ranking of alternatives in one step, you can compare and rank them in two. First, take each alternative and individually compare it on each criterion, putting aside its relative standing vis à vis other alternatives. In this way, you review each option and decide if it is likely to be highly, moderately, or not at all effective; very, somewhat, or hardly costly; and so on. Second, based on your assessment of how well each option fulfilled the objectives of each criterion, you can then

Step 1 in two-step comparative process: Individual rating of alternatives			
Alternatives	Effectiveness (More Leads to Higher Rankings)	Costs (More Leads to Lower Rankings)	Political Feasibility (More Leads to Higher Rankings)
Provide incentives to female faculty members in the sciences	Very effective	Very high	Very low
Provide incentives to female students entering the sciences	Effective	Modest	Modest
Providing information to change perception of the sciences	Somewhat effective	Very little	Very high
Step 2 in two-step comparative process: Ranking of alternatives based on individual ratings			
Alternatives	Effectiveness (More Leads to Higher Rankings)	Costs (More Leads to Lower Rankings)	Political Feasibility (More Leads to Higher Rankings)
Provide incentives to female faculty members in the sciences	Highest	Lowest	Lowest
Provide incentives to female students entering the sciences	Medium	Medium	Medium
Providing information to change perception of the sciences	Lowest	Highest	Highest

FIGURE 7.9 Example of Evaluative Process Using Two-Step Scorecard Rankings

rank the alternatives on each criterion in the way described in the previous subsection (refer to Figure 7.9).

Once you have assessed the alternative on each criterion, a useful strategy may be to assign numbers to the rankings or criterion-based assessment that you just completed. You can then simply choose the policy that has the highest score if higher numbers are associated with more favorable assessments. Recommend the option with the lowest score if lower numbers are associated with more favorable assessments. In comparing alternatives, be aware that an option may sometimes dominate the others on one criterion but may remain infeasible when other factors are considered. Thus, in recommending an alternative, you must decide if you will give further consideration only to those options that meet the basic requirements on all criteria.

Chapter Summary

When conducting policy analysis, you must figure out how to evaluate your options. A variety of criteria can guide your evaluation, including effectiveness, equity, costs, political feasibility, and administrative operability (the ability of the option to be implemented). You have to create measures of each criterion so that decision makers and other stakeholders have a clear idea of what "good" or "effective" looks like. You can then use quick analysis to systemize your weighting of the alternatives so that the bases of the evaluation are explicit. Regardless of the evaluative strategy employed, you must justify your decision. Because alternatives do not usually dominate all criteria, you need to address trade-offs, indicating how you came to the conclusions that you did. Once you have weighed the alternatives, you have laid the empirical foundation for recommending a particular course of action. However, who gets to decide which alternative rises to the top is essentially a political decision and requires normative arguments. The normative aspects of making a recommendation are the focus of the next chapter.

Review Questions

1. How would the evaluation process described in this chapter help you to weigh the different proposals described in the chapter-opening education vignette?
2. How is the evaluative process described here the same or different from processes you have used in the past?
3. The scorecard approach may also be used to evaluate candidates for particular positions. Suppose you are a member of the board for a large urban school district and you are conducting a search for a new superintendent.

As a group, you have decided that the salary requirements, urban savvy, education, and experience are the four main factors that will influence your choice of candidate. Create a scorecard that illustrates that process.
4. Review the chapter-opening education vignette. Create a scorecard to weigh each option on the appropriate criteria. Create a scenario that illustrates the same. Do you think that your decision is likely to differ depending on the evaluative approach used? Explain your response.

News Story for Analysis

"Teachers to tote guns in Texas; 'Embarrassing'."
National Post (f/k/a *The Financial Post*) (Canada).
August 19, 2008 Tuesday. National Edition.
BYLINE: Mary Vallis, *National Post*. SECTION:
NEWS; Pg. A3. LENGTH: 472 words

Teachers in Harrold, Tex., are bringing concealed handguns to class in an extreme attempt to keep the district's only school safe.

Harrold Independent School District is believed to be the first in the United States to allow teachers to carry arms. The policy was introduced in October, 2007, but is only coming to public attention now, re-igniting a debate over whether guns have a place in schools.

"I can lead my children from a tornado. I can lead my children from a fire. I can lead them from the railroad tracks that run about 400 feet from us. I can lead them from a toxic spill quickly. I cannot lead them from an active shooter," David Thweatt, the district's superintendent, said in a telephone interview. "We had to come up with a solution."

A Nevada-based firearms training center has offered every teacher in Harrold a free, four-day handgun course.

"Finally, a public school gets it right," said Ignatius Piazza, founder of the Front Sight Firearms Training Institute. "To prevent a school shooting massacre you must be prepared to stop the attack immediately. Placing a gun in the hand of a trained teacher is the answer."

The school, which has 110 students ranging from kindergarten to Grade 12, already has state-of-the-art camera and alarm systems, in addition to card-swipe entries and a button that locks all doors.

Mr. Thweatt insisted the gun policy is necessary because the school is about 30 minutes from the nearest sheriff's office in Vernon, Tex., 240 kilometers northwest of Dallas.

He believes declaring schools gun-free zones only makes them more attractive to potential shooters, who know they will not be challenged. The Amish school shooting in Pennsylvania convinced him all schools are vulnerable, not just urban ones.

The district's policy, which passed unanimously, allows school employees with proper licenses to carry concealed weapons while performing their normal duties. Mr. Thweatt would not comment on how many teachers carry guns.

Experts argue it would make more sense to hire private security or allow police officers into the school, but the superintendent believes his district's solution is better because it keeps guns out of sight, leaving students to remain focused on their studies.

Educators in Houston, where armed police regularly patrol schools, disagree.

Gayle Fallon, president of the Houston Federation of Teachers, called the policy "embarrassing" and "the stupidest move that I have seen done in public education.

"This is the sort of thing that puts us on late-night TV in Texas," added Ms. Fallon, who owns a .357 handgun.

She characterized the situation in Harrold as a tragedy waiting to happen.

"Whether they're rural or urban children, they have one thing in common: They are all fascinated by guns, and they will play with them if they find them," she said.

Source: Material reprinted with the express permission of: "National Post Inc."

Discussion Questions

1. What is the policy issue facing the education community described in the article? Who are the stakeholders?
2. Identify the different policy options that could have been chosen to address the problem identified.
3. What are the criteria implied for choosing among these options? Given the policy chosen, which criterion seems to be the most important?
4. Create scenarios for each option.
5. Create a scorecard to weigh the options. Provide a rationale for your response.

Selected Websites

U.S. Department of Education. Race to the Top Fund. Available at

http://www2.ed.gov/programs/racetothetop/index.html.

The official website of the Race to the Top initiative sponsored by the U.S. Department of Education. The website includes a description of the purpose of the program, applicants, scores, and reviewers' comments. It also provides details on how alternatives (states) were weighed and the criteria that underlay the decision. Education leaders may find this site helpful, not only because of the detail it provides on the process of this multi-billion-dollar program, but also because of the insight it offers on how criteria are used in weighing multiple options.

Growth and Justice. *Smart Investments in Minnesota's Students.* Available at

http://www.growthandjustice.org/education_report.html.

Part of the official website of Growth and Justice. The site provides a report, policy briefs, and research papers on what the literature indicates are cost-effective strategies for improving education outcomes. Education leaders may find this site helpful because it offers measures of cost for a variety of education strategies, including investment in early childhood education, class size reduction, and youth programs.

Selected References

Gandara, P., & Fish, J. (1994, Spring). **Year-round schooling as an avenue to major structural reform.** *Educational Evaluation and Policy Analysis, 16(1),* 67–85.

This article examines three policy options that school leaders pursued in their effort to extend the school year for their building. Education leaders may find this article interesting because of the information it provides on key education reform strategies, including the impact of these efforts on multiple criteria, including effectiveness (as measured by student achievement) and economic possibility (as measured by the cost effectiveness of the use of school facilities).

Peterson, W., & Rothstein, R. (2010, April 20). **Let's do the numbers: Department of Education's "Race to the Top" Program offers only a muddled path to the finish line (Economic Policy Institute Briefing Paper, #263). Retrieved from Education Policy Institute website: http://www.epi.org/publications/entry/BP263/.**

This policy brief published by the Economic Policy Institute reviews the decision process used to select states for the federal Race to the Top grant. Education leaders may find this article helpful because it highlights the importance of how the nature of the decision process has an impact on the credibility of the decisions that the process yields.

Simon, H. (1997). *Models of bounded rationality.* Cambridge, MA: MIT Press.

In this seminal text, Simon expounds on his discussion of satisficing as a means of choosing among alternatives. He argues that, given the constraints of individuals and institutions, the theoretical ideal of looking at all possible alternatives and choosing the best option (optimizing) is unlikely in reality. Education leaders may find this classic text valuable for its discussion on organizational decision making in a way that explicitly considers the limits of making optimal choices.

Make Recommendations

CHAPTER OBJECTIVES

After reading this chapter, you will be able to:

- Describe underlying normative issues when justifying recommendations
- Identify the varying roles of the analyst
- Identify the need for advocacy
- Describe approaches to making recommendations

EDUCATION VIGNETTE

You are a member of a school board. You have been asked to review several policies regarding the appropriate curriculum and adoption of textbooks in science, and you must decide from among three major proposals. One proposal updates the high school science curriculum previously taught in the district. It relies on a standard science text that incorporates the teaching of evolution. Another proposal requires the teaching of intelligent design along with evolution. It mandates the adoption of a text that supplements the traditional science curriculum and the reading of a statement emphasizing that evolution is just one of several theories. The third option requires that evolution not be taught at all. It requires the adoption of a new science text and curriculum.

How do you know which proposal is best? Should you be the one to decide?

TRANSFORMING TRADE-OFFS INTO PREFERRED RESULTS

You may wonder why this text distinguishes between weighing your options and ultimately making a recommendation. It may seem obvious that once comparison of the alternatives has been done, the preferred alternative would be the one to recommend.

Sometimes the recommendation step is overlooked, however, because the preferred option seems obvious or because some policy analysts consider the actual recommendation of policy outside their purview.

Chapter 7 focused on how you would *weigh* policy alternatives. This chapter focuses on how you *decide* on the appropriate policy. In essence, this chapter stands as a means of testing your work and ensuring the coherence of your evaluative argument. It also delves more deeply into the appropriate role of policy analysts in making recommendations.

This discussion is meant to emphasize the normative, multifaceted, and iterative nature of the policy analytical process. As noted by Dunn (2004, p. 216), when recommending policy action, you are essentially addressing the question of "What *should* be done?" [italics added]. In the public policy arena, the answer to this question often requires a complex model of choice in the presence of numerous stakeholders, uncertainty about outcomes, and the dynamic effect of time. It also requires a decision even when it is not always clear who should decide.

Beyond Eeny, Meeny, Miny, Moe

The rationale underlying policy analysis is choosing a strategy that will alleviate a negative social condition. Education leaders may decide that the choice is a political one best left to policymakers and the political process. Kingdon (1995) has written extensively on the political process, including agenda setting, policy formulation, and policy adoption. He notes that policymakers often determine the policy issues that make it to the formal agenda, but that it is policy analysts who often decide the components of the recommended alternatives. For example, state educational administrators create the specific rules for putting into practice the No Child Left Behind Act passed by federal policymakers.

Education leaders may decide that some major decisions are legal ones that are best left to the courts. For example, Superfine (2009) highlights the tensions among judicial, scientific, and democratic (i.e., political) decision making. Analyzing *Kitzmiller v. Dover*, Superfine explores the role of courts in education decisions. He notes that a plethora of factors influence whether an education decision should be a scientific, democratic, or judicial one. These factors include the wishes of the community, the public dimensions of the issue at hand, existing law, and so on. A comprehensive legal analysis is beyond the scope of this discussion; rather, this text looks at legal considerations as just one of several cues used by policy analysts to weigh a variety of options.

- Use the political (democratic) process.
- Let the courts decide.
- Let the analyst decide:
  - Choose randomly among a list of alternatives.
  - Optimize—consider all alternatives along all criteria and choose the best one.
  - Satisfice—choose the first alternative that meets your basic requirements.
  - Use a scorecard—weigh options based on overall assessment on key criteria.

FIGURE 8.1 Examples of Key Methods of Choosing Among Policy Options

ROLE OF THE ANALYST

Transform Values into Results

Policy scholars note that the role of the policy analyst is to work on solutions to specific policy problems. Formal policy analysis allows you to go beyond eeny, meeny, miny, moe. This discussion focuses on how education leaders and analysts choose the alternatives that they do and highlights the kind of information that you should seek when recommending alternatives. In proposing a policy, you explicitly transform trade-offs into preferred results. In doing so, you indicate that some outcomes are more valued than others. For instance, policymakers who favor liberty and individualism over equity may support school voucher programs for all students. An example of this is the proposal offered by governor-elect Rick Scott of Florida in 2010. He proposed that state education dollars follow all students to the schools of their parents' choosing, regardless of family wealth or school type (Matus, 2010). Education leaders who value equity over liberty tend to be troubled by untargeted voucher plans, fearing that this strategy will shift attention away from students in need and siphon resources from public schools. With contrasting objectives, education leaders may recommend those policies that most appropriately balance the values of key stakeholders. In some instances, leaders may decide simply to dictate those policies that reflect only their values. The recommendation strategy adopted depends on the political culture and structure of the community in which the leader operates.

Even if education leaders focus on the technical aspects of the problem, they already indicate their preferences by the objectives they choose to pursue. As noted in previous chapters, your choices are grounded in your value system, and how you prioritize your objectives has important normative elements. Dunn (2004), Patton and Sawicki (1993), and Heck (2004) all speak to the importance of values in the policy process. As an education leader, when you analyze the social problems that you face, your values may also influence the different conclusions you come to regarding your role.

Education Leader as Researcher, Bureaucrat, or Entrepreneur?

Citing Meltsner (1976), Patton and Sawicki (1993) indicate three types of analysts: technician (researcher), politician (bureaucrat), and entrepreneur. The **technician** focuses more on the analytical aspects of the policy process and pays little attention to its political constraints. By contrast, the **politician** focuses more on personal advancement and is overly concerned with the political ramifications of policy decisions. The **entrepreneur** balances both the analytical and political dimensions of the policy decision being made.

Nonetheless, given the complex nature of the policy analytical process, it would be incorrect to frame policy decisions as being either rational or political (e.g., Patton & Sawicki, 1993). This creates a false dichotomy suggesting that political decisions are never rational or that technical decisions are always apolitical. Dunn (2004) notes, for example, that rationality may be grounded in different values and is reflected in the diverse criteria that frame the analysis. Because analysts are not themselves free from politics, it is essential for them to identify their assumptions, keep accurate records, use multiple sources of information, and employ replicable methods and models (Patton & Sawicki, 1993). As noted previously in this chapter, whether analysts should merely present options to elected leaders, provide them with advice, or make recommendations depends on the political structure that is in place. As an education leader, your responsibility is to examine the facts surrounding the problem and inform the recommendation process by noting how well or how badly potential strategies advance your ideals.

Policy Analyst as Adviser and Decision Maker

Those analyzing policy problems at all stages of the analytical process will face moral pressure. This pressure is increased if your role is not simply to provide a description of available alternatives, but also to make recommendations on the most appropriate course of action. You should always keep in mind that policy decisions affect lives and the allocation of limited resources. You bear the responsibility for the consequence of your recommendation. Thus, when conducting policy analysis, you need to know yourself and to determine the ethical foundations on which you base your policy recommendations. As you reflect on the values presented in Chapter 1, consider again which values you identify with most closely. Ask yourself what "good" or "effective" looks like (outcomes), but also ponder what you think is the right thing to do (process). Education leaders must make choices that are not always popular, either because of the strategy recommended or the outcomes they yield. You should feel comfortable in the ethical grounding of the process that led to your decision. You should be clear about what you envision as ideal, and be able to justify your recommendations and persuade others that your recommendations are appropriate.

NEED FOR ADVOCACY

The arguments grounding the decision to pursue one set of policy actions versus another require making advocative claims. Dunn (2004) notes that advocative claims have four distinct attributes: They are actionable, prospective, value laden, and ethically complex. **Actionable** means that the assertions you make are not only calls for action; they can also be acted upon. Actionable recommendations are not meant to be "thought pieces." **Prospective** means that the claims you make in your recommendations are future-oriented; they are focused on what lies ahead. **Value laden** indicates that your claims reflect your values and philosophical orientations, either implicitly or explicitly. **Ethically complex** refers to the fact that the pursuit of one value is not always in tandem with the other values that you hold. Consequently, the standards that you use to make a policy decision on what is good and appropriate action are not always obvious or even straightforward.

The discussion in Chapter 7 focused largely on the actionable and prospective characteristics of advocative claims. It also focused on the analytical aspects involved in weighing options. I would like to focus the discussion in Chapter 8 on the value-laden and ethically complex nature of recommendations. This approach is tied closely to the opening discussion on values in Chapter 1.

Value-Laden Arguments

The crux of a logical argument is its claim and underlying warrants. **Warrants** are the pieces of evidence that support the assumptions held or assertions made. As an education leader making a recommendation, your task is twofold. You must provide substantial empirical support that the strategy you recommend will actually generate the forecasted results, *and* you must persuade the appropriate stakeholders that they want those results. To make your recommendation viable, you need to know what outcomes are valued by key stakeholders and to structure your arguments in a way that they find meaningful.

Fowler (2009) offers strategies that will allow you to frame your arguments in a way that fits the political context of your community. For example, if you are an education leader in a traditionalistic setting, you must identify and gain the support of the elite for any policy action that you prescribe. Settings are described as **traditionalistic** if key decision makers tend to be elite members of the community, and the community is generally supportive of the "old" ways of doing things (Elazar, 1984). Consequently, your recommendation will fare better if you draw on the traditions of the community.

If you are a leader in a moralistic setting, you must emphasize the transparency of the decision-making process. Communities or organizations that are considered **moralistic** tend to value government action as well as collective and open decision making (Elazar, 1984). Consequently, you should also allow multiple opportunities for stakeholder input and emphasize how the change proposed serves the common good.

If you are a leader in an individualistic setting, you should emphasize the efficiency implications of your proposed policy and the impact of the proposal on the local economy. Communities that are considered **individualistic** typically have a strong belief in the power of markets and the process of bargaining (Elazar, 1984).

It is unlikely that any community contains only one political culture. However, it is useful if you are aware of these general strategies and can modify your arguments to highlight the values that prevail. It is not surprising that, in 2009, policymakers in Texas, a state known for its traditionalistic culture, adopted accreditation rules that led to little obvious change in the status quo. These rules were targeted at degree-granting colleges and universities other than Texas public institutions. They were meant to provide greater transparency regarding the oversight of these institutions without changing the manner in which these institutions were overseen (Education Commission of the States, 2010). In Colorado, which scholars often characterize as moralistic, policymakers adopted a bill in May 2009 that also addressed accreditation concerns. Colorado bill SB-163 increased the transparency of the accreditation process by strengthening the alignment between accountability and accreditation procedures in that state. It also specified the role of the state board of education in that process (Education Commission of the States, 2010). In Missouri, which scholars often label as individualistic, the accreditation portion of Missouri bill SB 894, adopted in May 2006, seemed aimed at increasing efficiency. School districts that were unaccredited within the last 5 years and presently had only provisional accreditation would be allowed to "lapse" (Education Commission of the States, 2010). This is equivalent to the market allowing businesses to fail if they are not sufficiently efficient or profitable. (Note that the bill also contained provisions that allowed high schools to certify students as ready to work.)

Ethically Complex Arguments

As noted by Dunn (2004), certain stakeholders may consider a particular value a means to an end (extrinsic), but others may value that same attribute for its own sake (intrinsic). For example, many mission statements produced by educators include the value of diversity as a means of improving student performance, while others cite diversity as a valued outcome in and of itself. The difference between considering values as essential or simply as a means to an end influences whether certain choices are negotiable or not. Values considered to be intrinsic are non-negotiable, but this does not mean there is only one way of achieving these principles.

The decision about what values are essential and what values are strategic is an ethical one. Patton and Sawicki (1993) provide an excellent summary of ethical analysis, and their summary undergirds much of this discussion. While a thorough treatise of ethical theory is beyond the scope of this text, it would be useful for you to reflect deeply on the ethical beliefs underlying your decisions. Think about the kinds of principles you employ in justifying the choices that you make and the attention you pay to certain priorities. Are you more concerned with the *outcomes* of decisions than you are with the *process* used to reach those decisions? If you worry more about consequences than you worry about process, whose consequences do you consider most important? Are you more worried about the impact of policy on your personal situation, on others, or on society as a whole? Some of you may conclude that the consequences of the decision are not as important as making sure that you have followed a morally just process. In other words, you are more concerned about right and wrong than you are about benefit and harm. Others may reflect that both process and consequence are important to the decision, and the emphasis on either is context driven.

Is There One Best Way?

You may decide on a rule-based approach to decision making. This approach avoids the problem of having too many exceptions to the decisions that you support. If a rule-base approach is your choice, you will rely on your ethical principles to develop universal rules that guide your decisions in *all* situations. However, you may decide that this sort of approach is too rigid and inappropriate for the complexities of the public policy arena. You may opt instead to rely on specific ethical principles to guide your decision in *particular* situations. This decision may lead you to a more flexible approach to decision making, but one where it may become more difficult to justify your choices because of the number of exceptions that may result. The complexity of policy analysis often forces analysts to strike a balance between supporting policies where the "end justifies the means" and policies where "rules rule."

- Are you more concerned with the outcomes of decisions than you are with the process used to reach that decision? Does the end justify the means?

- If you worry more about consequences than you worry about process, whose consequences do you consider important?

  - Are you more worried about the impact of the policy on your personal situation?

  - Are you more worried about the impact of the policy on others? Who?

  - Are you more worried about the impact of the policy on society as a whole?

- Is your main concern that you have followed a morally just process? In other words, are you more concerned about right and wrong than you are about benefit and harm?

FIGURE 8.2   Reflective Questions to Ground Your Ethical Compass

Public policy has no hard and fast rule regarding the appropriate code of ethics that analysts should follow. Patton and Sawicki (1993) offer three guiding principles: (1) recognize an obligation to protect the basic rights of others, (2) acknowledge responsibility to support democratic processes, and (3) uphold academic and personal integrity. Patton and Sawicki (1993) argue for "thoughtful partisanship," where analysts make explicit their assumptions and biases (p. 41). However, Patton and Sawicki also recognize that in many instances, policy analysts are in an expert–client relationship, in which they may have the knowledge, but they do not have the final decision-making authority. Even when education leaders get to decide, they may still consult with other decision makers to ensure that their decisions balance key perspectives.

REFINE APPROACHES TO RECOMMENDATION

When conducting policy analysis, you must weigh options even if the political or legal process will be the final arbiter. To address a policy issue, you can elicit a list of alternatives and simply choose a policy option at random, but that approach is unlikely to be persuasive to a broader audience. You can also satisfice, choosing the first alternative that meets the basic requirements of solving the problem. After all, the constraints of time and other resources may make it difficult for you to optimize in the way called for by many economic models (March & Simon, 1958; Simon 1997). By satisficing, you explicitly recognize the limits to collective decision making and that investing further resources in finding the one best solution may be unproductive. That is, if you reject options in your quest to optimize, you may be constantly searching for perfection but not offering any policy action that is different from what was done before (e.g., Colander, 1991). By taking the first option that works, however, you may still find yourself wondering if a better choice could have worked within existing constraints.

Many students are uncomfortable with formally covering the steps of the policy analytical process because they think it is a strategy to mask the subjective nature of decision making. Much of the recent discourse on policy analytical studies rejects that concern. Public policy scholars, by and large, do not claim that the process is objective but argue instead for its transparency. Researchers generally agree that, despite the normative nature of the policy process, it can be improved by transparent and systematic analysis. Many policy researchers rightly note that ethical analysis is important because it forces us to acknowledge where we and others stand regarding a policy issue. This reckoning allows us to see what are disputes about facts and what are arguments about values (e.g., Denning, 2007; Patton & Sawicki, 1993). Education leaders need to be able to distinguish between the two types of conflict to know the proper persuasive tools. If the argument is about the appropriateness of specific values, it is unlikely that garnering the facts *sine qua non* will lead to substantive changes in behavior.

Testing the Credibility of Your Recommendation

To alleviate a negative condition, change often must take place. Making a recommendation regarding the fitting avenue for change requires decision makers (and analysts who advise them) to be persuasive that the change they prescribe will lead to a better world. A good step in that process is to test your recommendation against rival claims. You must be clear about the validity of your assumptions. Does the literature and professional experience support a rival claim regarding the causal relationship between

- Does the literature and professional experience support a rival claim regarding the causal relationship between the outcomes desired and the actions prescribed?

- How many informed researchers and stakeholders would agree with your assessment regarding the likely costs and effectiveness of the proposed policy? Is there general agreement in the field?

- Did you exclude any legitimate costs and benefits?

- Have you considered stakeholder needs?

- Are other actions more responsive and appropriate to the policy issue identified?

- Are you clear about the ethical considerations that drive your decision?

- Is the recommendation consistent with your stated ethical principles?

FIGURE 8.3 Questions to Test the Robustness of Your Recommendation

the outcomes desired and the actions prescribed? You also need to justify the costs and effectiveness you assume are associated with the recommended action. How many informed researchers and stakeholders would agree with your assessment? Did you exclude any legitimate costs and benefits? Have you considered stakeholder needs? Were any other actions more responsive and appropriate? Are you clear about the ethical considerations that drive your decision? Is the recommended action consistent with your stated ethical principles?

The case for going through this testing process is clear because policy analysis rarely comes with undisputed alternatives (e.g., Dunn, 2004). Indeed, the existence of multiple alternatives is the essence of defining a problematic condition as a policy issue. The multiple ways to address policy problems makes it is essential to follow the policy analytical process. In making recommendations, education leaders should be able to test the robustness of their decisions in a variety of policy settings. One way to do this is to consider, rather than ignore, conflicting claims and worldviews that may have generated different recommendations than the present recommendation process yielded.

Chapter Summary

The crux of policy analysis is to mitigate a negative social condition. You must figure out how to choose among several options. You can let the policymakers decide or let a court hand down a legally binding decision, or you can formulate your own recommendation. If you are responsible for making a recommendation, you can decide on the alternatives by choosing blindly, optimizing, satisficing, using a scorecard, or creating scenarios. Regardless of the strategy employed, you must justify your decision. Your justification must be based on both empirical and normative arguments. Because alternatives do not usually dominate all criteria, you must address trade-offs. Once you consider moral evaluations, you will not find an objectively right answer but you will still face coherent and incoherent arguments. You must be consistent within the ethical framework that you establish. When you have identified the alternative that has risen to the top, you may recommend it for implementation. How you choose to communicate that recommendation and persuade key stakeholders is the next step in the policy analytical process, and it is the subject of Chapter 9.

Review Questions

1. What do you think is the appropriate role of policy analysts in recommending policy action? Why?

2. What are the ethical concerns that would influence your policy recommendations?

3. What factors will help you choose among the alternatives described in the chapter-opening education vignette? Why?

4. Has your initial response to the chapter-opening education vignette changed after reading this chapter? If so, in what way? If your response has not changed, how does it parallel the discussion on decision making explored in this chapter?

News Story for Analysis

National Post (f/k/a *The Financial Post*) (Canada) April 21, 2007 Saturday National Edition Where there's smoke: A U.S. professor has brought a storm of controversy over tobacco funding to Alberta BYLINE: Kevin Libin, *National Post* SECTION: CANADA; in Calgary; Pg. A12 LENGTH: 1016 words

When Professor Carl Phillips relocated from the University of Texas to the University of Alberta [U of A], he brought with him two things: a $1.5-million U.S. research grant and a storm of controversy.

The grant came courtesy of an American tobacco company. The controversy [comes] from anti-tobacco groups that claim the funds sully the school's reputation and want U of A to refuse research funding from the corporations they oppose. Defenders of academic freedom argue that such pressure groups are the real threat, undermining the university tradition of academic freedom.

Corporate funding is standard business at universities. Oil companies, consumer-goods marketers, weapons manufacturers, all pay professors to research everything from climate change to the effects of fluoride on rat testicles. The U of A grant from U.S. Smokeless Tobacco Co., is the best kind—"completely unrestricted,"—says Mr. Phillips. "It's for anything I want it to be. They have no control over what I do, let alone what methods I use or results that I get. In theory, I could use it to do research on archaeology."

Actually, the Harvard-trained epidemiologist researches how to get smokers off cigarettes, a popular area of inquiry among his colleagues. But while others mostly focus on the effectiveness of cessation products (think Nicorette gum and Zyban pills) Mr. Phillips studies "harm reduction"—getting nicotine addicts unable to quit to at least switch to something less lethal than cigarettes: smokeless products, such as chewing tobacco or snuff.

Since arriving in Edmonton in 2005, the scientist has been a walking bull's eye for anti-tobacco groups crusading to push universities to ban tobacco money. "We do not want to be a part of anything that increases the social legitimacy and normalization of a product that technically should not be on the market because it's killing people," says Dr. Charl Els, a U of A psychiatrist and the Alberta director of Physicians for a Smoke Free Canada.

Dr. Els forced the issue into the spotlight when he applied for research funds from a federally funded organization last year (one administered by a former colleague and fellow anti-tobacco activist). It required applicants to submit an oath, signed by their department's chair, promising not to accept funds from tobacco firms. Though Mr. Phillips and his million tobacco dollars reside in the school of public health, not medicine, where Dr. Els works, his department chair nevertheless refused the pledge, disqualifying the doctor from the grant. When a local alternative newspaper caught wind of the school's refusal to swear off tobacco money, it suggested in a March 15 article, the school risked becoming known as "Tobacco University."

Days later, red-faced med school faculty hastily passed a policy outlawing tobacco funds. Now Dr. Els wants the university to follow suit, and go further, prohibiting faculty members from consulting to the industry. At the next board of governors meeting in May, he says he hopes the board will enact "a universitywide policy, sweeping in nature, to capture all research and any other funding."

But letting activists dictate research policies threatens the independence of universities, "whose primary function is the search for truth through the conflict of ideas," warns John Furedy, a University of Toronto professor emeritus and past president of the Society for Academic Freedom and Scholarship. "It destroys academic freedom and, of course, when an entire department at a leading university gives way to these activists, their power to harm both epistemology and practice only increases."

Attempts by anti-smoking groups to convince University of California administrators to block tobacco funds earlier this year were stymied when professors there stood fast for unfettered independence. "This cuts to the heart of what our job is all about," says Mr. Phillips. "It has to do with freedom of inquiry, and having an opportunity to say things, even though they may not be the most politically popular at the moment. All the things that make the university, as a thousand-year-old institution in the West, so critical."

Mr. Phillips acknowledges the industry has a dodgy scientific history, suppressing evidence of smoking risks. Still, U of A guidelines are clear: regardless of funding sources, researchers must "apply stringent standards of honesty and of scholarly and scientific practice in the collection, recording and analysis of data." The school's ethics committee reviewed and signed off on the smokeless grant.

Still, Mr. Phillips' critics insist tobacco money puts researchers in a "conflict of interest." Les Hagen, executive director of Action on Smoking and Health (where Dr. Els is also a director) compares it to accepting "money from the Hell's Angels to research organized crime."

But Mr. Phillips wonders why it's any different for scientists (such as Dr. Els) accepting money from drug firms, which have a vested interest in the quitting industry and their own checkered history of paying off scientists and suppressing evidence of drug risks. If anti-tobacco groups succeed today, Mr. Furedy worries which unpopular industries will be targeted tomorrow.

Mr. Phillips insists he is only trying to find ways of getting smokers off cigarettes. It just so happens that dozens of peer-reviewed studies demonstrate that smokeless tobacco is significantly safer than cigarettes for addicts who can't quit the nicotine habit. (In Sweden in recent decades, millions of smokers switched to a pouch-style smokeless tobacco called "snus," and rates of lung cancer, oral cancer and cardiovascular disease have plummeted to the lowest in Europe.)

Given the politically incorrect nature of his work, the industry is the only place Mr. Phillips says he has found funding. But unpopular or not, his research, he insists, must be allowed to proceed. "I fully accept the stipulation that these companies have done bad things. But we have to keep our eye on the prize. The goal here isn't to put Philip Morris out of business. The goal is to save people's lives."

Source: Material reprinted with the express permission of: "National Post Inc."

Discussion Questions

1. Identify the different alternatives facing the board of governors of the University of Alberta.
2. What are the ethical concerns highlighted in the newspaper article?
3. How do you think that Professor Phillips would respond to the questions in Figure 8.2? Would his response differ from that given by Dr. Els in the news story? Explain your response.
4. Who should decide what institutional policies are in place regarding the acceptance of grants? Why?
5. If you were advising the board of governors on a policy for accepting grants, what would you recommend? Justify your response.

Selected Websites

Education Commission of the States. (2010). Recent state policies/activities. Retrieved on March 8, 2011, from

http://www.ecs.org/ecs/ecscat.nsf/WebStateView? OpenView&Start=1&Count=30&Collapse=1#1.

This part of the Education Commission of the States website lists recent state policy activities in the United States. Education leaders may find this site helpful because it reflects the education policy recommendations of key policymakers across the country. In some cases, the description of the proposal can provide insight on the process used to find the recommendation or inform what outcomes are likely to emerge.

National Association of Educational Procurement. Code of Ethics. Available at

http://www.naepnet.org.

The official website of the National Association of Educational Procurement. Its members are primarily higher education purchasing officers in the United States and Canada. On the homepage, you can click on the tab that describes the organization. From that point, you can access a description of its governance and policy. Under that tab is a link to the code of ethics for the organization. Education leaders may find this site helpful because the code can provide guidance on the procurement strategies that would be recommended by the group. While many education leaders may not be involved directly in purchasing, reviewing the site can help them reflect on the development of rules that undergird official recommendations.

The American Society for Public Administration. Available at

http://www.aspanet.org/scriptcontent/index.cfm.

The official website of the American Society for Public Administration. Members include individuals working in or studying public service in the United States. Under the tab providing general information about the organization is another tab that gives you access to its code of ethics. Education leaders may find this site helpful because it provides another example of the code of ethics for a national organization. The code of ethics may be helpful to education leaders reflecting on the support that their recommendations might get from the broader public administration profession.

Selected References

Colander, D. (1991). The best as the enemy of the good. In David Colander (Ed.), *Why aren't economists as important as garbagemen? Essays on the state of economics* (pp. 31–37). Armonk, NY: Sharpe.

Colander has compiled essays that address the importance of nonoptimal solutions in public policy. Education leaders may find this chapter especially helpful as they think about recommending policy because they will realize that perfection is not expected from their decisions.

Kingdon, J. W. (1995). *Agendas, alternatives, and public policies.* (2nd ed.). New York: Addison Wesley Longman.

Kingdon provides a classic examination of how multiple streams influence how decisions are made in various policy arenas. Education leaders may find this book helpful because of the insight it provides on policy and decision making. It also offers persuasive explanations on the impact of the decision-making process on the policies that are recommended.

March, J. G., & Simon, H. A. (1958). *Organizations.* New York: John Wiley.

This text is a classic in the field of organizational theory. March and Simon examine important organizational theories and look at how organizations and the people within them actually work. They offered a less rationalized picture of how decisions are made and policies recommended than the conventional wisdom of that era. Education leaders may find this book interesting because it documents organizational features and captures the vagaries influencing the decision-making process in organizations.

Schwartz, S. (2007, November 25). Ethics and the university. University World News. Australia. Retrieved March 8, 2011, from http://www.universityworldnews.com/article. php?story=20071122150953605.

Schwartz provides a thoughtful treatise on the role of ethics in the development and pursuit of social policy, especially as it applies to higher education institutions. He highlights the potential trade-offs among actions that benefit the individual, those that benefit the university, and those that benefit society as a whole. Education leaders may find this article interesting because it offers guidance on how they can develop an ethical framework that can inform moral action.

Superfine, B. M. (2009, December). The evolving role of the courts in educational policy: The tension between judicial, scientific, and democratic decision making in *Kitzmiller v. Dover.* **American** *Educational Research Journal, 46***(4), 898–923.**

Superfine identifies the tensions among judicial, scientific, and political decision making. The article offers an examination of the answer to the question, Who decides? Education leaders may find this article interesting because of the perspective it provides on the factors that are important in determining which segment of the collective is the appropriate arbiter of decisions.

Persuade Your Audience

CHAPTER OBJECTIVES

After reading this chapter, you will be able to:

- Identify your audience
- Describe and conduct policy arguments
- Identify the context in which the argument is most credible
- Communicate clear analysis

EDUCATION VIGNETTE

You are the president of a leading research and land-grant institution in the United States. Budget cuts at the state level; the rising costs of attracting leading researchers, especially in the biomedical programs; and low persistence rates have forced you to consider a variety of strategic options. You want to raise the profile of your institution by emphasizing outstanding research and public engagement. However, key members of the urban community in which the main campus is located increasingly express distrust of university actions. Given your desire to cut costs and raise the status of the university, you have decided to eliminate the General College, which tended to attract poorer students as well as those who struggled academically. You face a backlash from some in the broader community who fear that your actions will make the institution more exclusive and who consider the General College closure a departure from the university's original mission. You have set up a series of forums directed at different audiences to explain your decision: the university community, high school advisers, and the community at large.

What do you tell them? Do you say the same thing to the audience in each forum?

THE ART OF COMMUNICATION

Before you can implement a policy, you have to persuade relevant decision makers about its suitability. In addition to reaching a decision regarding the appropriate policy, a key step in policy analysis is *communicating* that decision to key stakeholders (Bardach, 2009; Patton & Sawicki, 1993). This step differs somewhat from the second step identified in the policy analysis process. Making the case emphasizes assembling your data in order to support your problem statement and alternatives. The step described in this chapter looks more closely at communicating that information once the decision on the appropriate policy strategy is made. The focus of the two steps is different, so it is helpful to discuss separately the skills that help education leaders excel in the different persuasive stages of the process.

Research by Booth, Colomb, and Williams (1995) and Dunn (2004) suggest that an important part of communicating your analysis is being aware of the structure of policy arguments; knowing the different modes of policy arguments; and, perhaps most important, understanding your audience. Leach (2009, p. 2104) asserts that one must have a "strategic attitude to communication." She advocates translating knowledge gained from medical research into usable advice. She emphasizes the importance of both doctors and patients valuing communication even if they have different priorities. Leach (2009) writes that "flourishing communication relies on people valuing both process and content, both what is said and how to say it" (p. 2104). She admonishes researchers for being narrowly concerned with technical knowledge and argues that they must also be able to convey the practical implications of the research. Policy analysts in education must translate their analysis into meaningful advice. Preceding chapters focused on the content of the analysis, *what is said*, but this chapter discusses more fully *how to say it*.

How to Convey Your Analysis

The stereotype of an actor is that he prepares for his role by first determining the character's motivation. For policy analysts, an important step in preparing to communicate your analysis is knowing your audience. The advice offered by Booth and his colleagues regarding research in general is relevant here. They highlight six basic questions that give researchers an insight into their readers:

1. Who is your audience?
2. What do they expect you to do for them?

- Provide a simple description of the problem in words that non-experts can understand.
- Be clear about the purpose of your presentation. Does it inform, advise, promote?
- Provide a roadmap of the presentation so readers know where you are going.
- Be factual and consistent.
- Define all abbreviations.
- Justify your claims.
- Tailor your presentation to the delivery format.

FIGURE 9.1   Basic Rules for Communicating Analysis

3. How much do they know about your topic?
4. Do members of the audience already understand your problem?
5. How will they respond to your proposed solution?
6. In what forum will the audience encounter your report (Booth et al., 1995, pp. 26–27)

WHO IS YOUR AUDIENCE?   Your audience may be large or small, in general agreement or in conflict, decision makers or targets of the change. Its members may include the policymaker who inquired about the policy issue, the stakeholders who are affected by the problem, the stakeholders who are affected by the change that you propose, and the teacher who asked you to conduct the analysis. Regardless of the audience, you must summarize the problem in a descriptive statement that is grounded in facts. You must present a simple description of the problem in words that non-experts can understand. If you cannot summarize the policy issue in 30 words or less, you yourself may not be convinced that you have captured its essence. Think of your role as education leader. Would you be able to articulate the heart of the problem for the community you lead? Examples of succinct problem descriptions come from the press releases issued by the White House, state education departments, and other education organizations.

EXPECTATIONS OF AUDIENCE.   The parts of your analysis that you present will differ depending on the expectations of your audience. Audience members may want you to solve the problem for them, give them ideas on how to solve the problem, present information, or simply rubber-stamp the solution that they favor. Policy scholars describe the balance that analysts must attain in the presentation of their analysis: The presentation must often contain sufficient information to help the audience make sense of the recommendation without making them feel that their input is superfluous. Such a balance is seldom an easy task to accomplish. For example, the Minneapolis public schools faced a large budget shortfall, school closings, and district offices that policymakers considered to be unwelcoming to the community at large. Within that context, Minneapolis school board members considered the options of doing nothing different, refurbishing their existing building offices, or moving to another location. They decided to invite public input into their decision. During that process, however, strong criticism surfaced among some in the community that the board had already opted to move and that the community forums were simply pro forma. Instead of the forums leading to more unity between members of the community and members of the administration, it created another failure to communicate. One lesson to be learned from this Minneapolis public schools scenario is that you need to be clear about the purpose of your presentation. Do not raise expectations that you cannot fulfill. If you are merely presenting information, do not frame the presentation as if the analysis is ongoing. If you are inviting community input, make it clear how that input will be integrated into the final decision. Be transparent.

AUDIENCE KNOWLEDGE AND UNDERSTANDING.   When reviewing the facts for your analysis, you will learn a lot about the topic. You must decide how much of this information is already known by the audience and how much you will have to impart. Bardach (2009) warns against presenting too much background information. However, if your audience members are relatively ignorant about the key factors underlying your analysis, you must give them enough information to understand your point. Do not use abbreviations without first providing a definition. Avoid phrases like "as you all know . . ." because they may not know. While you do not want to talk down to the audience, you also do not want to share every fact that you learned or technical detail that you employed. A general rule of thumb is that you should provide more foundational information if the audience is not familiar with the topic. Your presentation *style* may differ with different audience expectations, but your *facts* should be the same. Do not contradict yourself. That is, while you may emphasize different facts with different groups, stating things differently is not a license for you to misrepresent reality. For example, do not tell the local chamber of commerce that you oppose teacher tenure and then meet with the teacher unions and inform them that you support tenure completely.

AUDIENCE RESPONSE TO THE SOLUTION. The justifications that you adopt for the problem depend on how much support or opposition you anticipate from key stakeholders. The more that people need to be convinced, the more justification you must provide regarding your problem definition and proposed solution. If you are presenting to an audience whose members wanted another problem tackled or who disagree with your position regarding why the problem exists, you must meet their concerns head on. You may not convince everyone, but you have to address all major concerns. For a mixed crowd (or an unknown one), at the very least, you must have a clear problem statement with three basic "so what" points provided. These points should be based on arguments taken from different points of justifications.

AUDIENCE FORUM. If you are presenting your analysis orally, you may have an opportunity to read body language or to take questions from audience members. If you have only the written word to communicate your concepts, you will not have the chance to explain any ambiguous claims. In either case, state your assertions simply. Use visual illustrations of your main points to ensure a quick, summative illustration of your analysis. Be careful that what you say in pictures matches what you say with words. While the key elements of your presentation will be the same, the finished product will look different depending on the needs of the audience. When possible, tailor your presentation to the audience. Use these questions and others that you find applicable to guide your presentation design: (1) Do you have a homogenous audience or a diverse one? (2) Are you preparing a complete report or an abridged version? and (3) Do you have a lot of time or just a little in which to present analysis?

HOMOGENOUS OR DIVERSE. Are you presenting your recommendations to a community forum or to an academic conference? If you are presenting to a community forum, you will likely have a broad range of interests and knowledge. Indicate what your conclusions mean for the community; describe explicit community impacts. If you are presenting to an academic conference, audience members may be more homogeneous in their support of academic and peer-reviewed journals. Detail the implications of your analysis for the field and for future research.

COMPLETE OR ABRIDGED ANALYSIS. Are you writing a report for your boss or sending a letter to the editor? When completing a full analytical report, you must provide sufficient information on the steps leading to the conclusion drawn. In writing a letter to the editor, you have less space. Go directly to the point and state your conclusion.

TIME.   Do you have 5 minutes to state your case in front of a legislative committee or a whole-day workshop? Legislators would likely be interested in the short version of your analysis. State your recommendations and indicate how they compare to recommendations made in similar communities. If you have a whole day to present your analysis, you have more time to lay out the steps in the process and the conclusions that you drew.

Making the Policy Argument

Just as audiences may differ, the arguments used to persuade them will also differ. Dunn (2004, pp. 395–418) identifies 11 main types of policy arguments: authority, method, generalization, classification, cause, sign, motivation, intuition, analogies, parallel case, and ethics. These justifications are not mutually exclusive, and it is likely that you will mix and match these policy arguments to enhance your ability to persuade your audience about the conclusions that you have drawn.

AUTHORITY.   Reasoning from authority is the social science equivalent of name dropping. By citing those "in the know," you lend credibility to the claims that you make and offer the audience some assurance that your analysis is not simply based on your opinion. Using arguments of authority are required when presenting to an audience knowledgeable about the field and may be especially useful at an academic conference or other forums for scholars. If your audience members do not place much credence in the experts you cite, your arguments are not likely to be persuasive. Finding the appropriate experts may be especially difficult if you are presenting to an audience with mixed knowledge and interest in the topic. In that case, you can rely on "expertise by association" by relying on the use of peer-reviewed journals or on power brokers within that community. Sometimes university personnel seem out of touch and lose the support of the broader community by referring to the "wrong" experts when justifying the decisions that they make.

METHOD.   If *who* you know does not work as a means of persuasion, *how* you know might. Making your argument by indicating that your assertions are based on knowledge gained from tried-and-true techniques may be helpful. Being able to match the methods that you use with the questions that you pursue is important (Heck, 2004, p.192). For instance, you may not be able to capture the nuances of a phenomenon and why it exists if you rely solely on statistical techniques. In describing the increased use of statistical analysis in the definition of educational adequacy, Guthrie and Rothstein (1999) write that statistical methods can obfuscate the practical implications of research findings. The authors assert that the precision of complex, statistically derived results may give its authors a false sense of security and still not be persuasive to their audience. They state, "We prefer the professional judgment approach, not because we believe it is more precise than statistical or inferential methods (it may not be more precise) but rather because its imprecision is more transparent" (p. 231). Consequently, if you rely on a method that is not suited for the questions that you ask or the conclusions that you draw, your arguments will not be convincing.

GENERALIZATION.   The underlying rationale when using generalization as a mode of argument is that what is true of the parts is also true of the whole. This assertion is credible if the parts are randomly selected from a broader population. Random selection

Table 9.1 Modes of Making Persuasive Policy Arguments

Type of Argument	Essence of Argument	Context in Which Mode Is Most Credible
Authority	Name dropping; reference to those "in the know" or experts.	Audience is knowledgeable about the field, especially those at academic conferences. Authority of experts is context driven.
Method	*How* you know matters	Appropriately matching the methods that you use to the questions that you address; for example, using qualitative analysis for answering why a phenomenon exists or how a process works.
Generalization	What is true of the parts is true of the whole	Credible assertion if parts are randomly selected from a broader population.
Classification	What is true of the whole is true of the parts	Credible only if there is no variation among the parts. The more diversity, the less credible the assertion and the more offensive the arguments may seem. Mode susceptible to accusations of stereotyping.
Cause	Established causal relationships	Assertion more credible if lots of empirical evidence exists to support existence of relationships. For example, the basis of economic analysis is the relationship between price and the quantity demanded or supplied of a good or service.
Sign	Indicators of a problem	Credible if there is empirical evidence that an association exists between indicators and the problem that is defined. Unlike causal arguments, there is no need to go beyond simple associations.
Motivation	Appeal to values held by stakeholders	Arguments are more credible the more it addresses the values of audience members.
Intuition	Persuasion by insight	Arguments are more credible if hard facts are less valued than the experience of players who are similar in characteristics to the audience members.
Analogy	Drawing comparisons between relationships in other contexts	Credible if the metaphor rings true in different policy arena.
Parallel case	Highlights the possibility of effective policies working within the same system but outside original implementation location	Arguments are more credible the more closely the original location resembles the new location where the policy is to be tried.
Ethics	Persuasion by motivation by appealing to principles of a just society	Arguments are more credible the more homogeneous the concept of what a just society looks like.

suggests that analysis of each part would yield the same results as analysis of the whole. Notwithstanding, because your conclusions are based on a sample and not the population, some will reject your line of argument by finding an exception to your claim. Your claim will be more robust if you follow research guidelines regarding sampling or if you provide so-called thick descriptions that allow people to make similar connections to the case outlined. For instance, in exploring the organizational capacity of states to respond to the federal No Child Left Behind Act (NCLB), Alexander (2006) justified looking at conditions in Massachusetts as a way to reveal conditions for the rest of the country. She assumed that if Massachusetts had difficulty responding to the act, then many other states would face similar challenges. She argued that the challenges would be particularly acute for some states because federal educators considered Massachusetts to be 1 of only 17 states in 2005 to be on track to meet the NCLB standards.

CLASSIFICATION.   Classification is akin to stereotyping because you reason that what is true for the population on average must also be true of individuals within that population. Be careful when using arguments relying on this mode of reasoning because they can be offensive. If you rely on classification to persuade your audience, state explicitly that you are aware that many individuals within the group do not share the group's average attributes. Many examples abound of presentations and analyses being rejected because of perceived stereotyping. For instance, a single mother, who happened to be white, professional, and wealthy, complained of the dire predictions made in the scholarship regarding the fate of children in single-family households. Similarly, a black professional objected to students of color being labeled "at risk." I have often seen researchers use *black* interchangeably with *poor* as if all black students are poor and all white students are rich.

CAUSE.   With the cause mode of persuasion, you try to persuade the audience about the soundness of your arguments by relying on established causal relationships. This mode of reasoning is more persuasive the more empirical evidence that exists in support of the presumed relationship. For example, general agreement exists that there is an inverse relationship between the price of a good and the quantity demanded of it. Thus, you may decide to rely on this economic "law" to persuade decision makers to offer scholarships in the sciences in order to increase the number of students who specialize in that field. Advocates of many federally sponsored programs designed to encourage students to enter the science, technology, engineering, and math fields took this approach.

SIGN.   You can try to persuade stakeholders that a problem exists by referring to the indicators, or signs, of a problem. This persuasive tool is useful because you do not have to convince your readers of the causal connection but simply that an association exists. For example, Singham (1998) argued as early as 1998 that the performance of black students is a harbinger of the performance of the system as a whole. He writes,

> It used to be that coal miners took canaries into the mines as detectors of noxious gases. If the canary died, then the miners realized that they were in a region of danger and took the necessary precautions. The educational performance of the black community is like the canary, and the coal mine is the education system. The warning signals are apparent. (p. 8)

MOTIVATION.   With the motivation mode of persuasion, you persuade by appealing directly to the values held by stakeholders. The history of education in the United States illustrates the plethora of arguments that have been used to encourage support for a variety of education strategies. Over the decades, policymakers have alternatively emphasized equity, excellence, and liberty (e.g., Fowler, 2009; Heck, 2004). The title of the No Child Left Behind Act illustrates an attempt to motivate stakeholders both from an equity and excellence standpoint. The duality of the arguments used to promote this act is reflected in the bipartisan support it received when it passed in 2002 and the bipartisan opposition to it today.

INTUITION.   The intuition mode of persuasion is persuasion by insight. In this day of data-driven management, however, it may be less persuasive to rely on your gut alone. Notwithstanding, in some contexts, especially when the people involved feel beleaguered, the insight offered from someone in the trenches can be more persuasive than hard facts. It is not unusual to hear teachers reject the authoritative or method arguments offered by researchers while embracing the guidance offered from one of their own.

ANALOGY.   With the analogy mode of persuasion, you try to persuade your audience by drawing on the impact of relationships in other contexts. This strategy is employed by many who propose market-based policies in the field of education. They argue that, because the market can allocate resources efficiently in the exchange of private goods, market mechanisms will be equally successful in allocating resources in the field of education. This line of reasoning dominates much of the federal and state policies that have been enacted since the 1990s. For example, market-driven policies have helped to spark a trend where states no longer serve as the primary source of funding for public higher education institutions and many leaders of public higher education institutions pursue marketing strategies that seem similar to their private counterparts (American Council on Education, 2005).

PARALLEL CASE.   Persuasion using parallel arguments highlights the possibility of effective policies working outside their original implementation location (Dunn, 2004, p. 396). Policymakers often look to their neighbors for ideas. For example, U.S. policymakers often point to the longer time spent in school by students in other industrialized countries as a reason for them outperforming students in the United States. The policymakers argue that the increased school time allows students from other countries to score higher than U.S. students on the Third International Math and Science tests. These arguments underlie the federal Time for Innovation Matters in Education (TIME) Act of 2008, which proposes federal funding to support states' efforts to expand the school day in pilot schools in each state.

ETHICS.   Persuasion using ethics is similar to persuasion by motivation, but it goes beyond the values held by individuals or groups and to the presumed principles of a just society (e.g., Dunn, 2004, p. 396). When you rely on ethical arguments to justify your conclusion, you are persuading by describing "the rightness or wrongness, goodness or badness, of policies or their consequences" (Dunn, 2004, p. 396). For example, when President George W. Bush expounded on the benefits of the No Child Left Behind Act, he urged U.S. citizens to abandon the "soft bigotry of low expectations." Also using ethical principles, Houston (2007) counters that

> [we should end] "the hard bigotry of inadequate resources" by developing a Marshall Plan for America's poor that provides adequate health care and preschool programs for those in need and creates "human enterprise zones" where large numbers of poor children live. (p. 747)

CHECKLIST FOR COMMUNICATING ANALYSIS

The preceding sections of this chapter focus on preparing for the presentation by knowing your audience and using appropriate arguments. This section is a check on the presentation itself. You should ask yourself the following six questions as a final test to see if you are prepared to communicate your analysis clearly:

1. Is your preparation and presentation of the materials timely?
2. Are the major findings of your analysis clear?
3. Is the presentation of information engaging?
4. Do you use visual displays?
5. Is the conclusion succinct and obvious?
6. Are the policy and research implications identified?

Timeliness

The factor of time refers both to having the report ready by the deadline established and also presenting the information within the time period specified. The audience may or may not recognize that there is a lot to cover, but it is your responsibility to gather, analyze, and report the facts within the time period allotted. Having a wealth of information at your fingertips is meaningless if it cannot be used. While it may seem unfair that you have to cover one year's worth of work in one month (or whatever the shortened timeframe), you will know that beforehand. Dive into the policy analytical process using the guidance presented herein to help you decide what tasks may be omitted and what tasks are necessary. Maybe you may have a lot to say and would love more than 10 minutes (or whatever the allotted time) to say it, but practice your presentation and cut it if you are over the allotted time. The key to understanding your analysis may be lost if you did not present essential information because you ran out of time.

Clarity of Findings

Be explicit. The audience members should not have to guess or infer the conclusions that you draw. Audience members should be able to follow the logic of your arguments, even if they do not agree with it. Sometimes a picture or graph illustrates your point clearly and quickly. Illustrations also serve to change the pace of the presentation and often allow it to be more engaging. However, do not use pictures for the sake of showing pictures. Their purpose is to move the presentation and the analysis along.

Your presentation must have a clear, concise identification of the policy issue with supporting evidence. While time constraints may prevent you from doing a complete stakeholder analysis, you should be clear about who are the major winners and losers. Identify the factors that helped you to reach your decision. Offer your audience a sound

- Is my preparation and presentation of the materials timely?
- Are the major findings of my issue paper clear?
- Is the presentation engaging?
- Did I use visual displays?
- Is the conclusion clear and succinct?
- Are policy and research implications highlighted?

FIGURE 9.2 Checklist for Communicating Analysis

explanation of the significance of each criterion and its measurement. Provide a clear description of the alternatives that you considered, indicating how you compared them. When preparing your presentation, try it with people who are not familiar with the topic. For that practice presentation, ask them to tell you which option rose to the top. If their response is the same as your conclusion, your findings and arguments are sufficiently clear.

So What?

Let the audience know where they should go from here. Highlight the implications for policy and research stemming from your analysis. Depending on the audience, you may conclude with future tasks, organizational changes that may result, or even unanswered questions in research.

Chapter Summary

Before you can implement a policy, you have to persuade relevant decision makers about its suitability. A key step in policy analysis, in addition to reaching a decision regarding the appropriate policy, is *communicating* that decision to key stakeholders. Previous chapters focused on the content of the analysis. Chapter 9 looked more closely at how you communicate that content in order to get things done. Knowing your audience and constructing strong justifications for the claims made are important persuasive tools. Your audience may be large or small, in general agreement or in conflict, decision makers or targets of the change. What you

tell them depends on what they already know and the forum in which you present your analysis. Tailor your presentation to fit their needs. It is not enough to know your audience and prepare appropriate arguments; you also have to be timely. Your analysis must be ready in time and delivered within the time given. For your analysis to be useful, its conclusions must be clear. When you have convinced the relevant stakeholders on the suitability of your policy option, you are now ready to think more deeply about its implementation. The creation of an implementation plan is the subject of Chapter 10.

Review Questions

1. Do you think drawing the "right" conclusion in policy analysis is as important as communicating your analysis to a broader audience? Explain your answer.

2. Which of the modes of argument described in Chapter 9 do you think is the most persuasive? Which mode do you tend to use in your professional life?

3. Return to the chapter-opening education vignette. Identify and analyze the different audience groupings that will be present at the forums. What kinds of argument would you use for each group? Why?

News Story for Analysis

"Board to review closing schools; Falling Enrollment." *National Post* (f/k/a *The Financial Post*) (Canada). October 29, 2009 Thursday. Toronto Edition. BYLINE: Kenyon Wallace, *National Post*. SECTION: TORONTO; Pg. A12. LENGTH: 523 words

Toronto District School Board [TDSB] trustees voted unanimously last night to begin a review of potential school closures and mergers in the face of dramatic declines in enrollment expected during the next 10 years.

The board will launch "accommodation review committees" for 36 schools in eight neighborhoods as part of education director Chris Spence's plan to eliminate under-used schools and bring scattered student populations together, allowing for more class choices and extracurricular activities. Any savings expected from school closures will also help the board tackle its $90 million capital deficit.

"These reviews don't necessarily mean school closures," said board chairman John Campbell. "They may make a recommendation for consolidation and even if a school does close, it is a temporary state of affairs and in some cases, doesn't mean the school would be sold."

Mr. Campbell cited the example of three schools in his own ward (Etobicoke Centre) that were closed in the late 1980s and early 1990s but were re-opened as a result of changing demographics.

Accommodation review committees take the form of public forums where trustees, parents and other stakeholders discuss the role of a local school in their community and what impact its closure would have on students and the neighborhood.

The plan to strike committees this fall—with more slated for January—is one of dozens of proposed initiatives put forward by Mr. Spence as part of his ambitious "Vision of Hope!", a broad set of directives aimed at keeping the board financially viable while providing quality education.

Last week, he called for the creation of an all-boys learning academy and boy-friendly classrooms to combat high male suspension rates and behavioral problems. He also announced his intention to hire a marketing manager to recruit students from private schools and foreign countries.

Board data show elementary school enrollment, currently at 177,000, is projected to drop by 30,000 to 60,000 students by 2030.

"The reality is that we have about 100 schools that are half empty," said Josh Matlow, trustee for St. Paul's. "That isn't being fiscally responsible with ratepayer tax dollars because it costs the same amount of money to keep the lights on, pay for gas and pay salaries in these schools as it does in full schools. If you want a better school, you have to deal with the reality that you can't have it half empty."

The last school to close in the TDSB was Timothy Eaton Business and Technical Institute in Scarborough, which was shut this year after enrollment fell to 200 (capacity was 750).

Not all trustees are sold on the review committees, however. Sheila Cary-Meagher (Beaches-East York) says people who live in lower income neighborhoods often don't have the knowledge of how the school system works or the language skills necessary to express their concerns over potential school closures.

"I have put the director on notice that I will be insisting that we provide each of these communities with an organizer who can work with families and residents to help give them the tools to do a competent job of making recommendations," she said.

Source: Material reprinted with the express permission of: "National Post Inc."

Discussion Questions

1. Describe the different audiences faced by the education leaders identified in this article.
2. How would you communicate favored policies to each audience group that you described in Discussion Question 1?
3. Would the mode of argument used differ based on the audience? Explain your response.

Selected Websites

American Council on Education. Available at *http://www.acenet.edu/AM/Template.cfm?Section=About_ACE.*

The official website of the American Council on Education (ACE). Its members include the leaders of accredited higher education institutions and affiliated higher education organizations in the United States. The site provides reviews of existing policy as well as policy briefs related to higher education in the United States. Education leaders may find this site helpful because of its in-depth look at policy that affects higher education institutions. Especially helpful are the publications made available under the tab labeled Government Relations and Public Policy and the press releases under the tab labeled News Room found on the homepage.

Time for Innovation Matters in Education Act of 2008. Available at *http://www.govtrack.us/congress/bill.xpd?bill=s110-3431.*

This website tracks the progress of the Time for Innovation Matters in Education Act of 2008. It contains the full text of the bill as well as its current status in Congress. Educators may find this site helpful for the information it provides on this particular bill as well as the insight it gives on parallel arguments used to justify it.

Selected References

American Council on Education. (2005, March). *Bridging troubled waters: Competition, cooperation and the public good in independent and public higher education.* (Third in a series of essays: *The changing relationship between States and their institutions.*) Washington, DC: American Council on Education.

This report, published by the American Council on Education, details the trends in context and policy faced by leaders of higher education institutions in the United States. Education leaders in higher education institutions may find this report especially helpful for its description of the changing role that states play in supporting higher education institutions and how education leaders respond to these changes. The insight it provides on how the language and values of business gets increasingly incorporated in the education discourse may be insightful as leaders consider how they can communicate with different audiences.

Houston, P. D. (2007, June). The seven deadly sins of No Child Left Behind. *Phi Delta Kappan*, **88**(10), pp. 744–748.

Houston is the executive director of the American Association of School Administrators and was critical of the strategies adopted by the No Child Left Behind Act. He wanted to persuade policymakers and other education leaders that the act was so badly flawed that they should not support even a modified version of it. Education leaders may find this article helpful for examining the ethical mode of argument employed to persuade policymakers that major policy revision is needed.

Leach, J. (2009, June 20–26). Valuing communication. *The Lancet*, **373**(9681), 2104.

Leach argues for the art of communicating details, indicating that this competence is often overlooked in the quest for honing technical skills. Education leaders may find this article helpful because it highlights the importance of being able to persuade and communicate even in a content-driven field like medicine.

Singham, M. (1998, September). The canary in the mine: The achievement gap between black and white students [cover story]. *Phi Delta Kappan, 80*(1), 8–15.

This article examines the achievement gap between white and black students, offering strategies that can help reduce the gap. Education leaders may find this article interesting for its use of signs as a mode of making a policy argument. Singham argues that the poor performance of black students is symptomatic of the poor performance of the education system as a whole. He also uses the analogy of the canary in the mine to make his point.

10

Implement the Solution

CHAPTER OBJECTIVES

After reading this chapter, you will be able to:

- Describe the context that sets the stage for change
- Identify the different underlying causes for unsuccessful implementation
- Identify the steps that go into successful implementation of policy
- Develop a strategic implementation plan
- Describe the different stages of implementation
- Identify leadership challenges in implementation

EDUCATION VIGNETTE

You are the minister of education for a large third world nation, rich in natural resources but poor in education funds. Almost two-thirds of your population is illiterate. Your nation has over 200 indigenous languages; three are dominant. Several changes in government and education policies have taken place over the past two decades. Everybody thinks that they know the right way to fix the education system, and policy leaders alternate between tinkering at the edges and endorsing radical reform. The leaders of your country enacted a law 2 years ago to improve the education system by focusing on the creation of informed, globally savvy, and highly skilled citizens. The law called for heavy investments in the science and technology fields, promotion of languages, the use of bilingual education, expansion of early childhood programs, and improving access to schools for all members of society. However, recent surveys suggest that many families, teachers, and headmasters still do not know the goals of the policy and the specific tasks noted therein. Several communities continue to school as they have always done. In the few places where educators initially tried to implement the policy, many abandoned the reform after the first year when they saw no immediate improvement in student performance.

What can you do to ensure that implementation is improved? What is your plan of action?

SETTING THE STAGE FOR CHANGE

Policy analysis often calls for change. Change is more likely to occur if you enact policies that are doable. For policies to have an impact, they must be carried out. While implementation is not equivalent to outcome, managing the implementation process bolsters the chance that the enacted policy will yield the results sought. Looking at Comer's School Development Program, for example, Gamse, Millsap, and Goodson (2002) find that assessing the feasibility of implementation models was important because it allowed education leaders to be better planners. They conclude that certain implementation strategies are more workable than others, and some plans are doomed to fail.

Why Won't It Work?

Enacted policies are not implemented for many reasons. Policymakers meant them to be symbolic (e.g., Edelman, 1995). Front-line workers and supporting staff members do not have the skill or the will to implement them. Organizations do not have the capacity to make the policy a reality. Communities do not have the necessary supports to commit to the changes called for in the policy option. In sum, Duke (2004) notes that successful implementation calls for "individual readiness, organizational capacity, and community capacity" (p. 123).

This chapter describes how to anticipate and tackle the implementation process to enhance the likelihood that the policy you recommend will produce the results that you seek. The chapter discusses how to create an implementation plan, including addressing the hurdles to implementation. Next, it provides an overview of the stages of implementation; a description of leadership challenges is infused throughout the discussion.

Creating an Implementation Plan

Creating an implementation plan does not supplant effective leadership. What it does is provide leaders with a means of anticipating more fully the potential pitfalls that lie ahead. An implementation plan creates a clear statement of why change is needed and offers a program of change that is doable. Education leaders must map out the future, indicating the changes in behavior that will make tomorrow different from today. The mapping process entails three steps: outline your plan, expand your outline, and check your plan.

OUTLINE THE PLAN. An implementation plan is a detailed description of the steps that you need to take in order to promote change in your organization or community (e.g., Duke, 2004, p. 138). The basic blueprint of that plan contains a description of the specific strategies that are needed, the personnel responsible for implementing these tasks, the resources needed to complete each task, evaluation provisions, and an overall timeline. Your plan essentially answers the questions of what, who, how, and when.

Why this plan? What are the problem definition and its obverse (goals and objectives)?			
What?	**Who?**	**How?**	**When?**
What are the tasks that need to be done to facilitate change?	Who will be responsible for overseeing or performing the specified activities?	How will the work be done? What resources, besides personnel, will be invested in completion of the task? How will you keep track?	When will the task be initiated? When will it be completed? What are your justifications for the timeline provided?

FIGURE 10.1 Example of Blueprint for Basic Implementation Plan

Let's say that you have defined a policy problem as high illiteracy rates. Among the several options available, you choose to mandate early childhood education for all 4-year-olds. Start by reviewing the goals and objectives of the analysis and indicating the connection between your policy choice and the goal sought. Next, define early childhood education and detail what that looks like. Do you have a list of all the early childhood programs that are presently available? Next, indicate *what* you need to change within the present system to align the current processes with desired ones. Does the system have the capacity to absorb additional pre-K students? If not, what steps will you take to increase that capacity? Are there sufficient teachers, classroom space, and educational materials available? *Who* will actually be involved in the implementation process? *How* will they be able to complete assigned tasks? What resources will you use to address the cost of enforcement and compliance of the recommended mandate? Who will pay for those resources? *When* will you start implementation of the various steps? When do you anticipate seeing the results of the implementation in terms of the procedures adopted and the goals achieved?

You do not create your implementation plan in a vacuum. Your earlier description of the basic components of the policy package serves as an outline of what needs to be done (see Chapter 6). Your implementation plan fills in that outline by expanding on your assessment of the administrative operability of the recommended policy. Make sure that your implementation narrative is consistent with your earlier overview of the alternatives. Address the opportunities and challenges to implementation that you identified when you first weighed the ability of the recommended option to be implemented (see Chapter 7).

EXPAND THE OUTLINE.   The outline of an implementation plan has the basic components already described, and your environmental scan of the organization influences how you expand the outline. The plan that you develop has to be dynamic and flexible in order to respond to changing needs. Your scan of the environment should alert you to likely areas of resistance and support. For example, policies that call for activities that diminish the power of the implementing agency are likely to meet more resistance from implementers than policies that enhance its power. Policies that increase the workload of the implementers with no increased benefit in prestige and resources are likely to be resisted. Policies that strain the resources of the implementing organization are not likely to be fully implemented (Cooper, Fusarelli, & Randall, 2004).

Why this plan?

Goal: To reduce high illiteracy rates (by promoting early childhood education)

Objectives:

- To increase the percentage of the population that is literate by 2012
- To increase the number of students participating in early childhood education from _____ to _____ by 2012
- To increase awareness of early childhood programs by 2012

What?	Who?	How?	When?
1. Create working definition of early childhood education programs. Count how many programs exist and count the number of children participating. Indicate percentage of eligible children who participate.	State department of education personnel will create baseline data by identifying all early childhood programs and their participants. They will create database with said data.	Computers and file storage systems will be available to store data. Existing personnel will be given time to check Internet sites, make phone calls, and do secondary analysis. No site visits.	This task will be done at the outset to make sure that baseline comparisons are available.
2. Provide incentives to families who participate in early childhood programs.	State department of education personnel will work with department of revenue personnel to create formula for providing incentives consistent with budget and law.	Incentives will be subsidized through deductions and credits noted on state tax forms. Ensure that sufficient funds are available to pay for participating families.	This task will be done the same year that baseline data are created and eligible programs are identified. This task is ongoing.
3. Start marketing campaign detailing the benefits of early childhood programs.	The communications arm of the state department of education will create public service announcements to inform state residents of the program. These spots will target families with children under age 5.	The use of websites and public alerts will limit the additional resources needed. Additional costs will be incurred with mailings and outreach to libraries and community centers.	This task will be done from the outset. Initial expenditures will be reduced as the program gets underway.
4. Provide support to eligible early childhood programs to ensure that capacity exists for expansion.	State department of education personnel will offer training to early childhood program educators to enhance capacity.	Provide ongoing professional development materials for staff members of early childhood programs.	This task will be done a year after the initial implementation of the policy to have a better understanding of the needs of the community.
Additional concerns:	• Does the system have the capacity to absorb additional pre-K students? If not, what steps will you take to increase that capacity? • Are there sufficient teachers, classroom space, and educational materials available? • What resources will you use to address the cost of enforcement and compliance of the recommended mandate? Who will pay for those resources? • If additional steps are warranted, when will you start implementation of the additional steps?		

FIGURE 10.2   Example of Basic Strategic Plan with Mandated Early Childhood Education as Recommended Option

Your environmental scan should document the distance between where the implementing organization is in terms of will, skill, and resources, and where you need it to be. The greater the distance between these two poles, the more resistance to implementation you should anticipate. The more resistance that you expect, the more detail your plan should contain regarding how you intend to implement the recommended option.

CHECK YOUR PLAN. Research on implementation (e.g., Fowler, 2009; Cooper, Fusarelli, & Randall, 2004; Duke, 2004; Louis & Miles, 1990) suggests that six key questions must be part of the checklist for your implementation plan. First, is there a direct connection between the implementation plan and the problem defined? If the plan does not seem to be addressing a solvable problem, implementers may consider the new policy to be simply a political tactic. Second, is the plan clear about its goals and objectives? If implementers are unable to understand why the goals and objectives reflect the organization's mission, they will be less likely to embrace the change in behavior that you require. Third, do the tasks listed present a clear pathway to the goal and objectives described? If you are not able to map the connection between the overall activities that you call for and the goal that you seek, then the activities may seem to be busywork. Fourth, are individuals identified for completing each assigned task? Because your plan likely calls for a change in the behavior of implementers, you need to be clear about their new responsibilities. If you do not specifically assign someone to a task, everyone may think that it is someone else's responsibility, causing key activities to be left undone. Fifth, is the timeframe for completion of the project noted and justified? While the actual timeline may change, you should have an idea of how much time is needed for each activity and program. Planning for time allows you to provide appropriate deadlines and priorities and to know when it is fitting to check with implementers and offer feedback. Sixth, is there a process for checking compliance? If noncompliance has no consequences, it will be difficult for you to encourage change. Meaningful consequences are impossible if you are unable to identify who is not doing what they are supposed to do.

Addressing the six questions on your checklist provides you with a workable plan of action that can be modified to fit more closely the actual circumstances that you face. Once you have created the outline of your implementation plan, you can expand on it by addressing specific hurdles to implementation.

- Is there a direct connection between the implementation plan and the problem defined?
- Is the plan clear about its goals and objectives?
- Do the tasks listed present a clear pathway to the goal and objectives described?
- Are individuals identified for completing each assigned task?
- Is the timeframe for completion of the project noted and justified?
- Is a process available for checking compliance?

FIGURE 10.3 Key Questions for Checking the Utility of Your Implementation Plan

IMPLEMENTING STRATEGICALLY

Major Implementation Challenges

Effective implementation does not occur by magic but through sound leadership and management. Complacency and resistance are ever-present hurdles. Leaders have to combat these twin obstacles while "inspiring commitment to change, and providing direction during the change process" (Duke, 2004, p. 183).

To combat complacency, leaders must be willing to examine their own performance as well as that of the organization. To do that, include clear feedback opportunities in the plan. Duke (2004) advises leaders to overcome resistance by identifying people who are resisters and noting their reason(s) for resistance. This knowledge will provide you with useful information on how to modify your plan to address important stakeholder concerns and to increase the ability of the policy to be implemented. Inspiring commitment allows you to deemphasize activities that are primarily geared toward control and compliance. One way of inspiring implementers is clearly articulating your vision for change and ensuring that tasks are meaningful, with clear connections to individual and policy goals (e.g., Duke, 2004; Cooper, Fusarelli, & Randall, 2004). To help provide direction, your plan should distinguish among the goals, objectives, and the activities that allow you to achieve them. We discussed goals and objectives at length in Chapter 3. Activities are the actions that you or others must take to achieve the goals and objectives. Your plan should be a constant reminder of the change sought; the activities assigned are simply steps to achieving your goal.

Bryson (1988) identifies four major categories of problems that may affect successful implementation of a strategic plan: human, process, structural, and institutional (pp. 199–215). Fowler (2009) uses similar groupings to categorize the challenges, indicating that implementation problems are largely people-, program-, or setting-related (p. 298). Education leaders must be able to recognize the challenges that they face and use that insight to overcome each of these potential hurdles to implementation.

HUMAN (PEOPLE-RELATED) PROBLEMS. Human problems arise readily when the implementation process is a jarring departure from present conditions and the learning curve for implementers is steep. If the radical nature of the change is what sparks the most resistance, your plan should include activities that temper the gradient of the learning curve. For example, a strong professional development component is part of Comer's school development programs to address the difficulty of implementing large-scale, whole-school reform (Comer 1988; Gamse, Millsap, & Goodson 2002).

Human problems can also arise when change is commonplace, and noncompliance does not have any real consequences. If the implementing organization believes that "this too shall pass," then your plan should include activities that shake things up a bit. For example, you could incorporate a variety of strategies to recognize different perspectives. This variety may come from integrating scholarly disciplines, collaborating with different departments, or crossing jurisdictional boundaries (Bryson, 1988, p. 204). For instance, the federal Investing in Innovation Fund (i3) program explicitly calls for cross-organizational partnerships to effect change.

PROCESS (PROGRAM-RELATED) PROBLEMS.   It is difficult to translate ideas into practice. Your plan should contain activities that make the implementing organization fertile ground for the acceptance of new ideas. Part of creating a sound strategic plan is recognizing the life cycle of ideas and managing their evolution over time. Your plan should establish procedures for which the implementing organization is both a producer and implementer of ideas (Bryson, 1988). Your plan should have a clear line of accountability for activities undertaken. To do that, your plan should reflect that organizations must be ". . . more like a university when they need ideas, and more like an army when they implement them" (Bryson, 1988, p. 210). Again, a similar duality exists in the federal i3 grant. That is, federal policymakers match their general call for innovative and flexible ideas with a specific plan for rewarding ideas that are put into practice.

STRUCTURAL (SETTING-RELATED) PROBLEMS.   You can enhance the effective implementation of policy when you do not divorce it from the policy planning process. Ensure that your plan is a cohesive document that ties together the different activities, and ties them to the resolution of the stated problem. Connections to the bigger picture must be clear to all facets of the implementing groups. For example, Miles and Frank (2008) find that when education practitioners improved the instructional coherence of their schools, students performed better. A key part of that instructional coherence was making the appropriate connections for the stakeholders, from the creation of targets to the means of reaching them, to knowing if you reached them (Miles & Frank, 2008). The interconnectedness needed for successful implementation reminds me of the famous children's story by Laura Joffe Numeroff (1985), *If You Give a Mouse a Cookie*. In that tale, Numeroff describes the sequence of events that evolve from the simple act of giving a mouse a cookie, ending right where she started. Education leaders do not necessarily want to end up where they begun, but they do want to clarify the connections between each set of activities described. Requiring activities that lead to a holistic look at implementation would be helpful to reform in K–12 schools and in other education arenas.

INSTITUTIONAL (PROGRAM-RELATED OR SETTING-RELATED) PROBLEMS.   Institutions are, by definition, organizations with "highly stable patterns of interaction" (Bryson, 1988, p. 214). Just like in the natural sciences, where stable bonds are hard to break, so it is in society and organizations, where creating new patterns of relationships is a daunting task. To address this difficulty, your implementation plan should have an explicit redefinition of purpose, indicating how this new purpose will infuse the organizational processes and structure. Your plan will not take the place of effective, transformative leadership, but it should help lay the groundwork for change and the reordering of priorities.

Referring to Louis and Miles (1990), Fowler (2009) argues that you can use technical, political, or cultural strategies to address the implementation challenges discussed in this chapter. *Technical strategies* call for an analysis of the problem and targeting the resources needed to solve it. *Political strategies* call on you to mobilize power. *Cultural strategies* focus on the shared beliefs underlying the problem. Fowler (2009) finds that technical strategies often yield better results than political or cultural strategies (p. 298).

STAGES IN IMPLEMENTATION

Knowing the phases of the implementation process also helps you to complete the details of an implementation plan. Fowler (2009) identifies three key phases: mobilization, implementation proper, and institutionalization.

Mobilization

Mobilization includes the time it takes to move a policy from recommendation to adoption, to planning. This initial phase can take from 14 to 17 months. As part of the mobilization stage, you must weigh the pros and cons of using a large or small steering committee to identify next steps. Large committees are more cumbersome, but they allow a wide array of interests to be integrated early in the process. Small committees may seem exclusive, but they are likely to be more efficient and may allow the policy to move forward more quickly to implementation proper.

Implementation Proper

Implementation proper includes the actual performance of the activities specified in the plan. Sometimes the policy is implemented quickly, and sometimes it takes several years. Quick implementation is not always best if it merely reflects a superficial commitment to the program for change. Initially positive outcomes may be reflecting the **Hawthorne effect**, where the novelty of the policy and the attention it garners is driving positive, short-term results. In time, as attention wanes and resources lag, outcomes may worsen. By contrast, initially negative outcomes may simply be reflecting an **implementation dip**, where implementers need time to learn new routines (e.g., Fullan, 1999). In time, as practitioners acquire the appropriate skills and the organization builds capacity, results may improve. Anticipate a lengthy implementation process if recommended changes require implementers to behave very differently compared to what they are accustomed to.

Your plan should include options for implementers to have ongoing assistance, with appropriate monitoring and feedback mechanisms built in. Create a timeline and expectations that are not overwhelming. Develop accountability mechanisms that both support and push implementers. For meaningful change to occur, consequences must be associated with behavior—both good and bad. For example, in examining the implementation of site-based management in New Jersey, Walker (2002) found that state policymakers did not have appropriate connections between goals and implementation mechanisms. State policymakers wanted to have site teams comprised of a balanced mix of community members, teachers, and administrators. However, their plan contained a ban on community members who are employed by the district. Because the district was a major employer in that community, many of its members were made ineligible. State policymakers also wanted the site team to be responsible for major decisions, but the timelines and training that they called for and that were offered in the plan inhibited local decision making.

Institutionalization

Implementation is an iterative process. When implementers consider activities outlined in the plan to be routine, new stable relationships form. To the extent that the new policy becomes the norm, it is *institutionalized*, which is the hallmark of the **institutionalization** phase of the implementation process. Leaders have the challenge of institutionalizing the recommended action but leaving the organization open to further change when needed.

Chapter Summary

Policy analysis often calls for change. Change is more likely to occur if you enact policies that are doable. This chapter describes how to anticipate and tackle the implementation process to enhance the likelihood that the policy you recommend will produce the results that you seek. Your plan essentially answers the questions of what, who, how, and when. It includes an overview of the tasks that need to be done, who will be responsible for doing them, and the timeframe in which they will be completed.

Your implementation plan must address the particular concerns of the implementing organization. Your environmental scan may uncover human, process, structural, and institutional obstacles to implementation. Document the distance between where the implementing organization is in terms of will, skill, and resources, and where you need it to be. The greater the distance between these two poles,

the more resistance to implementation that you should anticipate. The more resistance that you expect, the more detail your plan should contain regarding how you intend to implement the recommended option.

Do not be inflexible and wedded to the exact details of the implementation plan if some change is warranted when actual implementation occurs. Your implementation plan is a work in progress. Knowing the phases of the implementation process helps you to make appropriate modifications. Leaders must address a variety of implementation challenges, knowing that, even if they follow the plan, they still may not achieve the desired outcomes. The effectiveness of policy goes beyond its implementation. You must monitor its outputs and judge the success of its outcomes. Monitoring the outputs and evaluating the success, or outcomes, of the implementation plan are the subjects of Chapters 11 and 12, respectively.

Review Questions

1. Revisit the chapter-opening education vignette. Do your suggestions to the minister of education change after reading this chapter? If so, how? If not, how is your earlier response reflective of the chapter themes?
2. How would you revise the implementation plan in Figure 10.2 to address more fully

the implementation challenges described in later sections of Chapter 10?
3. Create an implementation plan for a policy that you recommended to address a particular policy issue.

News Story for Analysis

"Older pupils face larger class sizes: Kindergarten cap puts music rooms in jeopardy." *National Post* (f/k/a *The Financial Post*) (Canada). May 2, 2006 Tuesday. National Edition. BYLINE: Susan Kirwin, *National Post*. SECTION: NEWS; Pg. A1. DATELINE: TORONTO

TORONTO—Ontario's 20-student cap for primary classrooms has painful implications for the Toronto District School Board [TDSB] this September, with critics charging that schools must axe music classrooms, increase class sizes

for older grades, and in one case, consider putting children into a basement classroom.

The Toronto board will this fall begin enforcing the cap in junior kindergarten and kindergarten classes, and also enforce an average of 20.5 students in Grades 1 to 3, with a hard cap of 24 students per class.

By September, 2007, 90% of classes from JK to Grade 3 will have 20 students or fewer.

The burden of the well-meaning initiative is falling on students and teachers in Grades 4 to 8.

Music and other specialized classrooms may have to make way for additional primary classes. "We have told schools they need to use classrooms for classrooms," said Peter Gooch, the TDSB's director of policy, strategic planning and accountability. "How frequent that will be is under analysis now."

Music classrooms could disappear at Thorncliffe Park Elementary School in East York, Thomas L. Wells Public School in Morningside Heights and Northlea Elementary and Middle School in East York, according to reports from the Toronto District Music Coalition, a parent group.

"The first thing to go is music," said Cynthia Dann-Beardsley, an executive member of the coalition. "The music teacher is up on the block every year."

Ms. Dann-Beardsley said parents often find out too late to protest, and that school boards don't communicate enough.

"As soon as you don't tell people what you are doing it poisons the atmosphere," she said.

According to Annie Kidder, executive director of People for Education, Wilkinson Public School in Riverdale may create a classroom in its basement in 2007–08, which she said was "hardly tall enough for a grown-up to walk upright."

The Liberal government has added $2 billion to education spending over the last two budgets, bringing the total expenditure to $17 billion per year. About 2,000 new teachers have been hired to reduce class sizes, with some of the money going to a teacher-training program.

"I agree there are challenges in implementation," said Education Minister Sandra Pupatello. "But I'm happy to say those challenges are a result of the government's qualitative improvement.

"'We need to get class sizes down. It's absolutely essential to have smaller class sizes in the early years," Ms. Pupatello added.

But Ms. Kidder said the government is putting too much of a priority on enforcing the cap.

"It's one of those things that's really easy to sell politically," Ms. Kidder said. "Think about what you don't get [in order] to lower class sizes—if it means my kid isn't going to have a music teacher anymore or be in a big class later, is it worth the payoff?"

Though principals try to keep class sizes lower for Grades 4 to 6, Parents for Education said Grade 7 and 8 classes often have more than 30 students and that the averages are deceiving.

"A lot of Grade 5, 6, 7, 8 parents are worried about class size," said Ms. Kidder, who has received phone calls about class sizes in the mid-30s.

Principals in the Toronto District School Board have previously had a fair amount of autonomy on class sizes, but Mr. Gooch said they now must follow strict guidelines to implement the province-wide cap. The TDSB's average for Grades 4 to 8 in 2005–06 was 24.3 students, which is being increased to the provincial standard of 25 students per teacher.

Ms. Pupatello said the cap cannot be looked at as a stand-alone policy initiative. It is being combined with a teacher-training initiative that focuses on individual attention termed "differentiated instruction," whereby teachers will use multiple teaching methods to accommodate students' different needs.

Ms. Kidder said the primary cap is only making a marginal difference in primary class size, noting some studies say class sizes need to be at 17 or under to have a real effect.

Mr. Gooch said they may have to change attendance boundaries in the future or they may be able to solve the problem with poratables [sic] [temporary classrooms typically housed in trailers] and additions. He said the province has been recognizing the problems TDSB is facing.

"Part of making the cap work is making sure we have good classrooms," said Mr. Gooch.

Discussion Questions

1. How would you describe the implementation context facing the class size reduction policy described in the article?
2. Drawing on your knowledge of the different stages of implementation, which stages are relevant for the context highlighted in the article?

3. What are the implementation challenges to class size reduction implied by this newspaper article? Provide evidence for your response.
4. What activities would you recommend to address the implementation challenges you identified in Discussion Question 3? How would your response change if you were leading a school, district, state/province, or nation?

Selected Websites

U.S. Department of Education. Investing in Innovation Fund. Available at

http://www2.ed.gov/programs/innovation/index.html.

The official website of the U.S. Department of Education that describes the Investing in Innovation Fund, commonly referred to as i3. Education leaders may find this site helpful because it details the purpose of the grant and describes the application procedures, including eligibility. The information provided at this site offers useful insight on the factors that federal policymakers consider important in ensuring successful implementation of innovative education policies.

National Governors Association. Available at

http://www.nga.org/cms/home.html.

The official website of the National Governors Association (NGA). Membership includes the governors of the 50 states of the United States, its three territories (American Samoa, Guam, and the U.S. Virgin Islands), and its two commonwealths (Puerto Rico and the Northern Mariana Islands). Education leaders may find this site helpful for the information

it provides on the legislative agenda of key policymakers and the research it offers on best practices. By clicking on the tab labeled NGA Center for Best Practices, education leaders can access a plethora of information on what is happening in the states, and a description of major policy issues and initiatives highlighted by the organization.

Center on Education Policy. Available at

http://www.cep-dc.org/.

The official website of the Center on Education Policy (CEP). A key focus of the organization's stated mission is to help "Americans better understand the role of public education in a democracy and the need to improve the academic quality of public schools." Education leaders at the elementary and secondary levels may find this site especially useful for the information it provides on the history, facts, and leading issues facing public education. All leaders may find helpful the press releases and links provided on the progress made by states in implementing key education policies because of the insight those materials provide on implementation as it relates to organizational and community capacity.

Selected References

Fullan, M. (1999). *Change forces: The sequel.* **London: Falmer.**

This book is a classic look at organizations and the complexities involved in implementing sustainable reform in the education arena. Education leaders may find this book helpful because of the implementation challenges it highlights, and especially for the

insight it offers on how education leaders and organizations respond to change.

Louis, K. S., & Miles, M. B. (1990). *Improving the urban high school.* **New York: Teachers College Press.**

Though the empirical research is more than 20 years old, the findings remain relevant. Using case studies, the authors document and describe the education reforms that were implemented in selected U.S. urban high schools. Education leaders may find this book helpful because of the practical guidance provided and the insight it offers regarding the influence of time and other factors on the success of implementation.

Miles, K. H., & Frank, S. (2008). *The strategic school: Making the most of people, time, and money.* **Thousand Oaks, CA: Corwin Press and National Association of Secondary School Principals.**

Miles and Frank examine ways in which school leaders can act strategically in their particular school context. Education leaders may find this book useful as they consider the implementation of policy. The authors provide practical information regarding the prioritization of goals; the need to develop a coherent, systemic strategy for reform; and

the need to focus implementation efforts on student learning.

Walker, E. M. (2002, August 4). The politics of school-based management: Understanding the process of devolving authority in urban school districts. *Education Policy Analysis Archives, 10*(33). **Retrieved October 7, 2011, from http://epaa.asu.edu/ epaa/v10n33.html.**

Walker examines decentralization efforts in the state of New Jersey and highlights factors that contributed to the lack of effective implementation. She offers alternatives that can address some of these challenges and that can lead to what she considers to be more authentic, decentralized governance structures. Education leaders may find this article helpful because of the information it provides on the need for individual readiness as well as organizational and community capacity in setting the stage for successful reform.

11

Monitor Outputs

CHAPTER OBJECTIVES

After reading this chapter, you will be able to:

- Define and describe policy monitoring
- Identify the functions of monitoring
- Determine what data you should track
- Identify key methodological concerns of tracking

EDUCATION VIGNETTE

You are a newly elected governor and have made education the cornerstone of your leadership platform. Your state has not done well on most measures of education performance both by national and international standards. You call a meeting with your commissioner of education as well as other key education leaders in your state. At the meeting, you ask these educators for their analysis of why students are not doing better. A variety of responses emerge, but you are not sure what data prompted the responses, so you ask a few more questions. You want to know if most 5-year-olds are screened for disability and if that would make a difference. You are told that your state does not collect data on the percentage of students who are screened. You ask if there is any information on how many children attend early childhood education programs and, of these, how many go on to college; these data are also missing. You request clarity on how dropouts are counted. The response is different from what you expected. You ask if there are data on the percentage of teachers with national merit certification. Those data exist, but you are not able to connect those teachers with student performance statewide. You wonder if greater investment in libraries would be helpful, but no one is sure what percentage of students actually use public libraries and how many books the public libraries contain.

In frustration, you ask them how they know why performance is lagging if they are not keeping track of key variables? An awkward silence fills the room. Finally, a person puts up his hand and asks you what data you would like them to monitor from now on. What do you say?

WHAT IS MONITORING?

Webster's Encyclopedic Unabridged Dictionary of the English Language, 1989, defines *monitoring* as a process where you "observe, record, or detect an operation or condition with instruments that have *no effect upon the operation or condition"* [italics added]. This definition is not strictly true for the monitoring process in education because sometimes the mere act of monitoring changes behavior. Many teachers may have noticed that taking attendance can lead to students showing up more frequently, even if attendance is not a component of their grade. The publication of student performance in report cards has sometimes caused educators to allocate their time differently, even before high-stakes exams resulted in big consequences for teachers and schools. Consequently, the definition of monitoring offered by Patton and Sawicki (1993) is more fitting for education settings. They define policy monitoring as the "process of recording changes in key variables after policy or program implementation" (p. 368).

Monitoring offers information on what happened and can inform analytical decisions on how it happened and why. It is the penultimate step in the policy analytical process and connects the actions outlined in the implementation plan with policy objectives. Monitoring is descriptive and explicative, not judgmental. Notwithstanding, what you choose to monitor denotes your priorities. In other words, what you count lets us know what counts.

FUNCTIONS OF MONITORING

Policy analysis is about addressing a problematic condition. To know how effective your efforts are at resolving the problem, you have to document relevant aspects of its context. Manipulable and unmanipulable actions, as well as controllable and uncontrollable effects, are linked to the policy process (Dunn, 2004). **Manipulable actions** are those that vary and that policymakers can control; for example, principals can change the pickup location for students in their school. **Unmanipulable actions** are those that are outside the purview of policymakers. For example, principals in traditional public schools do not typically determine the demographic makeup of their student body. **Controllable effects** are related to manipulable actions and are outcomes that education leaders can influence. For example, education leaders can put procedures in place that may result in a decline of behavior referrals. In that context, the number of behavioral referrals is an example of controllable effects. **Uncontrollable effects** are related to unmanipulable actions and are outputs that are outside the command of education leaders. For example, school leaders may find that that they have little say in the effect of state and district cuts on their overall budget. By monitoring behavior and outputs associated with tackling the problem, you provide data for evaluation and prediction that informs knowledge on whether and why a policy produced the desired results. Consequently, there are four primary functions of monitoring: *compliance, accounting, auditing,* and *explanation* (Dunn, 2004).

Compliance

To address compliance, you have to produce data on whether people did what they were supposed to do. What were the actions of implementers? What was the behavior of targeted groups? These are process-oriented questions, and the implementation plan that you produced earlier will provide helpful guidelines on the variables that you should track. Determine how you will measure these activities and how you and others will know what denotes compliance. As part of that exercise, review your chosen measures to ensure that they reflect the activities called for and make sure that they contain data that are collectable. For example, Minnesota laws require charter schools to submit annual reports detailing their activities throughout the previous school year. A measure of compliance that state policymakers could use regarding charter school providers is to track the percentage of schools that actually submit the required forms.

Accounting

When monitoring focuses on the indicators of social change, it allows you to go beyond simple compliance and to track the results of that compliance and any existing preconditions. The outputs that you track will be tied to the objectives of the program and may be objective or subjective. **Objective outputs** are indicators that can be counted. For example, if you indicate that participation in early education programs is an important variable, then you would want to track the level of participation over time. Another objective indicator is the percentage of students who passed an exam. **Subjective outputs** are indicators that depend on the perspective and perception of those collecting and analyzing the data. For example, if you are concerned with the level of satisfaction that consumers have toward specific programs, you would have to measure that satisfaction. Another example of subjective data is the determination of whether or not a student passed the written portion of a language exam (e.g., Lussenhop, 2011).

Several domestic and international organizations provide data on crucial social indicators. On the national front, the National Center for Education Statistics offers important information on several indicators that reflect the condition of education in the United States. Internationally, the Organisation for Economic Co-operation and Development supplies useful economic, environmental, and social statistics for 30 democratic countries worldwide. The monitoring of indicators provides a useful context for measuring progress in those societies.

Auditing

Tracing the allocation of resources is important in assessing the effectiveness of policy and determining the efficiency of input use. **Effectiveness** looks at how the use of resources connects to goals. **Efficiency** refers to an absence of waste and is often described as the "bang for the buck" that you get for the investment that you make.

To determine if resources are allocated appropriately, you need to track whether they are reaching the intended target. For example, with increased interest in improving math and science participation and performance, educators want to know how much resources actually make it to these classes. New York State (NYS) is relatively unique among states in the United States in its collection of data that allows you to calculate how much student time was spent in particular subjects. For example, using the data provided in the NYS Basic Education Data Set, Alexander (1998) tracked changes in the per-pupil student hours spent in the core curriculum from 1975 through 1995. On a national scale, U.S. Department of Education (2004) tracked changes in course-taking patterns nationwide using the data available from the National Center for Education Statistics on high school transcripts.

Monitoring for auditing purposes is especially important because policymakers increasingly want more nuanced information on the efficiency implications of the policies that they enact. For example, would greater investment in the sciences lead to greater gains in student achievement than similar investment in other areas? One finding of the U.S. Department of Education high school transcript study is that, regardless of subject area, students struggle when the curriculum is wide (covering a lot of topics) rather than deep (addressing advanced subject matters).

To enhance the effectiveness and efficiency of the organization, policymakers may decide to change how resources are allocated. This change may require the monitoring of different or additional data from before. For example, the Elementary and Secondary Education Act (ESEA) of 1965 has always focused on addressing some of the negative impacts of poverty on student outcomes. However, poor students continue to fare badly on standardized tests relative to their more wealthy peers. More recent modifications of that act called for federal funds to be distributed to schools (not just districts) where poverty is at the levels defined by the federal government as being problematic. Previously once a district was eligible for Title 1 funds, district administrators decided which of their schools would receive the dollars geared toward addressing the challenges of poverty. For monitoring purposes, therefore, federal leaders will now have to track where the resources land *within* and not just *between* school districts. This approach targets more precisely the flow of federal funds. By monitoring the flow of these funds, policymakers have more useful data to determine if more targeted funding leads to more effective results.

Explanation

The focus of this monitoring function is to explain why the outputs that you track look the way they do or are the way they are. This goes beyond the simple act of describing and provides information on relationships. The explanation function of monitoring is essential for leaders to know how to proceed once they receive a description of their status. By tracking behavior and outputs, monitoring provides a needed feedback loop that helps to explain the connections among problem definition, program implementation, and success. After all, the reason that we care about compliance, accounting, and auditing is because we think that actions matter, that how we spend our time and money matters, and that the interaction between process and product determines the impact of policy. However, not all data are useful in clarifying relationships. Given the constraints on resources, you need to select what data you track, focusing on those data that help you understand and address more fully the problem you want to investigate.

WHAT SHOULD WE TRACK?

Functions, Data, and Data Sources

What you choose to track depends on the purpose of monitoring. If you are monitoring for compliance, you need to document the completion of tasks and their appropriate measures. You must balance the benefits of such measurements against the time and dollar constraints associated with collecting these data. For example, many schools have time cards to ensure that teachers arrive to work on time. In the case of traditional public schools in New York City, teachers are required to clock in if they arrive after the scheduled start time but not if they arrive before. The compliance data provided by this mechanism may be misleading, however. I know of a teacher who clocks in only when she is late; does not clock in when she is early; and does not clock out when she works overtime, which she does often. If she is typical of the other staff members, we would have inaccurate measures for determining how compliant teachers are in terms of the number of hours worked at school. As an education leader, you need to understand the rationale for compliance and be careful in your choice of measures for monitoring behavior. That is, education leaders need to enhance rather than diminish organizational effectiveness. Consequently, they must avoid rewarding just tightly confined behaviors by only tracking measures that are narrow definitions of professional responsibilities.

If you are tracking data to provide information on outputs, these data will be tied directly to the goals of solving the problem and to the objectives that you identified in your expanded problem statement. Policymakers can monitor changes in the indicators of what is valued by the community or organization. While data on compliance are process-oriented, data for accounting are results-oriented. Often, the product-oriented data make it to school report cards that are produced by districts and states annually. The data in these reports can be narrowly focused on academics, including proficiency rates on key state exams, percentage of students taking Advanced Placement courses, and so on. Increasingly, education leaders are also providing information on the climate of the school, as measured by surveys given to the staff members and sometimes to families and students.

If you are monitoring to ensure that resources are used appropriately, you need to provide information on the flow of resources within and outside the organization. Data from accounting and budgeting documents are helpful sources. Policymakers often employ accounting firms to monitor the use of resources in public agencies. In higher education settings, we often think of this process through the various accreditation processes that take place. Those who monitor organizations often look at the staffing and resources that are central to their core mission. These reviewers often try to determine if these resources are being employed in the way stipulated and if they are sufficient to meet the standards established by the accrediting agency. For example, the National Council for Accreditation of Teacher Education (NCATE) sends out examiners to review education programs that are seeking its accreditation. These reviewers examine the units in the higher education organization that are primarily responsible for preparation of professional school personnel, including teachers and other education leaders. While the language used on NCATE's website indicates that the site visits are evaluative, the review process is similar to the one that I describe for the auditing function of monitoring. That is, the NCATE examiners visit the organizations seeking accreditation and assess the capacity of each organization to deliver its program effectively.

If you are monitoring to provide information on the impact of the program, you need to provide information not only on the short-term outputs of the program but also on the long-term outcomes. For you to speak credibly about the impact of a program, you must explain the relationship between the outcomes and outputs documented and programmatic effort. Developing a service, effort, and accomplishment (SEA) plan based on a comprehensive literature review is helpful (e.g., Fountain, 1991). For example, leaders of the Governmental Accounting Standards Board (GASB) in the 1990s focused their efforts on producing reports that were more informative regarding the

Table 11.1　Relationship Among Functions of Monitoring, What to Track, and Data Source

Functions of Monitoring	What to Track	Source of Data
Compliance	Activities and tasks	Implementation plan
Accounting	Objectives of analysis	Problem and goal statement
Auditing	Resources and benefits	Budgets and accounts, accreditation documents
Explanation	Variables identified in theory of action	Evaluation reports, broad literature review

impact of governmental entities. One of the reasons these reports were valuable was that, along with the literature, leaders could see the connections among various activities, context, and the results that they produced. These types of connections are helpful in developing explanations about why certain education policies produced the results sought while other policies did not.

Three Key Monitoring Questions

Education leaders can often miss the importance of developing a systemic monitoring plan because the monitoring step is conceptually "stuck" between two major steps in the policy analytical process: implementation and evaluation. Practitioners tend to focus on the implementation phase because that is the phase over which they have the most control and for which they are regularly held accountable. Policymakers tend to focus on evaluation because they want to be assured that the policy worked the way that it was intended. However, the data from monitoring is what links these stages

- **Why am I tracking these data?**
  - Do they provide information on key aspects of the behavior I would like to see among implementers? How so?
  - Do they tell me something about the behavior or performance of the targeted group? How much do they tell me about these activities or outputs?
  - Does the information gained inform a key part of our mission?
- **Who should track the data being collected?**
  - Should I use someone inside or outside the organization to collect the data needed?
  - What do I gain from using an insider? What do I gain from using an outsider?
  - Is the person responsible for collection suitably trained to gather the information required?
- **How often should I track these data?**
  - How much information do I need to tell the story about compliance, results, or resource use?
  - What does the literature and practice indicate in terms of the data points needed?
  - Does the law dictate how often certain data need to be tracked?

FIGURE 11.1　Key Questions to Consider When Creating a Monitoring Plan

and these concerns. Consequently, education leaders must develop a plan for monitoring to ensure that they do not miss opportunities to collect appropriate data. The basic monitoring plan should address three questions: Why should we track these data? Who should track the required data? and How often should we track these data?

WHY SHOULD WE TRACK THESE DATA? If you are tracking a particular activity, it should be because it reflects key aspects of the behavior that you would like to see among implementers and the targeted audience. If you cannot think of a reason that you need that information, do not spend scarce resources collecting or analyzing those data. Your reasons for tracking select variables must be tied to accountability and fulfilling the functions of monitoring. You should be able to explain the rationale behind why specific data are important, and you should have a better reason for collecting and presenting data than "because it's there."

WHO SHOULD TRACK THE REQUIRED DATA? The data that you collect may be quantitative or qualitative, objective or subjective, as well as from primary or secondary sources. As noted in Chapter 4, *quantitative data* focus on numbers, while *qualitative data* focus on words. *Objective data* are reliable, often quantifiable, and do not change with the perception of the analyst. *Subjective data* vary with the perception of the analyst and are often associated with qualitative assessments. *Primary sources of data* are collected first hand, for example, the information learned in interviews and observations. *Secondary sources of data* are collected by someone else and are used to inform analysis. For example, if you rely on the data provided by the National Center for Education Statistics, you are using secondary sources.

The person or organization that you choose to collect those details must be sufficiently versed in gathering the appropriate information. With secondary analyses, the data have already been collected by an outside source and you simply have to analyze or present them. If you have to collect the data firsthand, you must weigh the pros and cons of contracting out or using inside personnel. In instances where the data may implicate the performance of your organization, it may be helpful to use outside personnel. By using external personnel, your data may be more credible to outsiders and less susceptible to distortion. For example, in the high-stakes testing environment in Texas in the 1990s, Houston school district officials undercounted the number of dropouts and overcounted the percentage of students who were college bound (Schemo & Fessenden, 2003). These errors called into question previous assertions regarding the success of high-stakes testing and the use of a basic curriculum in improving student performance. These findings are especially important because the expectations of the No Child Left Behind Act were grounded in the evidence produced from the Houston school district.

Although using outside personnel may be helpful, such use is not always the most appropriate choice. Education leaders may choose to use personnel inside the organization because it may be more cost-effective to do so. In addition, inside personnel may be more familiar with the organizational context and may have longstanding relationships with the implementers and benefactors of the policy. Consequently, inside personnel may be able to develop a more trusting relationship, which may encourage implementers and benefactors of the policy to be forthcoming in providing needed information.

HOW OFTEN SHOULD WE TRACK THESE DATA? You need to track data often enough to provide useful feedback to the implementers, participants, and evaluators of the program. The frequency with which you monitor key variables may depend on the policy questions that you seek to answer and the conceptual underpinnings of your theory of action. For example, if you are interested in the impact of summer breaks on the decline in student achievement, you must record student achievement at intervals before the summer as well as after (e.g., Cooper, Nye, & Charlton, 1996). Sometimes the law tells you the frequency at which you must monitor select data. For example, federal regulations require the annual monitoring of the academic progress of students in the United States. These data are reflected in the annually produced National Assessment of Educational Progress (NAEP). The NAEP scores are a nationally representative assessment of what U.S. students know and can do in specified subjects, and have been collected since 1969.

METHODS OF TRACKING

Establishing Baselines

Monitoring is not a one-shot deal. The value of monitoring in the policy analysis process is that it provides data on the impact of actions taken to resolve a policy issue. For those data to be meaningful, you need to establish appropriate baselines to gauge whether changes in behavior, outputs, and outcomes can be attributed to the enacted policy. In some cases, data already exist and you do not need to collect it, and baseline data are also readily available. What time period you choose to start your analysis depends on data availability and your theory of action. For example, examining high school transcripts, U.S. Department of Education (2004) documented the changes in course-taking patterns in secondary schools across the United States. Their analysis offers important insight on the relationship between curricula choices and student outcomes, which in turn had important policy implications.

- **Establish baselines.**
  - What time period will serve as a baseline?
  - Do you have a reason for choosing that time frame?
  - Are the baseline data already collected?
- **What change is being measured?**
  - What periods of time are being compared?
  - Which jurisdictions are being compared?
  - Are the comparisons credible?
- **What are the units of analysis?**
  - What type of change interests you? Are you interested in individual, group, organizational, or systems change?
  - What aspect of change is your focus? Are you interested in changes in input, process, output, or impact variables?
  - What measures will allow you to capture these changes?

FIGURE 11.2 Key Considerations When Determining Tracking Methods

Determining What Change Is Being Measured

A full description of methods to determine which change is being measured is beyond the scope of this book. Notwithstanding, education leaders must have an understanding of how one can use monitoring to determine what change is being measured.

MEASUREMENT ACROSS SPACE AND TIME.   Ideally, you will track changes both over time and across locations. Common analytical methods call for an **interrupted time series analysis,** where analysts document what happened before and after the policy treatment. Looking at changes in the patterns of key variables in locations with and without the policy also helps to distinguish the impact on behavior and outputs caused by the implemented policy versus other factors. By accounting for variations in time and space, researchers can control for some of the threats to validity common to social research. **Threats to validity** are factors that undermine the credibility of your findings. For example, critics may argue that it is the novelty of a policy that accounts for improved performance. Others may argue that teacher assistance during exams may have accounted for a rise in student test scores. Yet others may assert that, as students and teachers get used to a particular exam format, scores get better, even though learning per se may not have improved. As an education leader, you want to address as many of these concerns as you can. It is hard for community members to follow your lead if they do not believe the data support where you want to take them.

UNITS OF ANALYSIS.   The **unit of analysis** you use to measure change depends on how you defined the problem and the change in which you are interested: individual, group, organizational, or system. Consequently, you may find yourself tracking data for individual students, teachers, schools, districts, states, school systems, and so on. The variables that you measure may be tied to input, process, output, or impact. **Input variables** are used by the organization to fulfill its mission or to produce particular results. Looking at education organizations, these types of variables may include the number of teachers employed in schools, the curriculum being used, the dollars allocated, and so on. **Process variables** describe the way in which inputs are organized in order to produce the results sought. In education, they are sometimes referred to as treatment variables (e.g., Garner, 2004) and may include data on tracking, block scheduling, and so on. **Output variables** include tangible measures produced by the organization. Economists and others often refer to these variables as productivity measures, and these data tend to influence the ranking of schools at all levels of education. These data include graduation rates, the number of students who are proficient in particular subjects, the dropout rates, and so on. Data documenting impact tend to have longer-range implications than output data, but they may also be more difficult to track. **Impact variables** often reflect the long-term outcomes that education leaders would like to see. These data include information on employment, income earned, citizen participation, and so on.

DISPLAYING DATA.   To monitor the effect of policy, you can simply plot the measures of relevant variables over time and across locations using graphs, tables, indices, or statistical analyses (Dunn, 2004). Readers should be able to make the connection between what you monitor and the desired change you highlighted in your problem statement. In the end, monitoring is the basic means by which education leaders can check their work and document key information about their organization.

Chapter Summary

Monitoring offers recurring information on what happened and can inform analytical decisions on how it happened and why. It is the penultimate step in the policy analytical process and connects the actions outlined in the implementation plan with policy objectives. Monitoring is descriptive and explicative, not judgmental. By monitoring behavior and outputs, you provide data for evaluation and prediction that informs knowledge on whether a policy produced the desired results.

There are four primary monitoring functions: compliance, accounting, auditing, and explanation. To address compliance, you must produce data on whether people did what they were supposed to. To address accounting concerns, you document and keep track of subjective and objective indicators of social change. This work allows you to go beyond simple compliance and to track the results of that compliance. The outputs that you track will be tied to the objectives of the program. If you monitor to fulfill audit responsibilities, you must track whether invested resources are reaching the intended target(s). By tracking both behavior and output, monitoring provides a needed feedback loop that helps to explain the connections among problem definition, program implementation, and success.

Ultimately, you keep track of data because you want to know if you have made a difference. To address that question, you must do more than simply document measures of key variables; you must tie those measures to the problem statement. In other words, you must evaluate if your policy worked. The creation of an evaluation plan is the final step in the policy analysis process, and it is the subject of Chapter 12.

Review Questions

1. Why is monitoring an important step in the policy analytical process?
2. How does an implementation plan help in the development of a monitoring guide?
3. Is an implementation plan the same as a monitoring guide? Explain your response.
4. Return to the chapter-opening education vignette. Does your response to the question change after reading this chapter? If so, how? If not, how does your original response reflect the themes of the chapter?

News Story for Analysis

National Post (f/k/a The Financial Post) (Canada). February 16, 2007 Friday. National Edition. Better monitoring urged for overseas student placements: University of Waterloo: Student allegedly worked with terrorist group in Sri Lanka. *BYLINE:* Adrian Humphreys, *National Post*. **SECTION:** CANADA; Pg. A8.

A prominent Ontario university needs to better monitor its foreign placements after one of its students was charged with working for a banned terrorist group, activities alleged to have occurred during a co-op work term in Sri Lanka, according to an internal study by the school.

At the same time, the University of Waterloo says an independent audit of the finances of the Waterloo Tamil Students Association (WATSA) confirmed links between some of the men arrested in an anti-terrorism investigation in the United States and the student club but found no "inappropriate transactions" in the group's finances.

The university called for the probes after a series of arrests in Canada and the United States last August of Canadian men of Tamil descent on charges they were buying weapons and military hardware, laundering money and smuggling equipment in support of the Tamil Tigers.

None of the charges have been proven in court.

Four of those indicted in the U.S. were former or current students at the University of Waterloo; two had held executive positions with WATSA.

One, Suresh Sriskandarajah, is accused in the United States of being a Tiger operative named "Waterloo Suresh" who used his status as a student to hide his work for the Tigers.

Mr. Sriskandarajah completed a university co-op term in Tiger-controlled areas of Sri Lanka during the period covered by the FBI's allegations for an organization he created himself.

"The main thing is we are dealing with very small amounts of money. These clubs are operating on a shoestring," said Marin van Nierop, a university spokesman.

Auditors with Deloitte & Touche were hired by the university to analyze 10 years of funding and expenditures of WATSA, a recognized student club at the University of Waterloo.

During that period, the club reported $9,200 was received and disbursed for club activities, about $7,500 of which was raised by its members.

The remaining $1,700 came from the Federation of Students, which funds recognized student clubs, according to a summary of the audit provided by the university.

The school declined to provide the full audit to the National Post.

Approximately 60% of the money was spent on renting university facilities for events.

The rest was used to reimburse members for expenses and purchases, in small dollar amounts, and a donation to the Tamil Children's Endowment Fund.

The audit found that $100 of the club's money was given to one of those who was arrested to reimburse him for food purchased on behalf of the club. The person was not identified.

"Information provided by the university indicates that the university did not make any payments to WATSA, and that direct payments made by the University to individuals who were arrested pertained to normal course transactions for bursaries, scholarships, engineering endowment funds and student awards," the university's report says.

"The university is satisfied that there were no inappropriate transactions pertaining to WATSA or payments made to the individuals who were arrested, either through WATSA or directly by the university," the report says.

The university committee probing the work placement process found room for the school to tighten its oversight of students working abroad on placements that are self-generated.

The report said students working abroad need an on-site visit to authenticate the work and "address the risks."

Where it is not feasible for a co-op staff member to conduct such checks, a university faculty member travelling in the area, an alumni living in the area or staff at Canada's diplomatic missions might be able to assist, the report says.

The Liberation Tigers of Tamil Eelam, commonly called the Tamil Tigers or the LTTE, are fighting for a Tamil homeland separate from Sri Lanka and are notorious for their use of suicide bombings and assassinations. The group was declared a terrorist organization in the United States in 1997 and in Canada last year.

Those arrested are still before the courts, either waiting trial in the United States or free on bail in Canada fighting extradition requests to face trial in New York.

Source: Material reprinted with the express permission of: "National Post Inc."

Discussion Questions

1. What are the different functions of monitoring that are highlighted in this article? How do you know?

2. What information would you track if you were monitoring education organizations? Why?

3. If you were the leader of the university, how would you respond to the information garnered from the monitoring process? What would be your next steps?

4. Given the information provided in the audit, would you come to the same conclusions as the university spokesperson? Explain your response.

5. How would your response to Discussion Question 3 change if you were the leader of the country?

Selected Websites

Governmental Accounting Standards Board. Available at

http://www.gasb.org/.

The official website of the Governmental Accounting Standards Board (GASB). Its board members are appointed by the trustees of the Financial Accounting Foundation (FAF), which is an independent, private-sector organization responsible for setting financial reporting standards. The GASB is responsible for establishing accountings and financial reporting standards for U.S. state and local governments. Education leaders may find the information available under the Education tab on this site to be useful. Especially helpful is the PDF document on service, efforts, and accomplishments. It offers guidelines on the appropriate ways for governmental organizations (including schools and districts) to monitor and report key financial and output data.

Organisation for Economic Co-operation and Development. Available at

www.sourceoecd.org and http://www.oecd-ilibrary. org/.

The official websites of the Organisation for Economic Co-operation and Development (OECD). Education leaders may find these sites helpful for the plethora of data that they provide on indicators representing various aspects of a country's well-being. While policymakers may be impressed by the wealth of statistics provided on a variety of policy issues, education leaders may be especially interested in comparative data on education

statistics. Once on the websites, education data are easily accessible by searching for that term on the homepage.

The National Council for Accreditation of Teacher Education. Available at

http://www.ncate.org/.

The official website for the National Council for Accreditation of Teacher Education (NCATE). The organization is an accreditation agency and establishes standards for higher education organizations preparing teachers and other professional school personnel. Education leaders may find this site helpful for the insight it provides on how the auditing function of monitoring is realized in practical contexts.

U.S. Department of Education. Institute of Education Sciences. National Center for Education Statistics. Condition of Education. Available at

http://nces.ed.gov/programs/coe/.

The official website of the U.S. Department of Education, Institute of Education Science. It provides an online source of the annually produced *The Condition of Education*, published by that institute. The website contains a collection of the indicators and analyses published in *The Condition of Education* 2000–2010. Education leaders may find this site helpful in their monitoring process because many of the data they need may be available on this site. It gives education leaders useful guidance on what data should be tracked as they monitor the inputs, processes, outputs, and impacts of their organization.

Selected References

Cooper, H. M., Nye, B. A., & Charlton, K. (1996, Fall). The effects of summer vacation on achievement test scores: A narrative and meta-analytic review. *Review of Educational Research, 66*, 227–268.

Cooper and his colleagues examined the findings of 39 research articles to monitor the incidence of

summer learning loss among children. Education leaders may find this article helpful because it reflects the explanation function of monitoring. Synthesizing the data found in the articles reviewed, Cooper and colleagues document changes in learning associated with summer learning loss and offer explanations for this phenomenon.

Fountain, J. R. (1991, Winter). **Service efforts and accomplishments reporting. New approaches to productivity: Proceedings of the Fourth National Public Sector Productivity Conference.** *Public Productivity & Management Review, 15*(2), **191–198.**

Fountain describes the purpose of service, efforts, and accomplishments reporting, indicating that it is a means of increasing accountability. Education leaders may find this short article interesting because of the background it provides on efforts to create this reporting document. This article also describes the auditing and explanation functions of the monitoring process.

U.S. Department of Education. Institute of Education Sciences. National Center for Education Statistics (NCES-2004-455). (2004, March). The High School Transcript Study: A decade of change in curricula and achievement, 1990–2000.

This document is published through the National Center for Education Statistics and details changes in the high school curriculum-taking patterns in the United States. Education leaders may find this report interesting not only for the data it provides but the insight it offers on the use of indicators in the accounting function of monitoring.

12

Evaluate Outcomes

CHAPTER OBJECTIVES

After reading this chapter, you will be able to:

- Distinguish between monitoring and evaluating
- Identify the different foci of evaluation
- Describe the main types of evaluation
- Identify methodological concerns of evaluation

EDUCATION VIGNETTE

You are the education minister of a province. It is the end of the school year, and you are reflecting on the effectiveness of your programs. As part of that reflection, you look at the success of policies in other locales. You are particularly interested in the impact of a controversial education policy enacted in a neighboring province. This policy officially aims to improve the learning environment of alienated teens. It discourages teachers from penalizing students who turn in late or incomplete assignments if teachers feel that students have already met the requirements for a particular topic. Proponents of the policy argue that it allows teachers to think outside the box and promotes learning as a supportive, developmental enterprise with motivational, rather than punitive, pedagogical methods. They argue that this policy will be especially helpful for struggling students who may need more time to succeed. Policy opponents counter that the policy is a slap in the face to teachers. They object that the policy undermines the professional judgment of educators because it forces them to accept late work and to use complex bureaucratic formulas to determine student grades. Critics further accuse provincial policymakers of trying to inflate graduation rates at the expense of instilling important learning skills and discipline in students. They claim that this policy actually hurts struggling students because they put off important assignments and miss key learning opportunities.

What information will help you to know who is right? How will you know if the policy worked or not?

EVALUATING VERSUS MONITORING

Education leaders must marry facts and judgment in their evaluation of policy and programs. Evaluation is more than just monitoring. It is an explicitly value-laden phase of the policy analytic process. By contrast, monitoring is essentially empirical and is a prerequisite for evaluation. While you can monitor without evaluating, you cannot evaluate without monitoring. Monitoring provides descriptive information about what happened, how it happened, and why. Evaluation offers a normative assessment of what difference those actions made. In short, the distinction between these policy steps is the difference between a journalistic telling of a story and a critic's assessment of whether that story was good or bad. If you simply record the facts without offering judgment, you are monitoring. If you make meaning of those facts and offer a conclusion on their impact, you are evaluating.

FOCUS OF EVALUATION

Evaluation focuses on the achievement of goals and objectives. It is the production of information about the value of policy outcomes. In that process, you may revisit whether the original goals were worthwhile. However, evaluation is not necessarily about assessing the value of policy goals per se but gauging how well the policy actually achieved them. Revising the goals essentially entails a reevaluation of the problem statement, which is a function of the entire policy analytic process, not just the formal evaluative step.

Actual evaluation occurs after implementation (ex post), but it is imperative to have an evaluation plan from the onset. Ensure that the plan you develop allows you to assess if the policy addressed the problem fully, partially, or not at all. Provide clear guidance on what constitutes an improvement of the problematic condition. Will any movement in the desired direction suffice, or does a certain threshold have to be met? Justify your decisions. In other words, evaluation should be based on both *values* and *empirical* evidence. You should be able to provide *descriptive* and *normative* grounding for what counts as success. As noted, values are your underlying beliefs. Empirical evidence refers to data collected from reality. Descriptive grounding gets at statements of fact. Normative grounding gets at statements of values.

Stakeholders must find your evaluative framework relevant and credible. They need to connect your definition of success with your identification of the policy issue. Devote adequate resources to the evaluation process so that you can make plausible links among policy objectives, policy outcomes, and your conclusions. Evaluation is ultimately about assessing the impact of policy and determining its success at achieving policy goals. Along the way, evaluations can provide developmental information on whether programs are on track.

TYPES AND PURPOSES OF EVALUATION

Two types of evaluation are useful for this chapter discussion: formative evaluation and summative evaluation. Each one serves distinct purposes, which will be discussed separately in the next two subsections.

Formative Evaluations

Formative evaluations produce ongoing information that can help implementers of the program improve performance. They include feedback that allows implementers to choose different tasks or improve their performance on existing ones. A suggestion box is a simple means of getting instant feedback. For K–12 teachers, peer review through classroom observations by fellow teachers and principals is another example. The use of computer-based assessments (e.g., Yeh, 2009) is yet another. With rapid assessments, students use computers to complete assignments, and teachers can receive immediate diagnostic information on how students performed. This approach allows for quick and empirically grounded identification of student academic strengths and weaknesses. Principals can also use the overall results of a class to compare average classroom achievement (and teacher performance). By using computer technology, principals and colleagues can offer feedback that teachers can use and by which students can benefit before the school year is finished. Yeh (2009) found, for example, that class size reduction was 124 times less cost-effective than the implementation of systems that rapidly assess student progress in math and reading two to five times per week.

Summative Evaluations

Summative evaluations occur at the end of a program's life cycle, when enough time has passed to determine whether a program worked. They supply information on the extent that chosen alternatives contribute to the goals and objectives of the program. These findings, in turn, contribute to the expectations held of new or revised policy alternatives. Summative evaluations may be completed for individuals, groups, organizations, or systems. Summative evaluations of students include their end-of-year report cards. Summative evaluations for teachers include the principal's end-of-year evaluations. The summative aspects of those evaluations are more pronounced before the teacher's tenure and can play a large role in determining if their contract is renewed. Typically, the post-tenure evaluations of teachers have a more formative focus. Examples of summative evaluations of policies affecting organizations and systems include the No Child Left Behind (NCLB) Act. The act calls for policymakers to determine if schools and districts have made annual yearly progress. In turn, the policy itself is also evaluated to determine how well it led to improvements in student achievement and reductions in performance gaps between student groups. In education, we often offer summative assessments before giving education programs sufficient time to work. This can result in what Hess (1998) describes as "policy churn" or what Tyack, & Cuban (1995) called "tinkering towards utopia." **Policy churn** occurs when policymakers repeatedly try new policies for the prestige it brings rather than for the effectiveness of the policies.

- **Formative evaluations**
  - Ongoing assessments
  - Periodic review during the life of the program
  - Implementers are prime users
- **Summative evaluations**
  - Done at the end of the program's life cycle
  - Policymakers and researchers are prime users

FIGURE 12.1 Formative Versus Summative Evaluation

USERS OF EVALUATION

Stakeholders value evaluation for different reasons. Policymakers seek information about the success of programs to help determine if they should be dropped, continued, or modified. The type of evaluative information that policymakers appreciate tends to be *summative*. Practitioners, however, often want information on how to do their job better and prefer to get feedback when they can reasonably respond to it. Thus, implementers value *formative* evaluations. Beneficiaries of the program often want information about how to maintain or improve the services they receive. A program's clientele may want the opportunity to provide feedback on the services that they received so that policymakers and frontline workers may respond to their concerns. Researchers use evaluative results to inform their predictions on the likely workability of proposed solutions. The information sought by each stakeholder group is not mutually exclusive, and sometimes policymakers would like to have interim evaluations rather than simply an annual report. Similarly, sometimes implementers want to know the overall assessment of their program.

APPROACHES TO EVALUATION

Dunn (2004) describes three approaches to evaluation: pseudo-evaluation, formal evaluation, and decision-theoretical evaluation. **Pseudo-evaluations** describe policy outcomes in terms of the inputs and processes used to achieve them. These evaluations do not connect policy outcomes with the stated objectives of the policy. This evaluative approach brings to mind the old joke of the two individuals looking for money under a street lamp. They had lost their money elsewhere, but they looked for it under the streetlamp because they did not think they could find the money in the dark. Similarly, pseudo-evaluations make no credible connections between the goals sought (e.g. finding the lost money) and the actions taken. They use a variety of methods to describe the relationships among inputs, throughputs, and outputs, but they leave unanswered the one question of interest: Did the policy work? For example, Carnoy and others (2005) have criticized many of the charter school self-evaluations for reporting on parental satisfaction rather than on student productivity, a stated objective of charter school reform.

Formal evaluations go beyond pseudo-evaluations in that they try to link program outcomes with the stated policy goals and objectives. Like pseudo-evaluations, however, formal evaluations do not address underlying values. Engel (2000) criticizes

- **Pseudo-evaluations**
  - Am I describing inputs and processes but not outputs?
  - Have I omitted the stated objectives of the policy?
  - Have I overlooked any credible connections between goals sought and actions taken?
  - Have I answered the question, What works?
- **Formal evaluations**
  - Have I tried to link program outcomes with stated policy goals and objectives?
  - Do I take as given the underlying goals of the policy?
- **Decision theoretic evaluations**
  - Have I tried to link program outcomes to stated policy goals and objectives?
  - Do I examine the underlying goals of the policy?

FIGURE 12.2 Approaches to Evaluation

much of the evaluation of education reform for its emphasis on efficiency considerations rather than focusing critique on the value of the goals themselves. He writes:

> In short, the overarching belief seems to be that we are all in the same boat, rowing in the same general direction, divided only by differences in the course we wish to take. . . . This consensus is artificial and illusory. (p. 177)

Thus, a limitation of formal evaluations is that, while you may produce reliable and valid information on the connection between policy outcomes and policy goals, you do not indicate if those goals should have been the ones sought in the first place. An unquestioned assumption is that formally announced objectives are appropriate. In addition, you leave unexamined latent goals that are not voiced but that may be driving policy decisions (e.g., Chelimsky, 2009).

Decision-theoretic evaluations not only assess the success of policy vis-à-vis its stated goals; they also examine underlying values. Relying on descriptive methods, including stakeholder analysis, values are the centerpiece of this appraisal. This approach explicitly addresses the multiple political and personal considerations inherent in evaluation. While this type of evaluation goes farther than either the pseudo- or formal evaluation, it unearths, but it does not necessarily challenge, latent values.

Like Engel (2000), I think questioning the values of policy priorities and decisions is important. However, I think that inquiry is part of policymaking and policy writ large, not the function of the formal evaluative phase of the policy analytic process. The discourse regarding the role of evaluators in setting and questioning policy goals is an ongoing debate in the field of evaluation (e.g., Mark, 2001; Urban & Trochim, 2009).

METHODS OF EVALUATION

Components of an Evaluation Plan

Evaluation plans must contain at least four components: an explicit statement of policy goals and objectives, specification of policy actions that will achieve those ends, a clear description of methods for measuring the change that is achieved, and a clear description of methods for measuring and comparing the desired change with the change achieved. As part of your evaluation plan, determine the focus of the evaluation. Ask yourself the following types of questions: Are you simply describing outcomes? Will your evaluation be able to assess the success of the policy? How will you account for the political dimensions of the analytical process? Identify acceptable evaluation criteria, establish a timetable for evaluation, specify other protocols, and explain what can be expected from your evaluation. What data will your evaluation produce and how will they reflect the changes that you document? Is your chosen methodology appropriate for measuring impact? Will you use multiple methods of measuring change, or are you relying on only one? Will your feedback be during the course of implementation and be useful to implementers, or is it designed to provide information only to policymakers? (See, for example, Mintrop and Sunderman, 2009; Patton and Sawicki, 1993; Dunn, 2004; U.S. Government Accountability Office, n.d.).

I covered much of the first three components of the plan in earlier chapters of this text. This chapter focuses on using evaluative methods that allow you to present credible conclusions regarding programmatic impact. Your responsibility as an education leader is to be clear about the assumptions that link policy actions to policy goals. Making these assumptions and connections explicit is an important means of injecting integrity in your evaluation plan.

Analytical Considerations

A simple way of determining policy success is to compare the desired performance with what was achieved. If desired levels are reached or surpassed, you may deem the program successful; if not, the program failed. However, if your comparison of actual

- State explicitly the policy goals and objectives.
- Specify the policy actions that will achieve those ends.
- Determine the focus of the evaluation.
  - Are you simply describing outcomes?
  - Will your evaluation be able to assess the success of the policy?
  - How will you account for the political dimensions of the analytical process?
  - What data will your evaluation produce?
  - How will these data reflect the changes that you document?
- Identify acceptable evaluation criteria, establish a timetable for evaluation, specify other protocols, and explain what can be expected from your evaluation.
  - Will your feedback be during the course of implementation and be useful to implementers, or is it designed to provide information only to policymakers?
- Provide a clear description of methods for measuring the change achieved.
  - Will you use multiple methods of measuring change, or are you relying on one only?
- Give a clear description of the method for measuring and comparing the desired change with the change achieved.
  - Is your chosen methodology appropriate for measuring impact?

FIGURE 12.3 Important Tasks in Creating an Evaluation Plan, with Sample Questions That Help in Its Development

- Randomized control trials
- Direct controlled trials
- Quasi-experiments
  - Matching
  - Before-and-after comparisons
  - With-and-without comparisons
- Nonexperimental direct analysis
- Nonexperimental indirect analysis

FIGURE 12.4 Common Methods of Evaluative Assessments

versus planned outcomes does not adequately account for factors other than the policy intervention, your conclusions are vulnerable to rival explanations. Consequently, your evaluation plan must include methods that isolate the impact of policy.

Evaluators in the U.S. federal government have developed a diagnostic framework for assessing programs called Program Assessment Reporting Tool (PART). PART identifies five common ways to evaluate programs: randomized control trials, direct controlled trials, quasi-experiments, nonexperimental direct analysis, and nonexperimental indirect analysis. (I describe these methods more fully later in the chapter.) Critiquing the PART framework, the American Evaluation Association (AEA) offers a roadmap for "improving government through evaluation" (American Evaluation Association, AEA Evaluation Policy Task Force, 2009). Regardless of the methodological label applied, the main purpose of these evaluative methods is to establish credible connections among policy goals, policy intervention, and policy outcomes. The more you control for other influential factors, the more credible is your assertion that the policy intervention resulted in changes in outcomes.

A full discussion of research methods is beyond the scope of this text. What is important is that you create an evaluation plan that allows readers to believe your conclusions regarding the links among goals, actions, and outcomes. If you are evaluating the impact of policy, you must address other explanations of the outcomes measured, which is why, in the absence of random assignment, you control for time, locale, and other intervening factors. You want to address concerns that it was not the policy implemented that resulted in the changes that you observed but some other phenomenon or treatment. While statistical analysis can inform if change occurred by chance, you still have to determine if that change has practical as well as statistical significance. Evaluations must make sense and have meaning for stakeholders.

Common Methods of Assessment

RANDOMIZED CONTROL TRIALS. **Randomized control trials (RCTs)** are pure experiments where populations are randomly assigned to a control or treatment group. Random assignment provides assurance that differences observed between the groups are likely due to the impact of policy rather than to other factors. This method provides particularly credible evidence of policy and programmatic impact. Much of the recent U.S. education policy (e.g., NCLB and Investing in Innovation Fund) calls for use of this evaluative approach in determining the effectiveness of programs. However, federal evaluators also recognize the difficulty of using randomized control trials in much of social science research. They write,

> There are many programs for which it would not be possible to conduct an RCT. To carry out an RCT, there must be a possibility of selecting randomized intervention and control groups—those who will receive a program intervention and those who will not (or will receive a different intervention). For practical, legal, and ethical reasons, this may not always be possible ("What constitutes strong evidence . . . , n.d., p. 2).

The Tennessee Student-Teacher Achievement Ratio (STAR) Project is a notable exception, where the experimental project called for the random assignment of Tennessee elementary students in classes of different sizes. The researchers found that small class sizes have an advantage in the early primary grades for reading and math and that the benefits of smaller class sizes were most pronounced for children attending inner-city schools.

DIRECT CONTROLLED TRIALS. **Direct controlled trials** are not typical of social science research and are often used to test military equipment. With this method, many of the factors that could influence test results are controllable; controlling social contexts is a much more difficult endeavor. More common in social science research is the use of quasi-experiments.

QUASI-EXPERIMENTS. **Quasi-experiments** are good alternatives for addressing many of the threats to validity when they control for time, place, and other intervening factors. These evaluations try to minimize the differences between comparison groups from the outset so that you can reasonably attribute postintervention differences to the implemented policy. Quasi-experiments often entail the use of matching, before-and-after comparisons, and with-and-without comparisons using professional judgment and statistical analysis. Controlling for threats to validity using statistical tools instead of random assignment allows quasi-experiments to be more practical than pure experimental models.

MATCHING. **Matching** creates a comparison group through nonrandom assignment. Using a "natural" experiment, researchers may create a treatment and nontreatment group by matching participants on observable characteristics such as age, race, socioeconomic status, and so on. However, matching often misses nonobservable characteristics, such as motivation and drive, which may have caused different individuals to select program participation in the first place. Consequently, researchers may wrongly assess a policy action as being effective when it is not. For example, a comparison group design using matching of like students from similar schools indicated that career academies were successful at increasing graduation rates among middle and high school student participants. However, evaluators using randomized control trials found that participation in career academies did not significantly improve the graduation rates of participants ("What Constitutes Strong Evidence . . . , n.d.).

BEFORE-AND-AFTER COMPARISONS. **Before-and-after comparisons** include the collection of data from the same locale at different points in time. If patterns of change after the policy treatment are substantially different from the ones before, you could reasonably attribute that difference to the policy intervention that you evaluate. However, critics may argue that those outcomes would have occurred anyway with the passage of time and maturation of subjects. One way to address those concerns is to integrate pre-post tests with methods of with-and-without comparisons.

WITH-AND-WITHOUT COMPARISONS. **With-and-without comparisons** allow you to document changes across space by having information on different locales. If the patterns of change are different for places with the policy than for places without, it is plausible that this change is due to the policy intervention. This method does not eliminate selection bias concerns completely, but it does address more fully the threats to validity than methods using a single locale or single point in time. **Selection bias** occurs when changes in outputs may be linked to the particular attributes of participants rather than to the policy (treatment). For example, if motivated parents are more likely to participate in open-enrollment programs, achievement differences between those students who open-enroll and those who do not may reflect parental drive, not the policy itself.

NONEXPERIMENTAL DIRECT ANALYSIS. **Nonexperimental direct analysis** often looks only at differences in outcomes for a treated group over time and does not entail with-and-without comparisons. Findings using this method are suspect; they are vulnerable to challenges from rival explanations that another phenomenon besides the policy intervention being evaluated is responsible for changes in policy outcomes. This method is especially weak at assessing programmatic impact if researchers examine only post-intervention outcomes or rely only on cross-sectional data for the treatment group.

NONEXPERIMENTAL INDIRECT ANALYSIS. Another evaluative method is **nonexperimental indirect analysis**. The utility of this approach is primarily to get the insight of experts in the field on the potential success of a particular program. However, valid conclusions regarding actual programmatic impact will not be possible using this approach.

Political Considerations

Thus far, this chapter has focused on the analytical and informative function of evaluations. As Weiler (1990) and others have noted, however, evaluations are also political and can serve a legitimating function. Sometimes evaluations are not about the descriptive information that they provide but about the evaluative symbol that they represent (Weiler, 1990).

Like all political acts, evaluations are about relationships and the allocation of power and resources within them. Politics is the "struggle to have one's values backed by the authoritative role of government" (Wirt & Kirst, 1972, p. 4). The values that one uses to define policy problems and to establish policy goals and evaluative criteria reflect which individual or group was victorious in that struggle. The rise and fall of a policy depends on your definition of success.

Weiler (1990) notes, for example, that in the Netherlands, both opponents and supporters of comprehensive (vocational) high schools thought the government-sponsored evaluative results supported their point of view. Those individuals who favored the status quo and academic high schools pointed to the higher academic achievement produced by these institutions as a reason for preserving the status quo. Those who favored reform and the creation of comprehensive high schools pointed to the greater educational opportunity available to larger groups of less advantaged children in that educational environment (Weiler, 1990, p. 443). Both groups reflected the values of Dutch society (excellence and equity). However, to paraphrase George Orwell's (1946) *Animal Farm*, "[A]ll values are created equal, but some values are more equal than others." In the end, how the Dutch policymakers should proceed would depend on the priorities that win in the policymaking arena.

In her insightful look at the integration of evaluation units in the U.S. political environment, Chelimsky (2009) argues that three political pressures come to bear on three evaluative features. These pressures come from the political structure of government and the natural rivalry between the executive and legislative branches, the bureaucratic climate of an agency that may resent outside control, and the dominant professional culture of the agency that may prioritize different values from those of evaluators. **Political structure** refers to the legal balance of power between the executive and legislative branches of the government. **Bureaucratic climate** refers to the socialization of the professionals within the agency and their openness to being evaluated by outsiders. **Professional culture** is similar to political culture described in previous chapters. It refers to the prioritization of the values held by key actors within implementing units. These pressures independently and jointly affect the independence of the evaluative process, the credibility of its findings, and the morale of the evaluators involved in conducting the assessment.

In creating an evaluation plan, you must ensure that evaluation reflects the allocation of power, the strength of relationships, as well as the success of programs. An evaluation can, and does, do much more than assess if a program or policy worked or not. You must balance maintaining the credibility and independence of the evaluative study with understanding the culture of the people and program that you are assessing. Evaluation is the final, formal act of the policy analytical process, but it is also the beginning. The knowledge gained through evaluation helps to inform the political discourse that prompts the beginning of another policy analytical process.

Chapter Summary

Evaluation is an explicitly value-laden phase of the policy analytic process. It is the production of information about the value of policy outcomes. Actual evaluation occurs after implementation (ex post), but it is imperative to have an evaluation plan from the outset.

Evaluations serve formative and summative purposes. *Formative evaluations* produce ongoing information that can help implementers of the program to improve performance. *Summative evaluations* occur at the end of a program's life cycle, when enough time has passed to determine if a program worked or not. Summative evaluations supply information on the extent to which alternatives contribute to the goals and objectives of the program.

Stakeholders value evaluation for different reasons. Policymakers seek information about

the success of programs to help determine if they should be dropped, continued, or modified. Practitioners often want information about how to do their job better and prefer to get feedback when they can reasonably respond to it. Beneficiaries of the program often want information about how to maintain or improve the services they receive. Researchers use evaluative results to inform their predictions on the likely workability of proposed solutions. The information sought by each stakeholder group is not mutually exclusive.

Dunn (2004) describes three approaches to evaluation: pseudo-evaluation, formal evaluation, and decision-theoretical evaluation. *Pseudo-evaluations* describe policy outcomes in terms of the inputs and processes used to achieve them. *Formal evaluations* go beyond pseudo-evaluations in that they try to link program outcomes with the stated policy goals and objectives. *Decision-theoretic evaluations* not only assess the success of policy vis-à-vis its stated goals; they also examine its underlying values.

Stakeholders must find your evaluative framework relevant and credible. They need to connect your definition of success with your identification of the policy issue. Devote adequate resources to the evaluation process so that you can make plausible links among policy objectives, policy outcomes, and the conclusions that you draw. Evaluation plans must contain an explicit statement of goals and objectives, specification of policy actions that will achieve those ends, a clear description of methods for measuring the change that was achieved, and a clear description of the method for measuring and comparing the desired change with the change achieved.

Evaluations are also political and serve a legitimating as well as analytical function. Like all political acts, evaluations are about relationships and the allocation of power and resources within them. The values that one uses to define policy problems and to establish policy goals reflect which individual or group was victorious in having their values backed. In the end, evaluation is the final, formal act of the policy analytical process, but it is also the beginning of a new one.

Review Questions

1. How have you used evaluation assessments in the past? Using the information in this chapter, describe the types of evaluation that you found most productive.
2. Do you think assessment and establishment of values is meant for evaluators, policymakers, or both? Why?

3. Reread the chapter-opening education vignette. Create an evaluation plan that would help inform your decision on whether the policy worked.

News Story for Analysis

"The grade debate; Ontario plans to eliminate fall report cards. But is it a case of coddling kids or protecting them?" *National Post* (f/k/a *The Financial Post*) (Canada). December 23, 2009 Wednesday. National Edition. *BYLINE:* Matthew Coutts, *National Post. SECTION:* NEWS; Pg. A3.

While Ontario's education minister says a decision to eliminate fall report cards for elementary school students and replace them with kinder, gentler progress assessments is intended to give teachers time to evaluate students before issuing a letter grade, the change drew flak from critics who said pupils do not need to be shielded from the reality of grades.

A ministry memo sent this month said fall report cards would be replaced by progress reports, leaving the formality of issuing letter grades until January, six months into the school year.

The change, to take effect September 2010, is part of a shift in assessing student learning success that matches the industry's trend away from stringent grading systems toward a less abrasive system of evaluation.

Ontario will be the first region in Canada to issue two, as opposed to the unofficial standard of three, graded elementary school report cards. But many school districts across the country are now putting emphasis on "progressive" methods of evaluation.

Saskatoon school divisions started considering limiting the emphasis on high school marks last year, while elementary schools in the city's catholic school system focus on descriptive feedback. Similar projects are active in Alberta.

Quebec returned in recent years to report cards with percentage grades, leading teachers unions to push for a return to less specific general method.

Ontario says the new move is not one to reduce accountability, but to address a problem of timing.

"At the beginning of the year, do we want to assign a grade that indicates that somehow something has been completed, or do we want to say, 'this is the beginning of the process?'" Ontario education minister Kathleen Wynne said in an interview yesterday.

"In this first report card, what we want is a conversation between home and school."

Doretta Wilson, executive director of the Society for Quality Education, said she doesn't agree that professional teachers are unable to evaluate a student in that time, nor does she agree with the trend away from concrete grading.

"We keep trying to protect kids from these letter grades. We have to have a way of measuring. Are inches and centimeters harsh when we are talking about height? Or pounds and kilos when we are talking about weight?" she said. "I don't know why suddenly we have this sense that we shouldn't be measuring how kids do. How will we know how they do unless we measure where they are starting from?"

Annie Kidder, the executive director of the parent advocacy group, People for Education, said a number of concerns arise from axing the year's first report card. Among them is how to ensure parents are kept aware of their children's early progress.

But Mary-Lou Donnelly, president of the Canadian Teachers' Federation, and a former Nova Scotia teacher and principal, said that province has been using "progressive report cards" as opposed to a "set in stone" letter grade for years.

"Assessment is very complex,[sic] it's not just a right or a wrong and a test mark. It is an accumulation of how the student is doing in many, many different areas," she said.

"Letter grades make people feel good or they make people feel not good, depending on what the letter grade is, but a parent doesn't have an understanding of what the child can and cannot accomplish or what they are working toward."

Ontario's teachers' unions have long requested schools do away with the fall report card, suggesting they come too early in the year to properly gauge a student's level of growth.

The Elementary Teachers Federation of Ontario almost went on strike in 2005, the central issue being out-of-class prep time.

By killing the November grading process, teachers are expected to save 30 to 60 of those out of class hours, which will now be used communicating directly with the parent.

"[We] think it is a very positive step forward in terms of removing that fall report card and replacing [it] with a progress report," said Sam Hammond, president of the ETFO. "It has to do with the short period of time in the fall that teachers have to make a good assessment and evaluation of a student's progress and work."

Mr. Hammond said teachers only have a six- to eight-week period after students return to class in September to evaluate them and issue a letter grade in November.

The new progress report will be released in late November, issuing students an "excellent," "good," "satisfactory" or "needs improvement" in subject areas along with teacher comments about students' strengths and areas to work on.

Elementary school students will receive two letter graded report cards in January and June.

Source: Material reprinted with the express permission of: "National Post Inc."

Discussion Questions

1. How would you describe the focus, type, and approach to evaluation of the newly enacted law regarding report cards?
2. Which type of evaluative focus and type would you choose if you were the Ontario minister of education? Why?
3. How would you describe the political implications of the decision to change the required number of report cards from three to two?

Selected Websites

American Evaluation Association. Available at *http://www.eval.org/*.

The official website of the American Evaluation Association (AEA), whose membership includes professional evaluators across the United States and around the world. A prime purpose of the organization is to improve evaluative practices and use. Education leaders may find this site helpful for the guidance it provides on effective ways to evaluate programs, policies, and practices. Especially interesting is the tab about reading, available on the homepage. From that tab, education leaders can access the guiding principles to evaluation developed by the organization.

Centre of Excellence for Evaluation, Treasury Board of Canada, Secretariat. (1998). *Program Evaluation Methods: Measurement and Attribution of Program Results*. Available at *http://www.tbs-sct.gc.ca/cee/index-eng.asp*.

The official website of the Centre of Excellence for Evaluation (CEE). The center fulfills the evaluative function of the Treasury Board of Canada, Secretariat, to provide evaluative information on the federal government of Canada. The website contains information on the evaluation standards to be used by the Canadian government. Education leaders may find this site useful for the practical guidance it offers on effective evaluation methods.

Selected References

American Evaluation Association. *Evaluation roadmap for a more effective government.* **Downloaded on April 7, 2011, from http://www.eval.org/aea09. eptf.eval.roadmapF.pdf.**

This publication from the American Evaluation Association provides a roadmap to federal policymakers on effective means of program evaluation. Included on the site is a cover letter to the Director of the Office of Management and Budget and the report itself. Education leaders may find this publication helpful for the evaluative framework it provides for U.S. federal agencies.

Carnoy, M., Jacobsen, J., Mishel, M., & Rothstein, R. (2005). *The charter school dust-up: Examining the evidence on enrollment and achievement.* **Washington, DC: Education Policy Institute.**

The authors examine the performance of students attending charter schools versus students attending traditional public schools. They find that students attending charter schools did not perform significantly better than their traditional public school counterparts. Education leaders may find this book helpful for its use of quasi-experiments to determine the effectiveness of charter school policy.

Mark, M.M. (2001, Fall). Evaluation's future: Furor, futile, or fertile? *American Journal of Evaluation,* **22(3), 457–479.**

Mark highlights the major themes of evaluation research and practice. Education leaders may find this article helpful for the overview it provides of the field. By examining the primacy of historical issues raised for present evaluation policy and practice, education leaders will have better insight on the questions they may face in the development of their evaluation plans.

U.S. Department of Education. (2003, December). *Identifying and implementing educational practices supported by rigorous evidence: A user friendly guide.* **Downloaded April 7, 2011, from http://www. ed.gov/rschstat/research/pubs/rigorousevid/ rigorousevid.pdf.**

This is an official publication of the U.S. Department of Education, Institute of Education Sciences, National Center for Education Evaluation and Regional Assistance. Targeted to education practitioners, all education leaders should find this publication helpful. The report offers an excellent summary of data-driven evaluative approaches and the rationale for determining the credibility of the findings.

Urban, J. B., & Trochim, W. (2009). The role of evaluation in research practice integration working toward the "golden spike." *American Journal of Evaluation, 30(4),* **538–553.**

Urban and Trochim discuss the role of evaluation in spanning the bridge between research and practice. Education leaders may find this article helpful for the insight it provides on the responsibility of formal evaluations to provide a theory of action and to link the inputs, processes, and outputs to policy goals.

Weiler, H. N. (1990, Winter). Comparative perspectives on educational decentralization: An exercise in contradiction? *Educational Evaluation and Policy Analysis, 12(4), 433–448.*

Weiler presents a conceptual analysis of the effectiveness of decentralization policies in meeting their multiple, and sometimes contradictory, goals. In that context, Weiler discusses the political aspects of evaluation and asserts that the act of evaluation is always a political one because it entails the injection of values. Education leaders may find this article helpful as they consider the political dimensions of evaluation along with the technical guidance provided by many professional evaluative groups.

"What Constitutes Strong Evidence of a Program's Effectiveness?" Available at http://www.white-house.gov/omb/part/2004_program_eval.pdf.

This document details the evidence that federal policymakers would find compelling in their evaluation of the success or failure of policies and programs. Developed by the U.S. White House staff, education leaders may find this document helpful for its succinct description of the Program Assessment Rating Tool (PART), a rubric used by federal evaluators to assess programmatic effectiveness. By paying attention to this framework, education leaders can better develop and organize their evaluation plan to ensure compatibility with federal guidelines.

Yeh, S. (2009). Class size reduction or rapid formative assessment? A comparison of cost-effectiveness. *Educational Research Review, 4(1), 7–15.*

Yeh examines the cost effectiveness of class size reduction and rapid formative assessments in improving student achievement. Education leaders may find this article helpful in understanding the use of rapid formative assessments as well as the summative evaluation offered by the author of these two education policy alternatives.

13

Concluding Remarks

CHAPTER OBJECTIVES

After reading this chapter, you will be able to:

- Articulate the importance of policy analysis
- Summarize the steps in the policy analysis process
- Apply the steps in policy analysis to current policy

EDUCATION VIGNETTE

You are attending a large education summit that convened education leaders across the country and around the world. The keynote speaker is talking about the challenges and opportunities that lie ahead for educators around the globe. He closes his speech with a well-known African phrase, "So how are the children?" As you think about high-stakes tests, parent involvement, the global economic crisis, rising poverty, and community turmoil, you think that your children are not doing as well as you would like. The speaker has thrown out a challenge to make life better for these "little people."

You are fired up from the conference; as you fly home, you think, "What can I do to make the children's world better?" What should you do?

REMEMBER WHY WE DO POLICY ANALYSIS

We started this text by stating that policy analysis is a journey that begins with identifying something wrong with our surroundings and ends with a resolution or alleviation of that problematic condition. In this journey, education leaders may not always board at the same stop. Some may participate from the beginning and be in charge of defining the policy issue. Others may be responsible for developing alternatives, others are accountable for implementing policy strategies, and still others determine if those strategies worked. Some education leaders are along for the whole ride.

Educators have the difficult task of maximizing overall achievement without leaving some children behind—a difficult balancing act. Difficult because we as a society are not always clear about the goals we have for education, and even when there is consensus on the goals, we do not often agree on the policies that will get us there. Education leaders play an important role in addressing both those concerns. Policy analysis will not necessarily help you with the setting of goals, but it will assist you in choosing the appropriate policy once you (or others involved in the political process) have determined what those goals are.

Policy Analysis and You

Education leaders must be visionary. By looking toward the future, you can better prepare for it. You can anticipate and address potential challenges to successful resolution of a policy issue. In creating policy, you balance the facts, the context, and your judgment. Policy analysis offers a systematic way of determining how values and policy intersect.

What kind of education leader do you want to be? Sometimes your policy choices seem clear, and you are able to balance different community needs. Sometimes the choice is not obvious, however, and you may have to choose among options that lead to imperfect outcomes. You may find yourself having to select an alternative that maximizes overall achievement but does so at the expense of the outcomes of vulnerable groups. Sometimes your choice benefits students who are not well served by the status quo, but it does not help those children who benefit from the present system. What option will you choose? What are the ethical principles that will guide your decisions? While policy analysis will not establish your ethical foundation, it will help you to choose alternatives that are consistent with your moral grounding. It will help you make your choices transparent, both for yourself and the community that you serve.

Policy Analysis and the Community

The conditions that influence the educational adequacy of a community go beyond schooling. The broader community also has a role to play in supporting its children outside school at all levels of education. Regardless of the role of individual leaders, the purpose of policy analysis is to make the world a better place. This is not to say that the process is always idealistic; it is not. It is meant to remind and challenge us as education leaders to hold ourselves to that ideal.

In exploring the policy analysis process, we recognize more clearly that the heart of good policy is the resolution of a problem. Policy analysis is a reminder that policies are means, not ends. Education leaders can shape the policy discourse to ensure that the focus is not dominated by the strategies they choose but by their vision of a better place. To do this, education leaders must have a clear sense of the community that they serve, not only to identify problems appropriately but also to persuade others of their assessment. The heart of education leadership is vision and persuasion.

Policy Analysis and Change

Making things better requires change, and change can be hard. You and other stake-holders will sometimes wonder if the changes involved are worth the goals that you seek. Policy analysis will help you develop a reasoned response to these concerns. The more challenging the change, the more connected you should be with the members of your community to help them understand the changes being made. It is your responsi-bility to persuade others of the workability of your decision. Equally important, make sure your vision is workable. Policy analysis is a means by which you can accomplish both those objectives.

As an education leader, you must have a plan for monitoring the actions and out-puts of implemented policies. Without a plan, you will not know the significance of the changes that you see. Use monitoring strategies to collect data that inform your decisions on how and why programs changed or stayed the same. The policy analysis process helps you to anticipate the data that you will need to address your questions.

Policy Analysis and Evaluation

As an education leader, you bring your values to the table. When you come to a deci-sion about the success or lack thereof of a program, stakeholders must find your evalu-ative framework relevant and credible. They need to connect your definition of success with your identification of the policy issue. While evaluation is a political act, it does not have to be purely so. Policy analysis allows education leaders to emphasize that evaluation is not only about politics. By employing policy analytical information, you can use established evaluative techniques to determine what worked. To illustrate the ideas presented in this text, the remainder of this chapter discusses an important educa-tion policy in the United States through the lens of policy analysis.

THE STEPS IN POLICY ANALYSIS USING AN EXISTING POLICY EXAMPLE

Elementary and Secondary Education Act (ESEA)

Every policy represents a leader's choice of actions, even when that action reflects a compromise of values. The Elementary and Secondary Education Act (ESEA) of 1965 is no different. It was part of President Lyndon Johnson's War on Poverty. It has since been reauthorized and reshaped to fit the values of various U.S. administrations with mixed degrees of support and fanfare. For example, President George W. Bush put his own stamp on the act when he signed its reauthorization into law in January 2002. That iteration led to its most recent subtitle, the No Child Left Behind Act. In 2010, President Barak Obama announced his own plans to modify the act, leading many political observers to speculate about the possibility of NCLB: Act II (e.g., Klein, 2009; Sawchuk, 2010b). To date, the U.S. Congress has not yet voted to reauthorize the act, but the U.S. Senate Health, Education, Labor and Pensions Committee released draft legislation in October 2011. The debate on the bill in the U.S. Senate education committee is slated for October 19, 2011 (Robelen, 2011).

Throughout its policy life cycle, the ESEA has pumped billions of federal dollars into the education of America's children through programs such as Head Start, Even Start, and Title I. Because of its lengthy and colorful history, the ESEA (in its many forms) is a good springboard for examining how educational leaders explicitly or implicitly incorporated the steps of the policy analysis process. I will identify each phase and indicate how the most recent iteration of the act fits the highlighted analytical step.

DEFINE THE PROBLEM. Shakespeare's Hamlet proclaimed that there was something rotten in the state of Denmark. Similarly, proponents of the ESEA (now No Child Left Behind [NCLB]) also declared that something was wrong with the state of education in the United States. The titles and the policy actions promoted under the act offer insight into the variety of assumptions that policymakers held in their definition of what that something was. For example, Title I of the act calls for improving the academic achievement of the disadvantaged. This implies that policymakers defined the problem as low academic achievement among less privileged children. In earlier iterations of the ESEA, policymakers emphasized the role of poverty in hindering the success of children. The previous contents of the act focused on methods that would alleviate the impact of poverty on schools, including lunch programs. Now, the latest iteration of the ESEA, as reauthorized in the NCLB, emphasizes accountability, with the assumption that students are not doing well because of insufficiently prepared educators (Title II), old-fashioned pedagogy and governance (Title IV), lack of choice (Title V), and the inflexibility of the present school system (Title VI). That is, the remaining titles of the act are part of a diagnostic problem statement of why students are not performing better. Title II addresses the preparation, training, and recruitment of high-quality teachers and principals, which suggests that the problem of low academic achievement results partly from a deficiency in the preparation and recruitment of high-quality educators. Title V promotes informed parental choice and innovative programs, while Title VI calls for flexibility and accountability. These sections of the reauthorized ESEA suggest that federal policymakers think that more informed parents, more choice opportunities, and greater flexibility will lead to an improvement in schools and student performance (U.S. Public Law 107–110, 2002).

MAKE THE CASE. U.S. policymakers pointed to the large achievement gaps between student groups, their standing on international education standards, and mediocre National Assessment of Educational Progress (NAEP) scores across the nation as evidence that the system was not working. While a problem clearly existed, less easy to establish were connections between the policy issue and the solutions. President G. W. Bush pointed to the accomplishments of the Texas education system as evidence of a better path to student success than the one that was previously promoted by the federal government. The NCLB borrowed many of the programs from Texas, including greater emphasis on curriculum standards and more testing. As noted by Spring (2005) and others, however, little empirical grounding is available to support the link between more testing and higher student achievement.

ESTABLISH YOUR DRIVING VALUES. Several values underlie the enactment and reauthorization of the Elementary and Secondary Education Act. Each iteration of the law has led to a reordering of values. Earlier versions indicated a preference for school programs that focused on equality. More recent iterations indicate a preference for policies that emphasize liberty (e.g., choice), quality (scientifically based research), and economic growth (e.g., 21st-century schools and global competitiveness). Consequently, when policymakers today make choices among various policy options, they often promote alternatives that emphasize parental choice and market mechanisms, even at the expense of equity.

DEVELOP ALTERNATIVES. The present reauthorization of the act calls for alternatives that federal policymakers associate with education reform, student productivity, and accountability. These alternatives include greater support for charter schools; greater emphasis on math, science, and reading (e.g., Reading First grants); greater reliance on competitive grants; and the creation of Even Start, a program aimed at breaking the cycle of poverty and illiteracy.

WEIGH THE OPTIONS. The reauthorized ESEA has a strong emphasis on science-based research, with the implication that policymakers will weigh options based on the results of empirical evidence resulting from proven research methods. The law requires education leaders to evaluate the benefits of programs using empirical analysis and rigorous research methods.

MAKE RECOMMENDATIONS. The act is essentially an embodiment of the recommendation made and agreed upon by a majority of federal U.S. policymakers. While it heavily emphasizes accountability and science-based research, the law itself is a result of the compromise reached on the most appropriate way to balance the values of policymakers in their quest to improve education in the United States.

PERSUADE YOUR AUDIENCE. Advocates of the reauthorized ESEA emphasized the bipartisan nature of the policy to gain political and popular support. The updating of the short title to read *No Child Left Behind Act of 2001* also served as a symbolic tool. Who could oppose a policy that advocated that no child would be left behind? Critics of the law often had to defend themselves against the charge that they were not for the success of *all* children. If all children were not to meet a high standard, which ones were to be left behind? Framing the discourse in this manner took attention away from how the policy would help schools to support struggling students.

IMPLEMENT THE SOLUTION. The ESEA gives explicit instructions on when various portions of the law must be put in place, but it often leaves the details of implementation to administrators (McDermott, 2006). In implementing various aspects of the act state education leaders have changed their statewide examination system and have increased the number of grades in which they test students. Ironically, the flexibility called for by the law has led to greater centralization as states control more and more of the education production process in order to meet many of the standards set by the federal government.

MONITOR OUTPUTS. The act specifies the outputs that it expects state and local policymakers to monitor. These outputs include tracking the percentage of teachers that state policymakers consider to be highly qualified, the research-based instruction and materials being used, the achievement levels of children, the participation rates of children in specific programs, and so on.

EVALUATE OUTCOMES. Throughout the act are specific reporting and evaluation requirements. The evaluations sought are in the form of interim reports (formative) as well as summative assessments. If external evaluators find that the implemented program did not fulfill its stated purpose, the act calls for it to be terminated.

Chapter Summary

This concluding chapter serves as a prompt for reflection. It reminds education leaders of the overarching purpose of the policy analytical process. The process itself is a means of making the world a better place. This chapter describes the steps involved in policy analysis. The descriptions offered here should not replace the reflection of thoughtful education leadership. Remember that the process is iterative. Mastery of the process is a means to an end, not an end in and of itself. Ultimately, education leaders will find that policy analysis functions as a useful to-do list in the art of leadership.

Review Questions

1. How would you describe the importance of policy analysis in your role as education leader?
2. How would you apply the steps in the policy analysis process to an education policy in your state?
3. Refer to your response to Review Question 2. Would you have diagnosed the problem differently from the definition offered by the existing policy? Explain your response.
4. Discuss the implications of the diagnoses of a policy problem on the alternatives that emerge from the policy analytical process as reasonable solutions to the problem.
5. Reread the chapter-opening education vignette. Is your response to the questions following it different after completing this chapter and this book? If yes, how? If no, how is your response reflective of the themes discussed in this text?

News Story for Analysis

"More than one way to teach a child; Advocates, critics of early education agree the Finns do it best." National Post (f/k/a The Financial Post) (Canada). June 20, 2009 Saturday. All But Toronto Edition. **BYLINE:** *Natalie Alcoba, National Post.* **SECTION:** CANADA; Pg. A8. **LENGTH:** 1308 words

In the divisive debate surrounding how best to prepare our children for success at school, opposing views agree on at least this: Finland seems to know what it is doing.

Posting among the highest international test scores by 15-year-olds, worldwide educators seeking Nordic secrets have learned that Finnish students receive little homework, there are no gifted programs, and formal schooling does not start until age 7. The importance of early learning, however, is not lost, and the government provides a range of state-funded preschool programs that are open to infants.

The prescription is used to bolster both sides of the intense debate about early learning in North America—one that pits rival camps of educators and economists against one another, armed with competing research, contrasting pedagogical theories and class rhetoric, all in the name of giving children the best start.

The topic has most recently generated lively discussions in Ontario, where the government pledged this week to phase in full-day kindergarten.

In Canada and the United States, advocates of universal early learning programs say more is better at a younger age, provided there is the right balance of instruction and play. Detractors question the benefits of more government-funded preschool for all, saying it makes more sense to focus on those children that need the extra help the most.

There is research to support both sides.

Studies show early childhood education programs improve performance, regardless of socioeconomic background, although children from low income or single parent homes often reap greater rewards than their wealthier counterparts. In cognitive research, one study suggests the cognitive gains for some students may be offset by behavior and social issues. An analysis of one inner-city elementary school in Alberta found that full-day kindergarten students were further ahead than those enrolled in half-day programs, but a look at Quebec's subsidized day-care policy concluded that too much time in the institutional setting may be hurting the cognitive development of its charges.

The rhetoric, too, is equally divided.

Chester E. Finn Jr, chairman of the Hoover Institution's Task Force on K–12 Education at Stanford University, argues that universal preschool serves up a "windfall" to middle-class families already doing a good job of preparing their children, while creating inadequate programs for the disadvantaged students who need the help.

"The policy dilemma is inescapable: how important is it to expand participation in programs and services whose effects are unpredictable and uneven or that don't last?" he writes in his book, Reroute the Preschool Juggernaut.

It is an argument espoused by economists too, like the American, James Heckman, who said, "It is foolish to try to substitute for what the middle-class and upper-middle-class parents are already doing. I think that the evidence suggests that we can target pretty well, and we can certainly deal with the major problems, by starting first with children from disadvantaged families."

On the other side are advocates like Steven Barnett, a leading US early childhood educator, who says that providing only targeted programs would leave middle-class children behind. "In sheer numbers, there are more middle-class children who enter kindergarten poorly prepared to succeed than there are poor children who do so. One in ten will drop out of school. One in ten will fail a grade and be held back. These kids could benefit from preschool."

In its announcement of a blueprint for the most comprehensive early learning strategy in the country, Charles Pascal, the province's early learning advisor, described schools transformed into "community hubs," and a "seamless" approach to early learning that could start at 7:30 a. m. and flow right into an early learning program with a kindergarten teacher half of the day and full-time early childhood educators.

Students would have one cubbie hole; there would be one message book for parents.

The full day would not necessarily amount to more learning, but rather "deeper learning," according to Jane Bertrand, lead researcher for Mr. Pascal's team.

In response to the push-back from critics of such initiatives, Dr. Pascal clarified in an interview that this is not about replacing parents. "What's really key is for people to keep an eye on the notion that what we need is a high quality environment at home and a high quality environment when kids are outside the home," he said.

He will not brook the argument that good care at home can make up for a stimulating, child care environment. "Either/Or is actually silly," and, he says, completely misses the point.

"The truth is that three- and four-year-olds and five-year-olds are not home with the parents," adds Dr. Barnett, Co-Director of the National Institute for Early Education Research based in New Jersey. "So the question is, Are they going to be in a child-care center under the care of an adult who is not providing stimulation, who is not providing support for social or emotional development, who is not supporting the development of their executive function and self regulation, in which case what we have is a lost opportunity."

A study of a universal preschool program in Oklahoma—touted for being among the most widely subscribed in the country, employing certified ECE [Early Childhood Education] teachers who are paid the same as their classroom counterparts—found scores in letter identification, spelling and applied problems improved regardless of racial background or socioeconomic groups.

A larger 2005 study by the National Institute for Early Education Research measured the impact of state-run preschool programs on four-year-olds also looked at Oklahoma, plus Michigan, New Jersey, South Carolina and West Virginia.

Scores improved in all but one area, but they improved marginally more for disadvantaged youth compared to their more wealthy peers.

Meanwhile, research that is ongoing in Alberta has produced interesting results. Dr. Jose da Costa, Chair of the University of Alberta's department of Education Policy Studies, has been following a cohort of inner city Edmonton students who attended full-day kindergarten compared to half-day kindergarten.

He found that children from disadvantaged communities who attended full-day kindergarten were able to keep up with their more advantaged peers who were in a half-day program, and the literacy benefits carried through to Grade 5. Children from the better off homes who attended full-day kindergarten were :miles ahead" of everyone else, but their gains had faded by Grade 3. He noted that the children in disadvantaged situations had additional supports that may have enabled the long-lasting benefits.

Dr. Pascal believes his Ontario plan will make a difference because it comes at education from all sides, providing programming and support for parents, extending their leave at the outset and housing different child resources under one roof so that learning difficulties are diagnosed and addressed quickly.

"We don't live in the U.S.," he said. "The U.S. has a tradition of targeting the poor and targeted programs for the poor are usually poor programs."

He does look abroad, to France, for example, where 40% of the children enrolled in state-run child care programs have stay-at-home moms because they recognize the benefits of having their children develop and learn with other children.

He says the Finnish model, where more than one third of families opt for a government stipend that allows a mother or father to stay at home with their children, is another perfect example of how investing in early childhood education pays off.

"There is not just one way to do it, but [when] you look at country's [sic] that are successful, it's the level of the investment that they make," said Dr. Barnett.

Source: Material reprinted with the express permission of: "National Post Inc."

Discussion Questions

1. As an education leader, how would you use the research on early childhood education to inform your analysis of the policy issue and what worked?
2. How would you respond to Chester E. Finn's and Steven Barnett's remarks regarding the findings of early childhood education studies?
3. Given the data highlighted in the study, how would you say children are doing? What kinds of policies would you support to help children? Why?
4. What are the steps in the policy analysis process that are identified in this article? How do you know?

Selected Websites

Children at Risk. Available at

http://childrenatrisk.org/.

The official website for the Children at Risk nonprofit organization. The organization is focused on indicators that monitor the well-being of children in Houston, Texas. Education leaders may find this site helpful because of the information available on research and policy that affect the well-being of children in Texas. The site also contains information on the legislative policy agenda favored by leaders of the organization.

Higher Education Policy Institute. Available at

http://www.hepi.ac.uk/.

The official website of the Higher Education Policy Institute (HEPI), which is an independent think

tank based in the United Kingdom. It examines higher education policy issues. The organization publishes reports and arranges topical seminars and conferences targeted at policymakers and other stakeholders in the field. Education leaders may find this site helpful for the information it offers under its Publications tab, which provides leading policy analytical research on issues in higher education that affect the United Kingdom. Many of the highlighted issues are relevant to other contexts, too.

Selected References

McDermott, K. A. (2006, January). Incentives, capacity, and implementation: Evidence from Massachusetts education reform. *Journal of Public Administration Research and Theory: J-PART,* 16(1), 45–65.

This article looks at the implementation of standards-based reform in Massachusetts. The author finds that poorly thought-out incentive structures, lack of capacity, and lack of trust impeded implementation of the reforms. While policy leaders had a clear theory of action on how student achievement was related to standards, they did not consider the implementation implications or ground their assessment in purposeful analysis. Education leaders may find this article helpful because it emphasizes the importance of not skipping critical steps in the policy analysis process.

Spring, J. (2005). *Conflict of interests: The politics of American education* (5th ed.). Dubuque, IA: McGraw Hill.

This short text offers a strong point of view on the conflicting issues facing K–12 education in the United States. Educators may find it of interest because it addresses the values that we bring to education and offers an overview of the field.

Pullout Field Guide for Educational Leaders
Summary of Checklist of Each Step of the Policy Analytical Process

Now that you have covered all the steps in policy analysis, it is time to reflect on them as a whole. Think of the process like a decision tree, where you ask yourself a series of questions: Is the world perfect? If yes, stop. If no, can we do something about it? If no, stop. If yes, should we do something about it? If no, stop. If yes, commence the policy analysis process.

DEFINE THE PROBLEM

At the heart of the problem statement is a description of the condition and the use of data organized into meaningful evidence to support that there is a problem. Organize the discussion into a description of the condition, a discussion of the consequences of not solving the condition, and a review of the underlying factors causing the problem. By organizing the statement of the problem using these three components, you, as an educational leader, can go a long way in providing a clear definition of the problem. Your checklist for this step includes responding to the following questions:

- Did you include a *descriptive* statement of the condition, with accompanying evidence?
- Did you discuss the consequences of not solving the condition, also with accompanying evidence?
- Did you highlight the factors that led to the existence of the problem? Do the factors that you highlight have support in the literature as being linked to the problem you describe?

MAKE THE CASE

Policy analysis requires evidence-based strategies. Decision makers may rely on their gut, but your case is more convincing if you point to the facts. This step is largely about the process of assembling evidence, including the gathering of data and their ultimate transformation into persuasive proof. Your checklist for this step includes responding to the following questions:

- What data source are you relying on: people or documents, or both?
- Did you use quantitative or qualitative data? Which type does your audience find more credible?

- In assembling data for monitoring, did you include explicit indicators that allow you to know if and how the phenomenon that you describe has changed over time?
- In assembling evidence for prescriptions, did you document specific outputs regularly? Did that documentation reveal patterns, associations, and possible causation?
- In assembling evidence for evaluating, did you document the changes associated with the policy? Did these changes occur in the desired direction? Can these changes be linked to your policy actions?

ESTABLISH YOUR DRIVING VALUES

Reflect on the values that will help you choose among the various policy options available. The groups and individuals involved in the decision process influence the values that one ultimately uses to select among different policy alternatives. The political process and community mores determine whose values count and who participates. Once the desired vision for society has been established, this vision is explicitly reflected in the criteria used to choose among different policy options. Criteria are concrete, working definitions of the values driving the analysis. In selecting appropriate policy options, you will likely ask yourself these five questions:

- Does it work?
- Is it fair?
- Can we afford it?
- Will people support it?
- Who will implement it?

DEVELOP ALTERNATIVES

Develop strategies to identify policy options and modify existing solutions to broaden the alternatives that are available. In essence, you are seeking actions to change the condition that you found problematic. You can start from scratch or reinvent the old, making it something new. Here are the questions you need to ask yourself:

- How do the options identified address the underlying causes of the policy issue?
- What are the implications of the options identified for the success of children?
- Will the changes have an impact on the production process, governance structure, educational outputs, or individual behaviors?
- Who will be responsible for overseeing the change in action in your proposed alternative?
- How does the proposed funding differ from the status quo?
- Will the options under consideration promote flexibility for implementers?

WEIGH THE OPTIONS

Consider the merits of doing something different and ensure that it is compatible with the context that you face. You must create measures of each criterion so that decision makers and other stakeholders have a clear idea of what a "good outcome" looks like. From the start, you should think about the impact on key populations if the policy you propose does not work in the way that you imagine. Here are the questions you should ask yourself:

- What are the criteria that will undergird my choice?
- Why is it important to include these criteria?
- How will I know if I have more or less of a particular criterion?
  - What will "more effectiveness" look like? What measures allow me to know?
  - What will "more equity" look like? What measures allow me to know?
  - What will "more economical" look like? What measures allow me to know?
  - What will "more political feasibility" look like? What measures allow me to know?
  - What will "a greater ability to be implemented" look like? What measures allow me to know?

MAKE RECOMMENDATIONS

You must determine how to choose among several options. Because alternatives do not usually dominate all criteria, you must address trade-offs. An objective, right answer does not exist, but you can still present coherent and incoherent arguments. You must be consistent within the ethical framework that you establish. Ask yourself these questions to test the robustness of your recommendation:

- Does the literature and professional experience support a rival claim regarding the causal relationship between the outcomes desired and the actions prescribed?
- How many informed researchers and stakeholders agree with your assessment regarding the likely costs and effectiveness of the proposed policy? Is there general agreement in the field?
- Have you considered stakeholder needs?
- Are other actions more responsive to and appropriate for the policy issue identified?
- Are you clear about the ethical considerations that drive your decision?
- Is the recommended action consistent with your stated ethical principles?

PERSUADE YOUR AUDIENCE

Before you can move to the next step—implementing a policy—you must persuade relevant decision makers about its suitability. Knowing your audience and constructing strong justifications for the claims made are important persuasive tools. Tailor your presentation to fit the needs of the relevant decision makers. For your analysis to be useful, its conclusions must be clear. Here is a list of key questions to ask yourself:

- Am I timely in the preparation and presentation of the materials?
- Are the major findings of the presentation clear?
- Is the presentation engaging?
- Is the conclusion clear and succinct?
- Are policy and research implications highlighted?

IMPLEMENT THE SOLUTION

Your implementation plan essentially answers the questions of what, who, how, and when. It should include an overview of the tasks that need to be done, who will be responsible for doing them, and the timeframe in which the tasks will be completed. The following questions will help you check the utility of your implementation plan:

- Is there a direct connection between the implementation plan and the problem defined?
- Is the plan clear about its goals and objectives?
- Do the tasks that must be completed present a clear pathway to the goal and objectives described?
- Have I identified who will be responsible for completing each assigned task?
- Is the timeframe for completion of the project noted and justified?
- Is there a process for checking compliance?

MONITOR OUTPUTS

Monitoring is not a one-shot deal. It offers recurring information on what happened and informs analytical decisions on how it happened and why. It connects the actions outlined in the implementation plan with policy objectives. Monitoring describes and explains policy actions; it does not judge its impact. Here are some important questions to ask yourself:

- What data should I track to illustrate the workings of the policy?
- How do the selected data help to illustrate compliance and performance of implementers and other stakeholders?
- Who should track the required data?
- How often should I or others track these data?

EVALUATE OUTCOMES

Evaluation focuses on the achievement of goals and objectives. Stakeholders must find your evaluative framework relevant and credible. Devote adequate resources to the evaluation process so that you can make plausible links among policy objectives, policy outcomes, and the conclusions that you draw. Evaluations serve two main analytical purposes: formative and summative. *Formative evaluations* produce ongoing information that can help implementers of the program improve performance. *Summative evaluations* occur at the end of a program's life cycle, when enough time has passed to determine whether a program worked. In developing your evaluation plan, ask yourself these questions:

- Do I have an explicit statement of policy goals and objectives?
- Did I include specific policy actions that will achieve those ends?
- Am I simply describing outcomes?
- Does my research method allow me to assess the success of the policy?
- How did I account for the political dimensions of the analytical process?
- What data will my evaluation produce?
- Will I produce developmental feedback? What makes this feedback credible?
- What will lead people to believe my summative assessment?

REFERENCES

Alexander, N. A. (1998). *The impact of curriculum standards on student performance: The case of New York State*. Ann Arbor, MI: UMI Company. Unpublished doctoral dissertation. University at Albany, State University of New York.

Alexander, N. A. (2002). Race, poverty, and the student curriculum: Implications for standards policy. *American Educational Research Journal, 39*(3), 675–693.

Alexander, N. A. (2003, Winter). Considering equity and adequacy: An examination of student class time in New York State public secondary programs, 1975–1995. *Journal of Education Finance, 28*(3), 357–381.

Alexander, N. A. (2004). Exploring the changing face of adequacy. *Peabody Journal of Education, 79*(3) p. 81–103.

Alexander, N. A. (2006). Being on track for NCLB: Examining the capacity of Massachusetts public 8th grade programs. *Educational Policy, 20*(2), 399–428.

Alexander, N. A., & Schapiro, D. (2009, March). Seeking educational adequacy beyond the school walls: Public expenditures on children in urban communities. Paper presented at the annual American Education Finance Association Conference, Nashville, TN.

American Council on Education. (2005, March). *Bridging troubled waters: Competition, cooperation and the public good in independent and public higher education*. (Third in a series of essays: *The changing relationship between States and their institutions*). Washington, DC: American Council on Education.

American Evaluation Association, AEA Evaluation Policy Task Force. (2009, February). *An evaluation roadmap for a more effective government*, by William Trochim, Eleanor Chelimsky, Leslie Cooksy, Katherine Dawes, Patrick Grasso, Susan Kistler, Mel Mark, Stephanie Shipman, & George Grob. Retrieved from http://www.eval.org/aea09.eptf.eval.roadmapF.pdf

Bardach, E. (2009). *A practical guide for policy analysis: The eightfold path to more effective problem solving* (3rd ed.). Washington, DC: CQ Press.

Berne, R. & Stiefel, L. (1984). *The measurement of equity in school finance*. Baltimore, MD: John Hopkins University Press.

Biddle, B. J. (1996, December). Better ideas: Expanded funding for educational research. *Educational Researcher, 25*, 12–14.

Bishop, J. (1996). Incentives to study and the organization of secondary instruction. In W. E. Becker & W. J. Baumol (Eds.), *Assessing educational practices: The contribution of economics* (pp. 99–160). New York: Russell Sage Foundation.

Booth, W. C., Colomb, G. C., and Williams, J. M. (1995). *The craft of research*. Chicago: The University of Chicago Press.

Bryson, J. M. (1988). *Strategic planning for public and nonprofit organizations: A guide to strengthening and sustaining organizational achievement*. San Francisco: Josey-Bass.

Carnoy, M., Jacobsen, J., Mishel, M., & Rothstein, R. (2005). *The charter school dust-up: Examining the evidence on enrollment and achievement*. Washington, DC: Education Policy Institute, and New York: Teachers College Press.

CCSSO. (2010, March). *2010 Policy Statement on ESEA Reauthorization*. Available at http://www.ccsso.org/Documents/2009/ESEA_Task_Force_Policy_Statement_2010.pdf

Chelimsky, E. (2009). Integrating evaluation units into the political environment of government: The role of evaluation policy. *New Directions for Evaluation, 51*–66. doi: 10.1002/ev.305

Class Size. (2004, September 10). *Education Week*. Downloaded February 25, 2011, from http://www.edweek.org/ew/issues/class-size/

Coburn, C. E. (2001, Summer). Collective sensemaking about reading: How teachers mediate reading policy in their professional communities. *Educational Evaluation & Policy Analysis, 23*(2), 145–170.

Colander, D. (1991). "The best as the enemy of the good." Why aren't economists as important as garbagemen? In D. Colander (Ed.), *Essays on the state of economics* (pp. 31–37). Armonk, NY: Sharpe.

Comer, J. P. (1988). Educating poor minority children. *Scientific American, 256*(11), 42–48.

Cooksey, R. W., and Freebody, P. (1986, Spring). Social judgment theory and cognitive feedback: A general model for analyzing educational policies and decisions. *Educational Evaluation and Policy Analysis,* 8(1) pp. 17–29.

Coons, J., Clune, W., & Sugarman, S. (1970). *Private wealth and public education.* Cambridge, MA: Belknap Press of Harvard University Press.

Cooper, R. (1999, Spring). Detracking reform in an urban California high school: Improving the schooling experiences of African American students. *Journal of Negro Education,* 65(2), 190–208.

Cooper, B. S., Fusarelli, L. D., & Randall, E. V. (2004). *Better policies, better schools: Theories and applications.* New York: Pearson Education.

Cooper, H. M., Nye, B. A., & Charlton, K. (1996, Fall). The effects of summer vacation on achievement test scores: A narrative and meta-analytic review. *Review of Educational Research, 66,* 227–268.

Coplin, W. D., & O'Leary, M. K. (1998). *Basic policy studies skills* (3rd ed.). Croton-on-Hudson, NY: Policy Studies Associates.

Crace, J. (2006, July 11). Education: Could do amazingly: Gifted and talented children need special help in order to flourish, but with no dedicated funding, many schools wonder whether it's worth the effort. *The Guardian* (London), Final Edition, p. 1.

A decade of standards based education. Quality counts at 10. (2006, January). A special state-focused supplement, Minnesota. *Education Week.* Downloaded from http://www.edweek.org/media/ew/qc/2006/17shr.mn.h25.pdf

Denning, S. (2007). *The secret language of leadership: How leaders inspire action through narrative.* San Francisco, CA: John Wiley.

Duke, D. L. (2004). *The challenges of educational change.* New York: Pearson Education.

Duke, D. L., Bradley, W., Butin, D. Grogan, M., & Gillespie, M. (1998, April). Rethinking educational design in new school construction. *International Journal of Educational Reform,* 7(2), 158–167.

Duncan, A. (2011, January 14). Maintain diversity in schools. *Washington Post,* p. A20.

Dunn, W. N. (2004). *Public policy analysis: An introduction* (3rd ed.). Upper Saddle River, NJ: Prentice Hall.

Edelman, M. (1995). Symbols and political quiescence. In S.Z. Theodoulou and M.A. Cahn (Eds.). *Public policy: The essential readings* (pp. 26–33). Upper Saddle River, NJ: Prentice Hall. Originally published in Murray Edelman, *The symbolic uses of politics.* Urbana: University of Illinois Press, 1964, chapter 2.

Education Commission of the States. (2010). Recent state policies/activities. Retrieved from http://www.ecs.org/ecs/ecscat.nsf/WebStateView?OpenView&count=-1&RestrictToCategory=Texas.

Ehrenberg, R. G., & Mavros, P. G. (1995, Summer). Do doctoral students' financial support patterns affect their times-to-degree and completion probabilities? *Journal of Human Resources,* 30(3), 581–609.

Elazar, D. (1984). *American federalism: A view from the states* (3rd ed.). Harper & Row.

Ellis, R. D. (1998). *Just results: Ethical foundations for policy analysis.* Washington, DC: Georgetown University Press.

Engel, M. (2000). *The struggle for control of public education: Market ideology vs. democratic values.* Philadelphia, PA: Temple University Press.

Ferrer de Valero, Y. (2001, May–June). Departmental factors affecting time-to-degree and completion rates of doctoral students at one land-grant research institution. *Journal of Higher Education,* 72(3), 341–367.

Finn, C. E., Manno, B. V., & Vanourek, G. (2000). *Charter schools in action. Renewing public education.* Princeton, NJ: Princeton University Press.

Firestone, W. A. (1989, October). Educational policy as an ecology of games. *Educational Researcher, 18,* 18–24.

Fountain, J. R. (1991, Winter). Service efforts and accomplishments reporting. New approaches to productivity: Proceedings of the Fourth National Public Sector Productivity Conference. *Public Productivity & Management Review,* 15(2), 191–198.

Fowler, F. (2009). *Policy studies for educational leaders: An introduction* (3rd ed.). New York: Pearson Education.

Frase, L. E., & Streshly, W. (2000). *Top 10 myths in education: Fantasies Americans love to believe.* Lanham, MD: The Scarecrow Press (Technomic Books).

Fryer, R. (2010, April 8). Financial incentives and student achievement: Evidence from randomized trials. Harvard University, EdLabs, and NBER. Downloaded on April 13, 2011, from http://www.edlabs.harvard.edu/pdf/studentincentives.pdf

Fullan, M. (1999). *Change forces: The sequel.* London: Falmer.

Gamse, B., Millsap, M., & Goodson, B. (2002). When implementation threatens impact: Challenging lessons from evaluating educational programs. *Peabody Journal of Education, 77*(4), 146–166.

Gandara, P., & Fish, J. (1994, Spring). Year-round schooling as an avenue to major structural reform. *Educational Evaluation and Policy Analysis, 16*(1), 67–85.

Garner, C. W. (2004). *Education finance for school leaders: Strategic planning and administration.* Columbus, OH: Pearson, Merrill Prentice Hall.

Gillingham, L., Seneca, J. J., & Taussig, M. K. (1991, August). The determinants of progress to the doctoral degree. *Research in Higher Education, 32*(4), 449–468.

Grady, M. P. (1998). *Qualitative and action research: A practitioner handbook.* Bloomington, IN: Phi Delta Kappa Educational Foundation.

Grouping kids by ability harms education, two studies show. (2007, September 21). *ScienceDaily.* Retrieved February 12, 2011, from http://www.sciencedaily.com/releases/2007/09/070915104849.htm

Guthrie, J. W. (1983). Funding an "adequate" education. *Phi Delta Kappan, 64*(7), 471–476.

Guthrie, J. W., & Rothstein, R. (1999). Enabling "adequacy" to achieve reality. Translating adequacy into state school finance distribution arrangements. In H. Ladd, R. Y Chalk, & J. Hansen (Eds.). *Equity and adequacy in education finance* (pp. 209–259). Washington, DC: Committee on Education Finance of the National Research Council, National Academy Press.

Gutmann, A. (1990). Democratic education in difficult times. *Teachers College Record, 92*(1), 7–20.

Haller, E., & Kleine, P. F. (2001). *Using educational research: A school administrator's guide.* New York: Addison Wesley Longman.

Hanushek, E., Heckman, J., & Neal, D. (2002, Fall). Introduction to the JHR's Special Issue on designing incentives to promote human capital. *Journal of Human Resources, 37*(4), 693–695.

Heck, R. H. (2004). *Studying educational and social policy: Theoretical concepts and research methods.* Mahwah, New Jersey: Lawrence Erlbaum.

Hess, F. M. (1998). *Spinning wheels: The politics of urban school reform.* Washington, DC: Brookings Institution Press.

Houston, P. D. (2007, June). The seven deadly sins of No Child Left Behind. *Phi Delta Kappan, 88*(10), 744–748.

Hutchins, R. M. (2009). The basis of education. In J. W. Noll (Ed.), Taking sides: Clashing views on educational issues (15th ed.) (pp. 11–14). Dubuque, IA: McGraw-Hill.

Jones, C. (2000, November 16). Schools "lose out" in funding deal. *The Age* (Melbourne, Australia), p. 11.

Kaplan, A. (1998). *The conduct of inquiry: Methodology for behavioral science.* New Brunswick, NJ: Transaction Publishers.

Kelly, D. (1991, November 26). Programs for gifted students: Equitable or elitist? *USA Today*, p. 4D.

King, J. A. (1994). Meeting the educational needs of at-risk students: A cost analysis of three models. *Educational Evaluation and Policy Analysis, 16*, 1–19.

Kingdon, J. W. (1995). *Agendas, alternatives, and public policies* (2nd ed.). New York: Addison Wesley Longman.

Klein, A. (2009, December 9). Duncan aims to make incentives key element of ESEA: Education secretary weighs priorities for law's renewal. *Education Week, 29*(14), 1.

Kowalski, T., Lasley, T. J., & Mahoney, J. W. (2008). *Data-driven decisions and school leadership: Best practices for school improvement*. New York: Pearson Education.

Leach, J. (2009). "Valuing communication." *The Lancet*, 373(9681), 2104.

Leithwood, K., Louis, K. S., Anderson, S., & Wahlstrom, K. (2004). *How leadership influences student learning*. Learning from Leadership Project. The Wallace Foundation.

Lidman, R., & Sommers, P. (2005, September/October). The "compleat" policy analyst: A top 10 list. *Public Administration Review*, 65(5), 628–634.

Lim, S. (2010, July 30). Vouchers are on the rise. *St. Petersburg Times* (Florida). Special Report: Back to School, p. 8.

Louis, K. S., Febey, K., & Schroeder. R. (2005, Summer). State-mandated accountability in high schools: Teachers' interpretations of a new era. *Educational Evaluation & Policy Analysis*, 27(2), 177–204.

Louis, K. S., & Miles, M. B. (1990). *Improving the urban high school*. New York: Teachers College Press.

Louis, K. S., Thomas, E., Gordon, M., & Febey, K. (2008, October). State leadership for school improvement: An analysis of three states [Part of the special issue entitled Linking Leadership to Student Learning]. *Educational Administration Quarterly*, 44(4), 562–592.

Lowi, T. J. (1964, July). American business, public policy, case studies, and political theory. *World Politics*, 16(4), 677–715.

Lussenhop, J. (2011, February 23). Inside the multimillion-dollar essay-scoring business: Behind the scenes of standardized testing. Downloaded on April 7, 2011, from http://www.citypages.com/2011-02-23/news/inside-the-multimillion-dollar-essay-scoring-business/#.

March, J. G., & Simon, H. A. (1958). *Organizations*. New York: John Wiley.

Mark, M. M. (2001, Fall). Evaluation's future: furor, futile, or fertile? *American Journal of Evaluation*, 22(3), 457–479.

Marschke, R., Laursen, S., Nielsen, J. M., & Rankin, P. (2007, January/February). Demographic inertia revisited: An immodest proposal to achieve equitable gender representation among faculty in higher education. *Journal of Higher Education*, 78(1), 1–26.

Marshall, C., Mitchell, D., & Wirt, F. (1989). *Culture and education policy in the American states*. New York: Falmer.

Matus, R. (2010, December 11,). Schools shake up in store. *St. Petersburg Times* (Florida), p. 1A.

McDermott, K. A. (2006, January). Incentives, capacity, and implementation: Evidence from Massachusetts education reform. *Journal of Public Administration Research and Theory: J-PART*, 16(1), 45–65.

McDonnell, L. M. (1994). Assessment policy as persuasion and regulation. *American Journal of Education*, 102, 391–420.

McDonnell, L. M. (2009, August). Repositioning politics in education's circle of knowledge. *Educational Researcher*, 38(6), 417–427.

McDonnell, L. M., & Elmore, R. F. (1987, Summer). Getting the job done: Alternative policy instruments. *Educational Evaluation & Policy Analysis, 9*, 133–152.

Meltsner, A. J. (1976). *Policy analysts in the bureaucracy*. Berkeley and Los Angeles: University of California Press.

Miles, K. H., & Frank, S. (2008). *The strategic school: Making the most of people, time, and money*. Thousand Oaks, CA: Corwin Press and National Association of Secondary School Principals.

Mintrop, H., & Sunderman, G. L. (2009, June–July). Predictable failure of federal sanctions-driven accountability for school improvement: And why we may retain it anyway. *Educational Researcher*, 38(5), 353–364.

Monk, D. H. (1989, Spring). The education production function: Its evolving role in policy analysis. *Educational Evaluation & Policy Analysis, 11*, 31–45.

National Commission on Excellence in Education. (1983). *A nation at risk: The imperative of educational reform*. Washington, DC: U.S. Government Printing Office.

New Vision. (2007, April 15). Uganda; Secondary education vital for good health. *Africa News*.

New Vision. (2011, September 27). Uganda; women group seeks Sh200 million for girls school fees. *Africa News*.

Noll, J. W. (Ed.). (2009). *Taking sides: Clashing views on educational issues*. (15th ed.). Dubuque, IA: McGraw-Hill.

Numeroff, L. J. (1985). *If you give a mouse a cookie*. New York: Laura Geringer Books.

Oakes, J. (1990). *Lost talent: The underparticipation of women, minorities, and disabled persons in science*. Santa Monica, CA: Rand.

Odden, A. (2000). The new school finance: Providing adequacy and improving equity. *Journal of Education Finance, 25*(4), 467–487.

Odden, A., & Picus, L. (2009). *School finance: A policy perspective* (4th ed.). Boston, MA: McGraw-Hill.

Ogundare, F. (2010, July 21). Don tasks education managers on accountability. *This Day* (Lagos), np.

Okun, A. M. (1975). *Equality and efficiency, the big trade-off*. Washington, DC: The Brookings Institution.

Orfield, G., Frankenberg, E. D., & Lee, C. (2002/2003). The resurgence of school segregation. *Educational Leadership, 60*(4), 16–20.

Orwell, G. (1946). *Animal farm*. New York: Harcourt, Brace, and Company.

Patton, C. V., & Sawicki, D. S. (1993). *Basic methods of policy analysis and planning*. Englewood Cliffs, NJ: Prentice Hall.

Peterson, W., & Rothstein, R. (2010, April 20). *Let's do the numbers: Department of Education's "Race to the Top" program offers only a muddled path to the finish line*. Economic Policy Institute. Briefing Paper, #263.

Public Agenda. (2007, April 13). Africa; Countries fail to improve secondary education at the cost of development. *Africa News*.

Ravitch, D. (2010). *The death and life of the great American school system: How testing and choice are undermining education*. New York: Basic Books.

Reschovsky, A., & Imazeki, J. (2001). Achieving educational adequacy through school finance reform. *Journal of Education Finance, 26*(4), 373–396.

Robelen. (2011). Debate on ESEA bill slated for Oct. 19 Senate committee. *Education Week* blog.

Retrieved on October 14, 2011, from http://blogs.edweek.org/edweek/campaign-k-12/

Roellke, C. F. (1996). *The local response to state initiated education reform: Changes in the allocation of human resources in New York State schooling systems, 1983–1995*. Unpublished doctoral dissertation. Cornell University.

Sadovnik, A R., Cookson, P. W., & Semel, S. F. (2001). Exploring education: An introduction to the foundations of education (2nd ed.). Boston: Allyn & Bacon.

San Antonio Independent School District v. Rodriguez, 411 U.S. 1 (1973).

Sawchuk, S. (2010a). N.Y.C. school built around unorthodox use of time. *Education Week, 29*(2), 1.

Sawchuk, S. (2010b). Teacher plans stress competitive grants *Education Week, 29*(22), 1.

Schemo, D. J., & Fessenden, F. (2003, December 3). A miracle revisited: Measuring success; gains in Houston schools: How real are they? *New York Times*. sec. A, col. 1, p. 1.

Simon, H. (1997). *Models of bounded rationality*. Cambridge, MA: MIT Press.

Singham, M. (1998, September). The canary in the mine: The achievement gap between black and white students [cover story]. *Phi Delta Kappan, 80*(1), 8–15.

Spring,, J. (2005). *Conflict of interests: The politics of American education* (5th ed.). Dubuque, IA: McGraw Hill.

Superfine, B. M. (2009, December). The evolving role of the courts in educational policy: The tension between judicial, scientific, and democratic decision making in *Kitzmiller v. Dover*. American Educational Research Journal, 46(4), 898–923.

Thomas, S. L. (2000, September/October). Ties that bind. *The Journal of Higher Education*, 71(5), 591–615.

Tinto, V. (1997, November/December). Classrooms as communities: Exploring the educational character of student persistence. *Journal of Higher Education*, 68, 599–623.

Tyack, D. B., & Cuban, L. (1995). *Tinkering toward utopia: A century of public school reform*. Cambridge, MA: Harvard University Press.

United Nations Children's Fund (New York). (2011, September 27). Africa; governments urged to build on innovations, speed up inclusive education reforms for children with disabilities. *Africa News*.

U.S. Department of Education. (2011). Institute of Education Sciences. National Center for Education Statistics. *Trends in International Mathematics and Science Study (TIMSS)*. Retrieved October 17, 2011, from http://nces.ed.gov/timss/

U.S. Department of Education, National Center for Education Statistics. (2004). *The high school transcript study: A decade of change in curricula and achievement, 1990–2000*. NCES 2004-455, by Robert Perkins, Brian Kleiner, Stephen Roey, & Janis Brown. Project Officer: Janis Brown Washington, DC: 2004.

U.S. Department of Education. PowerPoint presentation of the No Child Left Behind Act of 2001. Retrieved October 17, 2011, from http://www2.ed.gov/nclb/overview/intro/presentation/index.html

U.S. Government Accountability Office. Retrieved October 17, 2011, from http://www.gao.gov/

U.S. Public Law 107–110, 2002—JAN. 8, 2002 115 STAT. 1425.

Urban, J. B., & Trochim, W. (2009). The role of evaluation in research practice integration working toward the "golden spike." *American Journal of Evaluation, 30*(4), 538–553.

Vanourek, G., Manno, B. V., Finn, C. E., & Bierlein, L. A. (1998). Charter schools as seen by students, teachers, and parents. In P. E. Peterson & B. C. Hassel (Eds.), *Learning from school choice* (pp. 187–212). Washington, DC: Brookings Institution Press.

Walker, E. M. (2002, August 4). The politics of school-based management: Understanding the process of devolving authority in urban school districts. *Education Policy Analysis Archives, 10*(33). Retrieved October 17, 2011, from http://epaa.asu.edu/epaa/v10n33.html

Wallace, K., & McDermott, V. (2010, November 20). How do you put a price on learning? Paying students for performance is a controversial idea. *National Post*. Toronto Edition, p. A19.

Wallace Foundation. (2006, September). *Leadership for learning: Making the connections among state, district and school policies and practices*. Wallace Perspective. The Wallace Foundation. Available at www.wallacefoundation.org.

Wang, Y., & Pilarzyk, T. (2007, Fall). Mapping the enrollment process: Implications of setting deadlines for student success and college management. *Journal of College Admission*, no. 197, 24–33.

Weiler, H. N. (1990, Winter). Comparative perspectives on educational decentralization: An exercise in contradiction? *Educational Evaluation and Policy Analysis, 12*(4), 433–448.

Weimer, D. L., & Vining, A. R. (1992). *Policy analysis: Concepts and practice* (2nd ed.). Englewood Cliffs, NJ: Prentice-Hall.

What constitutes strong evidence of a program's effectiveness?" (n.d.). Available at http://www.whitehouse.gov/omb/part/2004_program_eval.pdf

Willower, D. J. & Licata, J. W. (1997). *Values and valuation in the practice of educational administration*. Thousand Oaks, CA: Corwin Press.

Wirt, F. W. (1975/1972). *Political and social foundations of education/Frederick M Wirt, Michael W. Kirst* (rev. ed.). Berkeley, CA: McCutchan.

Wraga, W. G. (2006, February). *The heightened significance of Brown v. Board of Education* in our time. *Phi Delta Kappan, 87*(6), 424–428.

Yeh, S. S. (2006). Raising student achievement through rapid assessment and test reform. New York: Teachers College Press.

Yeh, S. S. (2009). Class size reduction or rapid formative Assessment? A comparison of cost-effectiveness. *Educational Research Review, 4*(1), 7–15.

Zezima, K. (2010, February 24). A vote to fire all teachers at a failing high school. *New York Times*, Section A, p. 12.

INDEX

A

Ability to pay, 86–87
Acceptability
  alternatives to different groups, 93
  factors influencing, 93
  measuring, 93–94
  of policy intervention, 94
Accounting, 167
Actionable attribute, 131
Adequacy, 83
Administrative capacity, 95–96
Adoption, policy, 37
Advocacy claims
  ethically complex arguments, 131, 132–133
  need, 131–134
  value laden arguments, 131–132
Affordability, 91
Agenda
  governmental, 34
  setting, 36
Alexander, N. A., 8, 69, 82, 83, 89, 103, 146, 167
Alternatives, 42–43
  ability (to be implemented), 120–121
  anticipating future, 117
  costs, 119–120
  customizing policy interventions, 106
  defined, 102
  developing, 42–43, 103–104
  distinguishing, 121–122
  effectiveness, 118–119
  equity, 119
  evolutionary models, 104
  ex ante analysis, 117
  generic, 105–106
  implementation plan vs., 102
  market models, 103
  objectives vs., 59–60
  outcomes vs., 102
  overview, 116–117
  packaging, 121
  political feasibility, 120
  production models, 103
  quick quantitave analysis, 122–125
  selecting criteria, 117–118
  single-step scorecard rankings, 123–124
  sources, 105–107
  two-step comparative process, 124–125
  variants, 102–103
American Council on Education, 147

American Recovery and Reinvestment Act (ARRA), 106
Analogy, 147
Analysts, in recommendations, 130–131
Anderson, S., 73
Animal Farm, 187
Arguments (policy), 144–148. See also Persuasion
  analogy, 147
  authority, 144
  cause, 146
  classification, 146
  ethics, 147–148
  generalization, 144, 146
  intuition, 147
  method, 144
  motivation, 147
  parallel, 147
  sign, 146
ARRA. See American Recovery and Reinvestment Act (ARRA)
Assembling, evidence, 65–67
Associated techniques, 118
Audience, 43, 142–143. See also Persuasion
  expectations, 142
  forum, 143
  knowledge and understanding, 142–143
  response to solution, 143
Auditing, 167–168
Authority, 144

B

Bardach, E., 5, 7, 29, 41, 49, 52, 53, 55, 66, 70, 71, 72, 81, 87, 88, 96, 102, 103, 104, 106, 122, 141, 142
Baselines, establishment of, 172
Basic Education Data Set, NYS, 167–168
Before-and-after comparisons, 185–186
Benefit cost ratio, 92
Benefits
  costs vs., 90
  principle, 87
  private vs. public, 88–89
Berne, R., 84, 119
Biddle, B. J., 66
Bishop, J., 69
Booth, W. C., 49, 52, 141, 142
Bradley, W., 102
Brown v. Board of Education, 31–32
Bryson, J. M., 94, 158, 159
Bureaucratic climate, 187
Butin, D., 102

C

Capacity-building policies, 95, 108–109
Carnoy, M., 89, 181
Cause mode of persuasion, 146
CCSSO. *See* Council of Chief State School
    Officers (CCSSO)
Change, and policy analysis, 194
Charlton, K., 172
Chelimsky, E., 182, 187
Civic virtue, 21
Classification, persuasion, 146
Class Size, 88
Clune, W., 35
Coburn, C. E., 67
Colander, D., 52, 134
Colomb, G. C., 49, 52, 141, 142
Comer, J. P., 158
Communicating analysis. *See also* Persuasion
    checklist for, 148–149
    clarity of findings, 148–149
    complete or abridged analysis, 143
    conveying, 141–144
    policy arguments, 144–148
    time, 144
Community, and policy analysis, 193
Compliance, 167
Comprehensive School Reform
    Demonstration, 106
Conditions, 6, 29–30
    as problem, 53
    statement, 52–53
Conflict theory, 17, 20
Controllable effects, 166
Cooksey, R. W., 116
Cookson, P. W., 14, 23
Coons, J., 35
Cooper, B. S., 155, 157, 158
Cooper, H. M., 172
Cooper, R., 57
Coplin, W. D., 93, 120
Cost analysis, 91
Cost-benefit analysis, 92
Cost effectiveness, 91
Costs
    counting, 90
    measuring, 119–120
    opportunity, 88
    transaction, 88
    vs. benefits, 90
Council of Chief State School Officers
    (CCSSO), 96

Crace, J., 84
Criteria, 80–85
    concept, 81
    conflict, 96
    values and, 80–81
Criterion-based approach, 124–125
Cuban, L., 49, 180
Cultural lens, 8
Cultural perspective, 57–58
Cultural strategies, 159

D

Data. *See also* Evidence
    assessing contexts, 71
    collection strategies, 72
    displaying, 173
    from documents, 73
    from people, 72–73
    primary sources of, 171
    qualitative, 73–74
    quantitative, 73–74
    secondary sources of, 171
    sources, 72–73
    subjective, 171
    tracking, 168–172
    transformation into evidence, 65–67
    use of, 71
    value, 70
Decision-theoretic evaluation, 182
Denning, S., 33, 134
Direct controlled trials, 185
Diseconomies of scale, 90
Distributive justice, 10
Distributive policies, 107
Documents, as data source, 73
Duke, D. L., 5, 102, 104, 105, 154, 157, 158
Duncan, A., 30
Dunn, W. N., 4, 6, 7, 8, 9, 29, 35, 36, 37, 38, 49, 50, 52,
    65, 66, 67, 68, 87, 102, 129, 130, 131, 132, 135,
    141, 144, 147, 166, 173, 181, 183, 184, 187

E

Economic growth, 11
Economics, 87–92
    cost analysis, 91
    cost-benefit analysis, 92
    cost effectiveness, 91
    costs *vs.* benefits, 90
    counting costs, 90
    decision tools, 91
    opportunity costs, 88

private *vs.* public benefits, 88–89
provision *vs.* production, 89
Economies of scale, 90
Edelman, M., 154
Educational philosophies, 9–23. *See also* Philosophy
   in schools, 22–23
   self-assessment worksheet, 18–19
   values. *See* Values
Education Commission of the States, 132
Effectiveness, 167
   measuring, 118–119
Efficiency, 11, 91, 167
Egoistic hedonism, 10
Ehrenberg, R. G., 56
Elazar, D., 132
Elementary and Secondary Education Act (ESEA),
   35–36, 168, 194–196
Ellis, R. D., 10
Elmore, R. F., 65, 66, 95, 96, 106, 107
Engel, M., 181, 182
Entrepreneur, 130
Equality, 11
Equity. *See also* Fairness
   ability to pay, 86–87
   benefits principle, 87
   horizontal, 84
   measuring, 119
   transitional, 86
   vertical, 84–86
Equivalent alternative, 122
ESEA. *See* Elementary and Secondary Education Act
   (ESEA)
Ethically complex arguments, 131, 132–133
Ethical relativism, 11
Evaluation, 8, 194
   alternatives. *See* Alternatives
   analytical considerations, 183–184
   approaches to, 181–182
   before-and-after comparisons, 185–186
   decision-theoretic, 182
   direct controlled trials, 185
   evidence for, 68
   focus of, 179
   formal, 181–182
   formative, 180
   matching, 185
   methods of, 182–187
   nonexperimental direct analysis, 186
   nonexperimental indirect analysis, 186
   outcomes, 44
   plans, 182–183

policy, 39–40
   political considerations, 186–187
   pseudo-evaluations, 181
   quasi-experiments, 185
   randomized control trials (RCT), 184–185
   selection bias, 186
   summative, 180
   users, 181
   vs. monitoring, 179
   with-and-without comparisons, 186
Evidence. *See also* Data
   assembling, 65–67
   data transformation into, 65–67
   for evaluation, 69
   for forecasting, 70
   for monitoring, 68
   for prescription, 68–69
Evolutionary models, alternatives by, 104
Ex ante analysis, 7
   alternatives, 117
Existentialism, 17
Explanation, 168. *See also* Monitoring
Ex post analysis, 7
Externalities, 89
Extrinsic values, 10

F

Fairness, 83–87. *See also* Equity
Far circle participants, 54
FAWEU. *See* Forum for African Women Educationists
   Uganda (FAWEU)
Febey, K., 67, 72
Feedback, 33
Ferrer de Valero, Y., 57
Fessenden, F., 171
Finn, C. E., 82, 89
Firestone, W. A., 37
Fish, J., 119
Focusing events, 33
Forecasting, 7
   evidence for, 68
   safeguards in, 117
Forgotten players, 55
Formative evaluation, 39, 180
Forum for African Women Educationists Uganda
   (FAWEU), 85
Fountain, J. R., 169
Fowler, F., 11, 31, 32, 35, 36, 40, 49, 73, 80, 93, 95, 109,
   132, 147, 157, 158, 159, 160
Frank, S., 159
Frankenberg, E. D., 30, 32

Frase, L. E., 14
Fraternity, 11
Freebody, P., 116
Free ride, 88
Fryer, R., 56
Fullan, M., 160
Fusarelli, L. D., 155, 157, 158

G

Gamse, B., 154, 158
Gandara, P., 119
Garner, C. W., 58, 173
GASB. *See* Governmental Accounting Standards
     Board (GASB)
Generalization, 144, 146
Gillespie, M., 102
Gillingham, L., 56
Goals, 81
   of policy analysis, 6
   of solving policy problems, 58–60
Goodson, B., 154, 158
Gordon, M., 72
Governmental Accounting Standards Board (GASB),
     169–170
Governmental agenda, 34
Grady, M. P., 73, 74
Grogan, M., 102
Guthrie, J. W., 83
Gutmann, A., 21

H

Haller, E., 71
Hanushek, E., 8
Harlem Children Zone (HCZ), 2, 105
Hawthorne effect, 160
HCZ. *See* Harlem Children Zone (HCZ)
Heck, R. H., 4, 6, 7, 8, 9, 33, 49, 54, 55, 65, 72, 74, 92, 93,
     130, 144, 147
Heckman, J., 8
Hess, F. M., 180
Hidden participants, 36
Horizontal equity, 84
Hortatory policies, 109–110
Houston, P. D., 148
Human (people-related) problems, 94, 158
Hutchins, R. M., 15

I

Idealism, 14–15
If You Give a Mouse a Cookie, 159
Ill-structured problems, 49

Imazeki, J., 83
Impact variables, 173
Implementation, 43
   human problems, 158
   institutional problem, 159
   major challenges, 158–159
   process (program-related) problems, 159
   stages, 160
   structural (setting-related) problems, 159
Implementation dip, 160
Implementation plan, 154–157
   checking, 157
   expanding outline, 155
   outlining, 154–155
Implementation proper, 160
Indicators, 33
Individual freedom, 21
Individualism, 11
Individualistic setting, 132
Individuals with Disabilities Education Act, 109
Inducements, 108
Input variables, 173
Insiders, 54
Institutionalization, 160. *See also* Implementation
Institutional perspective, 56–57
Institutional (program-related or setting-related)
     problems, 94, 159
Interdependence, of problems, 50–51
Interrupted time series analysis, 173
Intrinsic values, 10
Intuition, 147
Issue definition, 35–36
Issue rhetoric, 49

J

Jacobsen, J., 89, 181
Jones, C., 86
Justice
   distributive, 10
   retributive, 10

K

Kaplan, A., 71
Kelly, D., 84
Kentucky law 704 KAR 3:390, 20
King, J. A., 90
Kingdon, J. W., 3, 33, 34, 35, 36, 54, 129
Kitzmiller v. Dover, 129
Klein, A., 194
Kleine, P. F., 71
Kowalski, T., 71, 72, 73

L

Lasley, T. J., 71, 72, 73
Laursen, S., 123
Leach, J., 141
Leaders, 34, 35, 130–131
  entrepreneur as, 130
  and policy analysis, 2–3, 29
  politician as, 130
  technician as, 130
  visible or hidden participants, 36
Lee, C., 30, 32
Legislators, 36
Leithwood, K., 73
Lexiographic ordering, 122
Liberty, 11
Licata, J. W., 117
Lidman, R., 67
Lim, S., 89
Louis, K. S., 67, 72, 73, 157, 159
Lowi, T. J., 107
Lussenhop, J., 167

M

Mahoney, J. W., 71, 72, 73
Mandates, 95, 109
Manipulable actions, 166
Manno, B. V., 82, 89
March, J. G., 134
Mark, M. M., 182
Market failures, 88
Market models, alternatives by, 103
Marschke, R., 123
Marshall, C., 54, 92
Matching, 185
Matrix, 122
Matus, R., 130
Mavros, P. G., 56
McDermott, K. A., 196
McDermott, V., 56
McDonnell, L. M., 34, 65, 66, 95–96, 106, 107
Measures, 81
Meltsner, A. J., 130
Merriam-Webster's Collegiate Dictionary, 14
Method, persuasion, 144
Miles, K. H., 159
Miles, M. B., 157, 159
Millsap, M., 154, 158
Mills v. Board of Education, 109
Mintrop, H., 183
Mishel, M., 89, 181
Mitchell, D., 54, 92

Mobilization, 160. *See also* Implementation
Monitoring, 7, 43
  concept, 166
  evidence for, 68
  functions, 166–168
  key questions, 170–172
  measuring change, 173
  vs. evaluation, 179
Monk, D. H., 103
Moralistic setting, 132
Motivation, 147

N

NAEP. *See* National Assessment of Educational
    Progress (NAEP)
National Assessment of Educational Progress
    (NAEP), 172, 195
National Center for Education Statistics, 167
National Commission on Excellence in Education, 34
National Council for Accreditation of Teacher
    Education (NCATE), 169
A Nation at Risk, 34
Nature, of problem, 49
NCATE. *See* National Council for Accreditation of
    Teacher Education (NCATE)
NCLB. *See* No Child Left Behind (NCLB)
Neal, D., 8
Near circle participants, 54
Net present value, 92
New Vision, 85
New York State (NYS), 167–168
  Basic Education Data Set, 167–168
Nielsen, J. M., 123
No Child Left Behind (NCLB), 4, 20, 109, 171, 195
Noll, J. W., 14, 15
Nondominated alternative, 122
Nonexperimental direct analysis, 186
Nonexperimental indirect analysis, 186
Norm-based approach, 123–124
Numeroff, L. J., 159
Nye, B. A., 172
NYS. *See* New York State (NYS)

O

Oakes, J., 70
Objective outputs, 167
Objectives, 81
  of solving policy problems, 58–60
  vs. alternatives, 59–60
Objectivity, transparency *vs.*, 8–9
Odden, A., 7, 83, 84, 119

Ogundare, F., 33
Okun, A. M., 96
O'Leary, M. K., 93, 120
Opinions, 118
Options. *See* Alternatives
Order, 11
Orfield, G., 30, 32
Organisation for Economic Co-operation and Development, 167
Orwell, G., 187
Output, monitoring. *See* Monitoring
Output variables, 173

P

Packaging alternatives, 121
Paired comparisons, 122
Parallel arguments, 147
Pareto efficiency, 91
PART. *See* Program Assessment Reporting Tool (PART)
Participants
  hidden, 36
  visible, 36
Past policies, assessment of, 67
Patton, C. V., 4, 7, 29, 41, 58, 70, 81, 82, 87, 88, 89, 90, 104, 105, 106, 117, 118, 120, 122, 130, 133, 134, 141, 166, 183
Payment, 86–87
  progressive system, 86
  proportional system, 86
  regressive system, 86
People, as data source, 72–73
Personalism, 10–11
Personal *vs.* policy problems, 50
Personnel support, 95
Persuasion, 2–3
  analogy, 147
  authority, 144
  cause, 146
  classification, 146
  ethics, 147–148
  generalization, 144, 146
  intuition, 147
  method, 144
  motivation, 147
  parallel, 147
  sign, 146
Peterson, W., 116
Phenomenology, 17
Philosophy
  conflict theory, 17, 20
  defining, 14
  existentialism, 17

idealism, 14–15
  phenomenology, 17
  postmodernism and critical theory, 20–21
  pragmatism, 16–17
  realism, 15–16
Picus, L., 7, 84, 119
Pilarzyk, T., 57
Policy adoption, 37
Policy analysis, 192–196
  change and, 194
  community and, 193
  complexities of, 31–32
  crafts, 41
  defined, 5
  evaluation and. *See* Evaluation
  example, 194–196
  goal, 6
  leaders in, 29
  as policy problems, 29–32
  process, 31
  roadmap, 41–44
  stepping-stones of, 44
  steps, 42–44
  types, 6–9
  users, 3–5
  vs. policy making. *See* Policy making
Policy evaluation, 37–38. *See also* Evaluation
Policy formulation, 36–37
Policy implementation, 37. *See also* Implementation
Policy interventions, 106
Policy issues, 6, 30
Policymakers, 32
Policy making, 32–38
  phases in, 33–35
  stages, 35–38
Policy mechanism, 107–110
  capacity-building policies, 108–109
  hortatory policies, 109–110
  inducements, 108
  mandates, 109
  system change policies, 109
Policy options
  distributive policies, 107
  redistributive policies, 107
  regulatory policies, 107
Policy problems, 6
  causes of, 55–58
  characteristics of, 49–52
  condition as, 53
  condition statement, 52–53
  dynamic nature of, 52
  goals and objectives of solving, 58–60

ill-structured problems, 49
interdependence of, 50–51
personal *vs.*, 50
policy analysis as, 29–32
scope of, 54–58
structuring, 49–53
subjectivity and artificiality of
    structuring, 51–52
writing a clear description of, 49
Policy stream, 34–35
Policy talk, 49
Political culture, 20, 94
    individualistic, 132
    moralistic, 132
    traditionalistic, 132
Political feasibility, measuring, 120
Political strategies, 159
Political structure, 187
Politician, 130
Politics stream, 34
Pragmatism, 16–17
Prescribing, 7
Prescription, evidence for, 68
Present values, 92
Primary sources of data, 171
Private *vs.* public benefits, 88–89
Problem. *See* Policy problems
Problem stream, 33–34
    feedback, 33
    focusing events, 33
    indicators, 33
Process (program-related) problems,
    94, 159
Process variables, 173
Production, 89
Production models, alternatives by, 103
Professional culture, 187
Program Assessment Reporting Tool
    (PART), 184
Progressive system, 86
Proportional system, 86
Prospective, 131
Provision, 89
Pseudo-evaluations, 181
Public *vs.* private benefits, 88–89

Q

Qualitative data, 73–74
Quality, 11
Quantitative data, 73–74
Quasi-experiments, 185
Quick quantitave analysis, 122–125

R

Randall, E. V., 155, 157, 158
Rankin, P., 123
Rational lens, 8
Rational perspective, 56
Ravitch, D., 103
RCT. *See* Randomized control trials (RCT)
Realism, 15–16
Recommendation, 43
    approaches to, 134–135
    credibility testing, 134–135
    questions to test robustness, 135
Redistributive policies, 107
Regional Conference on Secondary Education in
    Africa (SEIA), 85
Regressive system, 86
Regulatory policies, 107
Reschovsky, A., 83
Resources, 95–96
Retributive justice, 10
Robelen, 194
Roellke, C. F., 69
Rothstein, R., 89, 116, 144, 181
Randomized control trials (RCT), 184–185

S

Sadovnik, A R., 14, 23
Safeguards, in forecasting, 117
Sampling, 118
*San Antonio Independent School District v.
    Rodriguez*, 93
Satisficing, 122
Sawchuk, S., 108, 194
Sawicki, D. S., 4, 7, 29, 41, 58, 70, 81, 82, 87, 88, 89, 90,
    104, 105, 106, 117, 118, 120, 122, 130, 133, 134,
    141, 166, 183
Scenarios, 117
Schapiro, D., 83
Schemo, D. J., 171
Schroeder. R., 67
Scorecard, 122
    creating, 122–123
Secondary sources of data, 171
SEIA. *See* Regional Conference on Secondary
    Education in Africa (SEIA)
Selection bias, 186
Self-assessment worksheet
    educational philosophies, 18–19
    values, 12–13
Semel, S. F., 14, 23
Seneca, J. J., 56

Serrano v, Priest, 35
Severity, of problem, 49
Sign, 146
Simon, H. A., 134
Singham, M., 146
Single-step scorecard rankings, alternatives, 123–124
Sometimes players, 54–55
Sommers, P., 67
Spring, J., 14, 17, 20, 55, 195
Stakeholders, 54
Standards alternative methods, 122
STAR. *See* Tennessee Student-Teacher Achievement Ratio (STAR) Project
Stiefel, L., 84, 119
Streshly, W., 14
Structural lens, 8
Structural problems, 94, 159
Subjective data, 171
Subjective outputs, 167
Sugarman, S., 35
Summative evaluation, 39–40, 180
Sunderman, G. L., 183
Superfine, B. M., 129
System change policies, 109

T
Taussig, M. K., 56
Technical strategies, 159
Technician, 130
Tennessee Student-Teacher Achievement Ratio (STAR) Project, 185
Thomas, E., 72
Thomas, S. L., 57
Threats to validity, 173
TIME. *See* Time for Innovation Matters in Education (TIME) Act of 2008
Time for Innovation Matters in Education (TIME) Act of 2008, 147
Timeliness, 148
Time series analysis, 118
Tinto, V., 8, 57
Transitional equity, 86
Transparency *vs.* objectivity, 8–9
Trochim, W., 182
Two-step comparative process, alternatives, 124–125
Tyack, D. B., 49, 180
Type III error, 38

U
Uncontrollable effects, 166
United Nations Children's Fund, 85
Unit of analysis, 173
Unmanipulable actions, 166
Urban, J. B., 182
U.S. Department of Education, 168, 172
U.S. Government Accountability Office, 183
U.S. News and World Report, 6
Utilitarianism, 10

V
Value laden arguments, 131–132
    individualistic, 132
    moralistic, 132
    traditionalistic, 132
    warrants, 131
Values, 42
    in action, 21
    criteria and, 80–81
    economic growth, 11
    efficiency, 11
    equality, 11
    extrinsic, 10
    fraternity, 11
    individualism, 11
    intrinsic, 10
    liberty, 11
    order, 11
    quality, 11
    self-assessment worksheet, 12–13
    transforming into results, 130
    worldviews, 10–11
Vanourek, G., 82, 89
Variables
    impact, 173
    input, 173
    output, 173
    process, 173
Vertical equity, 84–86
Vining, A. R., 105, 106
Visible participants, 36

W
Wahlstrom, K., 73
Walker, E. M., 160
Wallace, K., 56
Wallace Foundation, 73
Wang, Y., 57

Weiler, H. N., 37, 186
Weimer, D. L., 105, 106
Williams, J. M., 49, 52, 141, 142
Willower, D. J., 117
Wirt, F. W., 32, 54, 92, 186
With-and-without comparisons, 186
Wraga, W. G., 32

Y
Yeh, S. S., 39, 180

Z
Zezima, K., 106